Praise for

Landscape Urbanism and its Discontents

Herein one can find the most articulate and insightful debate
on Urbanism to surface in decades. The issues raised should be at
the heart of any serious dialog about the human prospect.

—Peter Calthorpe, author, *Urbanism in the Age of Climate Change*

Landscape Urbanism propaganda famously vaunts its own
doctrinal incompleteness, indeterminateness, openness, while
paradoxically broadcasting a possible maturation. In this unique
compendium formidable antagonists pay the LU gobbledygook
more attention than it is capable to sustain and scrupulously
expose the extent to which LU is but old modernist wine
presented in new greenwashed bottles.

—Leon Krier, Louis Kahn Visiting Professor, Yale University

This important collection of essays lays bare the
comprehensive wrongheadedness at the foundation of Landscape
Urbanist theory, from its apparently unconscious preference of the
symbolic over the real to its surprisingly outdated conception of man's
proper relationship to nature. We've known for decades that the best
way to protect the landscape is to stay the heck away from it, collecting
ourselves in dense, walkable cities. Any alternative to this time-tested
model is still carbon-belching sprawl, however well it drains.

—Jeff Speck, author of *Walkable City: How Downtown Can
Save America, One Step at a Time*

Landscape Urbanism and its Discontents

Dissimulating the Sustainable City

Landscape Urbanism and its Discontents

Dissimulating the Sustainable City

Edited by Andrés Duany and Emily Talen

new society
PUBLISHERS

Cover design by Diane McIntosh.
Top image: Master Plan for the Cornell Unviersity/Technion Institute's
Applied Science Campus, Roosevelt Island, New York.
Image courtesy of SOM. © Skidmore, Owings & Merrill LLP.
Bottom image: The High Line, New York courtesy of Bruce Donnelly

Printed in Canada. First printing March 2013.
Paperback ISBN: 978-0-86571-740-4
eISBN: 978-1-55092-536-4

Inquiries regarding requests to reprint all or part of *Landscape Urbanism and its Discontents* should be addressed to New Society Publishers at the address below.

To order directly from the publishers, please call toll-free (North America) 1-800-567-6772, or order online at www.newsociety.com

Any other inquiries can be directed by mail to:

New Society Publishers
P.O. Box 189, Gabriola Island, BC V0R 1X0, Canada
(250) 247-9737

New Society Publishers' mission is to publish books that contribute in fundamental ways to building an ecologically sustainable and just society, and to do so with the least possible impact on the environment, in a manner that models this vision. We are committed to doing this not just through education, but through action. The interior pages of our bound books are printed on Forest Stewardship Council®-registered acid-free paper that is **100% post-consumer recycled** (100% old growth forest-free), processed chlorine free, and printed with vegetable-based, low-VOC inks, with covers produced using FSC®-registered stock. New Society also works to reduce its carbon footprint, and purchases carbon offsets based on an annual audit to ensure a carbon neutral footprint. For further information, or to browse our full list of books and purchase securely, visit our website at: www.newsociety.com

Library and Archives Canada Cataloguing in Publication

Landscape urbanism and its discontents : dissimulating the sustainable city / edited by Andrés Duany and Emily Talen.

Includes index.
ISBN 978-0-86571-740-4

1. Urban landscape architecture. 2. City planning. 3. Sustainable development. I. Duany, Andres II. Talen, Emily, 1958-
SB472.7.L35 2013   712.09173'2   C2012-908588-X

To Jane Jacobs and Rachel Carson,
neither of whom ever confused the urban with the natural.

Contents

Preface

THIS BOOK PROBABLY SHOULD HAVE BEEN WRITTEN 15 YEARS AGO. As there has never been a group of people so ready for intellectual engagement, the essays in this collection seem to have exploded from the pens of their authors.

This book wrestles with one of the greatest unresolved debates in modern urban history: what is the position of humans – and the physical structures they require — in nature? This question is central for anyone concerned with the future of cities.

The 20th century American urban experience increased the urgency of the question. American society forced the issue by committing itself to auto-dependent suburbia and the host of technologies that enabled it. We invented a symbiotic system of financing, marketing and administration, that became, for fifty years, virtually the only way America was built. The promise of open space, a private house, the freedom to drive (and park) for everything — to shop, to go to school, to socialize — independent of proximity — was a fantastic one, and temporarily fulfilled. We became a country so wealthy that we could pay for simple-minded policies and then pay to patch over the problems they created.

The New Urbanism offered a highly public counter to this calamity. But it was heavily scrutinized: the charters, congresses and manifestos they presented, and particularly the built projects, added up to, in the minds of some, a hegemony that needed to be challenged.

This challenge fueled the emergence of another paradigm, called Landscape Urbanism. In contrast to New Urbanism, it had no official organization or annual congress, and this made it much less visible, at least initially. It was led by a very able and organized polemicist named Charles Waldheim, who was invited to Harvard to make the landscape architecture department the preeminent intellectual authority. Its treatise was a book of essays organized somewhat loosely as *The Landscape Urbanism Reader*, published by Princeton Architectural Press in 2006. Later, a major conference at Harvard produced the essays for a closely aligned venture, *Ecological Urbanism* (Lars Müller Publishers, 2010). Both books included explicit and implied doses of criticism aimed at New Urbanism.

The New Urbanists were accustomed to critique, but the Landscape Urbanist opposition involved something more fundamental. Most prior opponents of the New Urbanism had deliberately misrepresented the movement, requiring only a rebuttal of simple factual correction. But the Landscape Urbanists were different. Their counter-proposal rested on an alternate model to claim the same territory: utilizing different power bases, different methods of implementation, and different and incompatible techniques. The only thing the two movements had in common was that both proposed to be the principal urban planning solution to the environmental crisis.

The New Urbanists were slow to realize that in some important arenas Landscape Urbanism had methodically taken over the sustainable city discourse — in the academy, in competitions, and as the main preoccupation of the high-design establishment. After a couple of decades of disciplinary cultivation, they had also gathered enough weight to capture the hearts and minds of students, who the New Urbanists had long counted on as unwavering champions of the Jane Jacobs vision.

And yet, in our view, all of this amounted to a very welcome intellectual challenge. The contrasting position provided an unambiguous basis upon which to debate the future course of urbanism. The New Urbanists fear fire, as carbon emissions warm the planet and melt the icecaps, while the Landscape Urbanists fear water, if it does not flow directly to aquifers. The New Urbanists focus on the importance of streets defined by disciplined frontages, believing them to be an essential component of walkability, while the Landscape Urbanists are more concerned with maintaining a very high proportion of greenspace, irrespective of its effect on street life. The New Urbanists connect to the market, the regulators, and the anthropocentric environmentalists who value Smart Growth, while the Landscape Urbanists connect to design competitions, academia, elite patrons, and the biophilic environmentalists. The New Urbanists focus on the middle class and its housing, while the Landscape Urbanists are attuned to large-scale civic infrastructure. The New Urbanists gain acceptance through populism and proven method, while the Landscape Urbanists gain acceptance via high-culture and experimentalism.

We don't want to lose the ability of these contrasts to energize our thinking. In a profession over-ridden with meta-theory, many are accustomed to disengagement and delimited discourse, and this may be understandable. But there are smoldering issues that should not be glossed over. Our hope is that this book will bring clarity to these positions, helping to advance the debate on the still-unresolved question of the human presence in nature.

The essays in this collection range in polemical intent. Some rashly endeavor to convince the practitioners of Landscape Urbanism of errors in their position. This outcome is unlikely, as a theory so well conceived is impervious to mere evidence. Some will likely serve to hearten those emergent minorities in the design studios and the competition juries who are skeptical of this new orthodoxy. This, too, is unlikely, as the goal often is not reason, but power. However, we hope that all of these essays will prove consequent to those committed to effective environmentalism — those for whom the problems at hand are too important to be satisfied by symbolic gestures, however critically intended and cleverly conceived.

We are deeply indebted to our contributors, some of whom cared enough to control their adrenaline, and write seriously about this topic.

Andrés Duany, Miami, FL
Emily Talen, Tempe, AZ

I

Looking Backward:
Notes on a Cultural Episode

ANDRÉS DUANY AND EMILY TALEN

IN THE MIDDLE YEARS OF THE LAST CENTURY, Jose Luis Sert summoned designers and critics to Harvard with the intention of defining a discipline to be called urban design. Records of the annual meetings show reams of tentative disquisition.[1] That no conclusions were drawn, even though the gatherings took place in the presence of the exemplary urbanism of Cambridge, signaled from the outset that empirical evidence was to be held outside the discourse.

Not until 2010, with the semicentennial proceedings commemorating Sert's quest, did it become clear that his legacy to urban design, at least in the academy, had been a consensus to avoid consensus. This clarification arrived by way of contrast, as a replacement paradigm became visible: the highly focused academic agenda called Landscape Urbanism.

Meanwhile, outside the academy, another consensus had become dominant, this one based specifically on the empirical observation of places like Cambridge. It was called the New Urbanism.[2]

By the end of the century, the practicing design professions had come to support the principles of the New Urbanism (by its several names) with remarkable unanimity: Americans should drive less and live more compactly because of concerns related to pollution, health, economics, social equity, and energy use.[3]

The particulars were still in debate, but that basic outline of the human habitat had largely been settled. The instruments to achieve it would be based on the pedestrian shed, an urban pattern in which the basic needs of daily life are within walking distance. These would be integrated to regional and transportation patterns for access to the complete repertoire of special needs. The buildings would not be megastructures, but multiple and compatible and designed sequentially in response to evolving circumstances, under the guidance of the existing administrative protocol of codes — which would be re-written accordingly.[4] From this model would ensue what was then known to be sustainable for both the human and the natural habitat.[5]

The New Urbanism was close to supplanting the tenacious paradigm of suburban sprawl, which had been the unintended consequence of a century's search for the "true synthesis" of the social and natural realms. The original proposition, called the Garden City, had dissipated long before — when geographic discipline was made unnecessary by the ubiquity of the automobile. But the New Urbanism, especially through Transect-based codes and LEED-ND (for Neighborhood Development), was poised to become a new standard. Rather than administering protection of nature, the new strategy would be projective, enabling an urbanism that humans needed and desired, and would therefore be loath to abandon. And it was to be market-oriented: those who could choose would not *want* to inhabit suburban sprawl.

As the Congress for the New Urbanism conceived the campaign, the effort seemed to provide enough intellectual content to support research, stimulate debate, and keep reform-minded designers well occupied: How much compactness should be expected, with development driven also by market expectations? To what extent could natural processes be accommodated without undermining human prerogatives? How could the socioeconomic segregation enabled by the automobile be reversed? Should urban growth be bounded as conceived by Howard, or channeled as proposed by McKaye? How to incorporate food production, energy sourcing, and the inevitable impoverishment into an urbanism adapted to the twenty-first century? These proposals would have to be implemented within then-current bureaucracies, through the friction of an angry and confused public, a venal political system, a development industry programmed for simplistic solutions, and — as it turned out — the opposition of the design academy.

At the turn of the century it became clear that the more intellectually compelling debate was no longer against conventional suburbia, but between the New Urbanism and Landscape Urbanism, two paradigms with differing visions of nature and society. Landscape Urbanism had managed to overcome the reflex that had kept the academy uncommitted for half a century — not by challenging Sert's discourse, but by unifying the academies against an opponent: explicitly taking on the threat of New Urbanism and proposing to "undermine its certainties, explode its limits, ridicule its preoccupations."[6]

The New Urbanists did not initially engage the challenge. Ann Spirn's early critique in *The Granite Garden* — that there had been "a fundamental lack of understanding of how natural processes shape cities, towns and regions" — was dismissed with the facile retort that Commonwealth Avenue, which appeared on the cover of her book, could not be built following the prescriptions of the text within.[7]

In retrospect, the New Urbanists' failure to assimilate Spirn's prescient and reasonable message was a strategic blunder. Years of practice complying with mandatory federal standards had coarsened their ecological sensibility. The natural processes, which were accommodated only as required by law, had not been *polemicized*. A withering emphasis on socially determined designs for public space opened New Urbanism to the accusation that it was dismissive of nature. New Urbanists, responding to the architectural critiques of Jane Jacobs, William White, Jan Gehl, and Oscar Newman, were both socially and environmentally responsible, yet did not *appear* to be so.

For years, the emergent challenge had been overshadowed by a distracting debate over architectural style. It seemed that academic architects would not go along with a New Urbanist standard of a contextual architecture cooperating toward spatial definition. The *discipline* was seen as an intrinsic constraint on their creativity. New Urbanism had underestimated their profound discontent. Not even the spectacular success of modernist buildings within a New Urbanist discipline, of HafenCity in Hamburg (opened in 2015), could assuage the avant-garde architect's prerogative of unfettered innovation.

In strategic contrast, Landscape Urbanism sought favor within the architectural academy by providing refuge from urban *discipline*. Nature's "indeterminacy and flux"[8] was understood to allow freely designed buildings as freestanding objects within a landscape both buffering and unifying their individualism. A brilliantly argued and lavishly illustrated agenda to restore unconstrained form-making was on offer[9] — in exchange for the dominant position within Sert's old Urban Design triad of architecture, urban planning, and landscape architecture, where landscape architecture had been the junior partner.

Rather than an urban fabric based on the spatial definition by buildings, landscape would be the "structuring medium." "The look and shape of the city" was to be a matter of "open space within which buildings are set."[10] When Stan Allen stated that "designers can activate space and produce urban effects without the weighty apparatus of traditional space making,"[11] it was a radical proposition only against the then-consensus that a disciplined building frontage was the primary component of a successful urban outcome — and its absence a catalyst for failure.

This "critical" position forced Landscape Urbanism to discard *all* the constituent elements of the dominant paradigm, leading to a *deformation professionelle*. With an aplomb unique to the academy, there would be an exploration of density, without reference to "traditional" models. This was simply *hors le discours*.

As Landscape Urbanists had transcended Harvard's 50 years of dithering by systematically asserting whatever positions were contrary to the New Urbanism,[12] the design syntax was backed into the categorical rejection of grids, blocks, sidewalks directly associated to building frontages, primary ground planes, standard-issue pavement, trees coinciding with paths, multiple buildings accreting to define public space, and *any* of those design techniques that could promote and reconcile the super-adjacency of disparate social and functional programs.

This position was, at least, unambiguous — far from Sert's confusion of coveting the forbidden traditional city, a self-imposed distance from the exhausted CIAM, and reluctant avoidance of the glamorous but non-Harvard brand of Team 10. The one continuity with Sert was the prerogative of high design. Indeed, the exceptional quality of Landscape Urbanism's designs would long obscure the evidence that attracting free-willed pedestrians required disciplined frontages. Until it was proven otherwise by the built projects, trust would be placed in the swarms of Photoshopped pedestrians.

Given the decisive failure of *espace vague* in the last half of the twentieth century, the belief that street frontages were dispensable required a kind of deliberate amnesia that could be effected only within a delimited academic discourse. Evidence was buried that the attempts at a non-spatial, landscaped, public realms at the earlier touchstone urbanisms of Vallingby, Stevenage, Toulouse-le-Mirail, Firminy-Vert, Don Mills, Brasilia, Pruitt-Igoe, Tyson's Corner, Columbia and Hansaviertel, without exception, had failed to support pedestrian activity at levels approaching those of the nearby corridor streets, which — unless they had been economically undermined or demolished — stood as their permanent indictment.

New Urbanists believed that walkability was the essential element that made urbanism intrinsically sustainable — and that, conveniently enough, it was also urbanism's greatest competitive advantage. Why would one choose to live in higher density if not for the *street life*? The compensation for the absence of a private yard out the back door was to be the vitality teeming out the front door. Even the omni-skeptical New York critic Michael Sorkin could not deny the delights of the spatially defined street. In his autobiographical *Twenty Minutes in Manhattan,* there was nothing but the *rue corridor* to salve his quasi-penitential apartment.[13]

The discourse of the Landscape Urbanists was unusual in excluding Manhattan, otherwise the *maison mère* of the architectural avant-garde. But...Manhattan's urbanism was a model for New Urbanism. A list of its differences from Landscape Urbanist principles would be quite long. Proportionally (height to width), Manhattan's streets were the opposite of *espace vague* and — above all — the natural and the urban were radically juxtaposed as in Central Park — and not in the least interspersed. Indeed, in those years, when a modernist object-building within Manhattan (or any other historic core) was seen to support pedestrian life, it was predictably embedded into and braced by the pre-existing urban fabric. This had been the case with the Seagram Building and Foster's Gherkin, neither of which had exterminated pedestrian activity. This was a reason that the "starchitects" increasingly *demanded* inclusion in the historic urban areas of London, Milan, St. Petersburg, Washington, and Paris — rather than accept sites in such then-new enclaves as La Defense and Crystal City. Modernist buildings succeeded only when they were parasitic on traditional urban fabric. Among other object-buildings, they coalesced into a *strada comica*, as Rem Koolhaas eventually demonstrated with his Starchitect Collage.[14]

Just as CIAM (and Team 10) had done previously, Landscape Urbanists banned the *rue corridor* for ideological reasons, and the result eventually proved to be the same. Proscribed from emulating the world's stock of functioning urbanism, only the dreary social housing and suburban sprawl would have remained as the models. The disinterment of the unverifiable projects like Usonia and Hilbersheimer had necessarily to follow.

Besides, as modernist housing schemes were demolished or gentrified, the evidence of failure was fortuitously eliminated. The demolition of the Robin Hood Gardens at the turn of the century was not permitted to have the devastating effect on Landscape Urbanism that Pruitt-Igoe had on CIAM's legacy. A new justification, *environmentalism*, was brought into the avant-garde discourse for the first time, replacing the failed social commitment. The high proportion of *espace vague* became justified, not as social space: Landscape Urbanism never succeeded in conceptualizing an *integral* social agenda (see Talen: "The Social Apathy of Landscape Urbanism," *Landscape Urbanism and Its Discontents*, 2013), but as the locus of environmental mitigation through bucolic implantations. Surrogate hill and dale, prairie, woodland, and stream embalmed the residue between buildings. The result was highly appealing visually, and endowed Landscape Urbanism with the appearance of superior environmental performance.

These audacious and untested propositions were dissimulated by an attack on the New Urbanists' purported inability to deal with the realities of practice. Thus James Corner defined Landscape Urbanism as "a response to the failure of traditional urban design and planning to operate effectively in the contemporary city." The "out of control" metropolis was "not a weakness but its strength."[15] A crossover vocabulary of "indeterminacy," "openness," and "flux" was developed to affirm the unwillingness to engage the American planning system, contradicting the ideal of predictable outcomes through codes and standards *because* the New Urbanists had done so. The incompletion and temporality of nature became the "antidote to the implicit finitude" of New Urbanist planning tools, not acknowledging similarities with the successional and parametric technology of the widely used Rural-to-Urban Transect, which was the basis for the SmartCode freeware.

While the social agenda was elusive, the treatment of the "ecological" landscaping was curiously honest: there would be no pretending that the plantings were natural. Landscape Urbanism's design tropes were careful to signal that even the layout of "native species" would be on the artificial order of a plant nursery. Naturalistic planting, when unavoidable, would be as quotation — to be framed literally and physically. Anything that might be confused with the natural was proscribed. Olmsted's successful replicants were ignored in general and avoided in detail.

A greater difference permeates the ethos of both movements. For Landscape Urbanism the environmental crisis was not a scientific reality to be mitigated, but an incubator of metaphor. As an example, one proposal presented at a conference on Ecological Urbanism held at Harvard in 2010 involved the replacement of a street intersection in downtown Berkeley by a plug of landscape. That this intervention clipped the street grid, reducing transportation capacity and thereby density, was an externality. The concept was to provide an explicit allusion to a coastal wetland some miles distant. This was understood as a "critical" position by the cognoscenti present, but taken as effective environmentalism by the trusting elsewhere.

James Corner dismissed even McHarg's foundational overlay maps because they attempted to impose measures. In the absence of metrics, the kind of *technical* arguments deployed by New Urbanism in favor of compact urbanism could be ignored.[16] There would be no accounting for suburbia's dismal ecological performance. Only one metric was retained for its scientific gloss: hydrology. Water filtered to the aquifer was elevated to a rhetorical position whose merits were beyond verification. Eventually hydrology came to be mandated — ironically, for those disapproving of fixed standards — by federal policy.

The perverse implications of hydrological privilege gradually became evident. Manhattan and Charleston emerged as polemical counterexamples. What would the effect be on Manhattan's transportation network if the nearly 3,000 streams and wetlands then in pipes were to have remained "riparian corridors" as per Landscape Urbanist praxis? How much street connectivity would be interrupted, thereby severely reducing density? How many thousands of square miles of actual, functioning, wilderness would have been consumed by the dwellings, stores, and offices of the millions of consequently dispersed Manhattanites — all adding their lower-density carbon footprints to the global crisis?

But this argument failed to have an effect — as it missed the point of Landscape Urbanism. An ethical commitment — even to ecology

— could not alone provide a decisive argument within the then-current relativistic discourse — where power would be the only objective verification. Landscape Urbanism could not be successfully analyzed as a design movement, or even an environmental reform strategy. Its peculiar combination of agendas would be finally understood as a campaign to amass power.

Landscape Urbanism had enlisted the support of constituencies that the New Urbanists had either ignored, annoyed, or anathemized. Among them were: 1. The profession of Landscape Architecture, whose design concerns had been made subordinate to social determinants; 2. Environmentalists, specifically those seduced by the visual foregrounding of "nature"; 3. Academic faculty, otherwise constrained by New Urbanism's research agenda which privileged proof over speculation; 4. Architects, who would be able to retain their prerogatives to formal innovation; 5. Infrastructure purveyors, confronting NIMBYs, eager to underwrite the high cost of visual mitigations; and 6. Unpopular suburban sprawl developers, who could be made to, literally, "look good." These groups were strategically embraced by Landscape Urbanism.

First among these constituencies were the architects, to whom Landscape Urbanism offered a reprieve. They rediscovered that interspersed "nature" could provide the visual shock absorber between the mutually destructive shapes of their buildings. The New Urbanist proposition had required a collective discipline and a formal cooperation. Architects could retain the prerogatives of untrammeled formalism in exchange for ceding urban design to the Landscape Urbanists. This finally slipped the Beaux-Arts assumption that architecture was the master art. Furthermore, there was something to be gained by aligning with an agenda that was exclusively ecological — there would be no further need to sustain the tiresome CIAM/New Urbanist commitment to social equity.

In symbiotic relationship, architects supported the "ecological projection" of Landscape Urbanism by evolving a formal repertoire that provided an "urban" metaphor equivalent to the "natural" one. There was a *look* that identified the corresponding architecture: the quality of the carefully *random* — from arbitrarily complicated repertoire of materials and a diverse massing to a laborious misalignment of details such as walls, columns, openings, and mullions. This architectural syntax, which had previously emerged to express the uncertainty inherent in the relativist discourse, was re-framed as a surrogate for the complexity of urbanism. The visual multiplicity provided camouflage for what were in fact functionally homogenous buildings. The "critical" method privileged appearance as the expression of intention — and so representation trumped the evidence of an absent functional and social diversity.

The timing of the architectural alliance was fortuitous. By that time a generation of students had been educated having had no exposure to the necrotic European New Towns or the narcoleptic American Planned-Unit Developments, or to the social failure of H.U.D., which together had extinguished what was left of modernist planning's reputation. All reference was lost of the mercy killing that had once come from every direction: *Collage City, Delirious New York, Townscape, Architecture Rationelle, The Golden City, Jane Jacobs, the Krier brothers, Defensible Space, the Charter of the New Urbanism.* There was only revulsion for the "postmodernist" episode, when the practitioners, the academy, the publications had experienced the rare moment of consensus that whatever may still have been viable about modernist architecture, nothing could survive of modernist planning. But that consensus had occurred in the 1980s. A full generation of amnesia had since been stage-managed.

The trusty *rue corridor*, which was the *one* weapon the executioners all held in common, was slated once more for the trash heap of history[17] (further proof of Jane Jacobs' observation that the "pseudoscience of planning seems almost neurotic in its determination to imitate empiric failure and ignore empiric success"). Jacobs herself was replaced by her nemesis, Robert Moses — with reputation refurbished from a scourge of cities to the builder of infrastructure. His achievements would be tapped by Landscape Urbanists as another means of connecting to the infrastructure constituency. This became an important agenda, manifested in the aestheticizing of the arterials, highways, stormwater facilities, and parking lots. The traffic impact and carbon emissions that such auto-dependent transportation systems induced were statistical externalities to the ecological discourse. If there was a gloss of "science," it was at the scale of advancing plant-bed technology in unnatural locations: on roofs, decks, walls, and high slopes.

"Cutting-edge" design was essential to Landscape Urbanism's academic credentials, but it was a fiction that could not be maintained indefinitely, even within the highly edited history curriculum pioneered by Michael Hays at Harvard. One of the requirements of an avant-garde position, duly achieved, was the sidelining of the pioneers like Anne Whiston Spirn and Ian McHarg (while still alive and in academia!). But the enormous threat remained: the indisputable and ineradicable evidence of Olmsted's success under a virtually identical agenda.

As the establishment of a suitable prehistory became a priority, Charles Waldheim, the *eminence grise* of Landscape Urbanism, put forth three decoys — Andrea Branzi's Agronica, Frank Lloyd Wright's Usonia, and Hilberheimer's New Regional Pattern — taking recourse in three unbuilt concepts that could not therefore be challenged by objective measurement. But all three resisted resurrection until they were bundled with an emergent aspect of ecology — food self-sufficiency. This development coincided with an important New Urbanist initiative, becoming a first instance of agreement between the contending parties. The contemporaneous *Theory and Practice of Agrarian Urbanism*[18] could have become a Landscape Urbanist text had the illustrated buildings been flat-roofed. Yet another point of agreement became the hydrology agenda, not as metaphor but as the utilitarian, cost-effective Light Imprint technology formulated by the New Urbanist Tom Low.

When the national debt finally curtailed the infrastructure projects, the environmentalists became the principal Landscape Urbanist constituency. The seeds had been long-ago planted. A century and a half earlier, the American environmental movement had emerged from the campaign to create the National Parks. This agenda held wilderness as the ideal. Humans and their activities were thereby necessarily conceived as other than nature (per Woody Allen: "Nature and I are two."). As the toolbox limits the craft, Landscape Urbanism's pervasive rustication of the city was recognizable, while New Urbanism, with its focus on density, connectivity, and contiguity, could not be conceived as anything but a clipper of green corridors, purveyor of impervious surfaces, and creator of heat islands.

The New Urbanist response was technical: that the application of visual greening de-tuned those attributes of urbanism that supported walkability and hence *lowered* the environmental performance by fostering vehicular traffic. This argument was forcefully engaged in the compendium *Landscape Urbanism and its Discontents* (2013).[19] But it was too complex a discourse for the time — lacking the reflexive appeal of visual biophilia.

Besides, politically, the "green" aesthetics continued to provide the most effective vaccine against NIMBYism. The otherwise unpopular suburban sprawl could be re-packaged. Sprawl developers had long been adverse to New Urbanism, so the new alliance with Landscape Urbanists became a direct existential affront. Conventional development had been reduced by the thirty-year campaign of the New Urbanism — by government-administered protocols like the SmartCode and private ones associated with LEED-ND. But this kind of legalistic and technical progress was invisible to designers. The superb design associated with Landscape Urbanism managed to (somewhat) refurbish the reputation of suburbia, a pattern that had not only been failing economically and environmentally, but *looked* as if it were. The social, economic, and environmental consequences of the old "unprecedented typologies" such as big-box retail were camouflaged by green roofs, plant-laden screens, and porous-pavement parking lots. Landscape Urbanists were so skillful that most failed to recognize they were protracting the car-dominated, sociofugal places that few outside the then-ascendant Tea Party/Agenda 21 alliance could continue to condone.

Landscape Urbanism settled into arranging buildings that were urban in their statistical density, but not in their performance: "an expansive form of urbanism," disaggregated, not only to accommodate the automobile but also to become "integrated with nature and agriculture," dispersed under a "sustainable energy grid".[20]

And there was a further bonus for the architects: the elusive phenomenon of making modernism widely marketable. Landscape Urbanism had delivered at long last a connection to the *populus*. As any Visual Preference Study[21] will show, human biophilia is such that an image of anything with leaves will tilt the selection in its favor. Americans accepted "green" modernism from the same stimulus that had enamored them to the original suburbia embedded in landscape. For managing acceptance by the middle class, as much as the ecological benefits claimed by its rhetoric, was the reason Landscape Urbanism first gained disciplinary preeminence *outside* the academy.

That other great constituency, the regulators of a scientific persuasion, principally at the U.S. Department of Environmental Protection, did not at first discern that the biophilic visuals of native plants, enhanced topography, and ground plane permeability had scant measurable effect on performance. They had been thoroughly seduced by the practice to re-present the metrics of their studies in gorgeous graphic formats, displayed as totems justifying the actions of the designers. Landscape Urbanists evolved a brilliant escalation in the representational quality of scientific analysis. The once-lugubrious environmental reports were aestheticized. Analytical drones had been promoted to protagonists, while the New Urbanists had done no more than follow their rules.

The Landscape Urbanists thus succeeded for a time in avoiding scientific verification. When the effective environmental performance was eventually revealed, the benefits proved to be paltry, and — because of the extremely high cost of producing natural effects where they did not naturally occur — counterproductive. Vignetted nature was expensive to install and maintain.

This problem had been obscured for a time by the propensity to apply Landscape Urbanist technique only to civic space — which justified the higher investment. But with both the economic and environmental crises becoming truly serious, the counter-doctrine emerged that ecology was effective only where natural systems were preserved or restored in substantial areas — not as implants between buildings. Ecology as a science could not validate Landscape Urbanist theories and techniques.

While Landscape Urbanism made a bucolic contribution to civic space, it was ultimately incapable of delivering ordinary urban fabric. The claim that it was a comprehensive theory of urbanism was more than it could bear. The fundamental rhetoric of "process" failed because there were no means of coordinating the sequence of urbanization. The problem was technical and intrinsic: when an infrastructure of nature permeated between, above, below, and within, both private buildings and public spaces had to be designed and built simultaneously. There was no possibility of successional protocols. The coding that would have permitted the sequential generation of urbanism, by many, over time, belonged to the New Urbanism, and was therefore outside the Landscape Urbanists' discourse. The avowed aspiration to flux and indeterminacy was reduced to the prerogative of choosing sympathetic architects to design the grey voids between the landscaped areas on the plan. A planning method based on the designer's and patron's personality could not be sustained in the long-running timeline of urbanism, which exceeds the human and the political.

The conceptualized "quotations" of implanted nature gradually became a physical necessity. The puritanism of "native species" rather than the exotic hardy urban ones required that the "frame" become actual railings and planters to keep humans from trashing the landscape by walking on it. The landscape could be gazed upon, but that was all. An enormous amount of urban open space was thereby removed from its primary recreational purpose — at the very center of cities where it was most necessary. After the first sections of the High Line were completed, a prophylaxis of "temporary" fencing and signage became necessary. Subsequent sections had to include the "exotic" common lawns that could actually be used by humans in the original, Olmstedian function.

Another well-known failure came out of Portland, Oregon, with the juxtaposition of New Urbanist Jamison Square from the 1990s and the Landscape Urbanist Tranner Springs Park, one block away and a decade later. Jamison is usually packed with people of all ages, while Tanner is virtually devoid of humans whose feet and posteriors would crush the prairie grasses. In yet another square in Portland, the restoration of "woodland" resulted in objections — not so much to the outdoor sexual activity enabled by the mask of dense landscape, but to the residue that dogs would find when they were walked in the mornings. The New Urbanist Transect would have prevented such misfits of human nature and Nature.

Slowly, the reputation of Landscape Urbanism would have eroded exactly like the ethanol initiative, which arose concurrently — both driven by elegant intention rather than practical effect — had it not been subjected to the Rural-to-Urban Transect. This taxonomic engine absorbed Landscape Urbanism's techniques wherever they were contextually appropriate and effective. Not being ideologically proscribed, New Urbanists were able to assimilate Landscape Urbanism at the sub-urban end of the Transect. They refurbished those aspects of their own open space design where it had been weak. The Urban Center and Urban Core Transect Zones remained intact, as Landscape Urbanism had never really engaged either. The *rue corridor* survived after all.

New Urbanists absorbed the compelling polemical vocabulary as well. Using Lars Lerup's "areas of stimulation," or "stim," within the "unfortunate economic residues," or "dross,"[22] was more interesting than what New Urbanists had been calling "sprawl retrofit" and "districts."

But above all, Doug Farr's compendium, *Sustainable Urbanism*,[23] as an operational manual across the entire field, exposed that the hydrological concerns, in the end, were primarily a formalist design agenda.

The Landscape Urbanist episode within the New Urbanist discourse became important, as it shared the fate of other intelligent alternatives: assimilation. The effective techniques were absorbed as a matter of pragmatism. The result was a truly Ecological Urbanism that dealt with a greater range of constituencies, wielding a more extensive design repertoire, cultural as well as natural.

The perennial avant-garde at Harvard, as expected, moved on. The demands of the times do not necessarily coincide with the interests of the academies — nor should they, despite the difficult century that is still upon us.

Endnotes

1   Sert was president of the Congrès International d'Architecture Moderne (CIAM) from 1947 to 1956, and Dean of Harvard's Graduate School of Design from1953 to 1969. See Mumford, Eric. *Defining Urban Design CIAM Architects and the Formation of a Discipline* 1937-69, Yale 2009.

2   Krieger, Alex and William Saunders, Eds. 2010. *Urban Design.* University of Minnesota Press.

3   By evidence, as reported in, e.g., Bartholomew, K. and R. Ewing. 2009. Land Use-Transportation Scenario Planning: A Meta-Analysis. *Journal of the American Planning Association*, 75, 1: 13–27; Ewing, R., K. Bartholomew, et al. 2008. *Growing Cooler: The Evidence on Urban Development and Climate Change.* Washington, D.C.: Urban Land Institute, Washington.

4   See *The Charter of the New Urbanism*, Michael Leccese, Kathleen McCormick, Congress for the New Urbanism, Eds. 1999, McGraw-Hill.

5   Mumford, Lewis. 1956. The Natural History of Urbanization. In William L. Thomas, Ed., *Man's Role in Changing the Face of the Earth.* Chicago: University of Chicago Press. Pp. 382–400; Jacobs, Jane. 1961. *The Death and Life of Great American Cities.* New York: Vintage Books; Cronon, William. 1996. The Trouble with Wilderness; or, Getting Back to the Wrong Nature. In William Cronon, Ed., *Uncommon Ground.* New York: W.W. Norton & Company. Pps: 69–90.

6   Koolhaas, R. 1995. Whatever Happened to Urbanism? In *Design Quarterly* 164: 28-31.

7   Spirn, A. W. 1985. *The Granite Garden: Urban Nature and Human Design* (1st ed.). New York: Basic Books; Spirn, A.W. 2000. New Urbanism and the Environment. Places 13, 2: 2–79.

8   Corner, J. 2006. Terra Fluxus. In Charles Waldheim, Ed., *The Landscape Urbanism Reader.* New York: Princeton Architectural Press. Pp. 21-33; see also Wall, A. 1999. Programming the Urban Surface. In *On Landscape Urbanism.* Austin, TX: Center for American Architecture and Design University of Texas at Austin School of Architecture. Pp. 182–93. Mostafavi, M., Ed. 2010. *Ecological Urbanism.* Zurich: Lars Muller Publishers.

9   Waldheim, Charles. 2006. *The Landscape Urbanism Reader.*

10 Ibid.

11 Allen, Stan. 2009. Practice: *Architecture, Technique and Representation.* London: Routledge.

12 See *Urban Design* by Alex Krieger and William Saunders (2009, University of Minnesota Press). A passing dismissal of the New Urbanism is one of the few themes common among the 21 papers.

13 Sorkin, Michael. 2009. *Twenty Minutes in Manhattan.* New York: Reaktion Books.

14   See Mostafavi, Mohsen, and Gareth Doherty, Eds. *Ecological Urbanism*. Zurich: Lars Muller Publishers, p. 56.

15   Talen, Emily. "The Social Apathy of Landscape Urbanism". Duany, Andres and Talen, Emily, editors, *Landscape Urbanism and its Discontents*. 2013. Canada: New Society Publishers.

16   Corner, James. 1991. Landscape Architecture and Critical Inquiry. *Landscape Journal*, Fall, 10, 2: 155–170.

17   At a jury at SciArch, Duany mentioned the striking similarity between a student's social housing project and Pruitt-Igoe. The hapless student asked, "What is a Pruitt go?"

18   Duany, Andres. 2011. *Theory & Practice of Agrarian Urbanism*. London: The Prince's Foundation for the Built Environment.

19   Duany, Andres and Talen, Emily. *Landscape Urbanism and its Discontents*. 2013. Canada: New Society Publishers.

20   Crawford, Margaret. 2010. In Mostafavi, M. and G. Doherty, Eds. 2010. *Ecological Urbanism*. Zurich: Lars Muller Publishers, p. 143.

21   See Anton Tony Nelessen, anelessen.com/.

22   Lerup, L. 1994. Stim and Dross: Rethinking the Metropolis. In *On Landscape Urbanism*. Austin, TX: Center for American Architecture and Design University of Texas at Austin School of Architecture. Pp. 94–107.

23   Farr, Douglas. *Sustainable Urbanism: Urban Design With Nature*. 2008. New Jersey: John Wiley & Sons, Inc.

Transcript of a Debate ca. 2011

Edited by Sandy Sorlien and Bruce Donnelly

Andrés Duany

THE HIGH LINE IS THE LATEST OF THE SILVER BULLETS. In chronological order:

1. Civic Centers ("Burnham plans")
2. Urban Highways
3. Towers with Rotating Restaurants
4. Pedestrianized Main Streets
5. Convention Centers
6. Festival Market Places
7. Aquariums
8. Bilbaos
9. River Walks
10. High Lines

Assign a dateline and you will see the accelerating desperation of an *architectural* profession that does not have a clue about urbanism. It will do anything but the hard work of reconstituting the socially based urban fabric.

Dan Solomon

Andrés, your metaphor is gloriously mixed. It is you who have the Brace Beemer part in the remake: *From out of the days of yesteryear, thundering hooves and a hearty cry....*

Only instead of careful aim with a pair of six shooters, you have an AK-47 spraying everything in sight, including innocent High Line, whose beauty lies in the experience it provides of "socially-based urban fabric".

Michael Mehaffy

Let's think about cost. There are plenty of reasons to worry about the maintenance costs of little slivers of nature, which have a notorious reputation already: green roofs that die without very careful maintenance, small samples of ecosystems that don't have the sufficient scale of "real" ecosystems to sustain and regenerate them (like "Biosphere II"), etc. Permaculturists have been "doing nature" for a long time, and even they have varying success. They have a cardinal rule: "Go with what nature already wants to do." I think Landscape Urbanism essentially inverts that.

Paul Crabtree

Witold Rybczynski reported that the first two phases (about one mile) of the High Line cost $152 million. That's about $30,000 per lineal foot.

Andrés Duany

Paul, for comparison, what is the price of a first rate urban street 32 feet wide, including sidewalks, granite cobbles, light and drainage, London plane trees, 30 ft. on center. And so on?

Paul Crabtree

$700 per lineal foot. That's based on recent East Coast contractor estimates. Green art is expensive. The ratio ($30,000:$700) is around 40:1.

San Francisco did an answer to the High Line that was much less expensive. The 1700 block of Newcomb Avenue between Phelps and Newhall Streets is a streetscape retrofit that has atypical costs including undergrounding of utilities, chicanes, the removal of existing sidewalks and paving, and a program to help residents upgrade their building facades. Its questionable costs and designs include gold-plated "Low Impact Development" stormwater structures, the chicanes, and its excessive removal of existing paving in good condition. Still, Newcomb's costs are $2,500 per lineal foot while the High Line cost $30,000 per lineal foot. That's twelve blocks of street retrofit for every one block of High Line retrofit. I would argue that an even more frugal, *original green*,[1] streetscape retrofit would achieve better results at a third of the cost of Newcomb.

Dao Doan

Paul, I appreciate the fact that cost is a serious consideration in achieving the most sustainable solutions for the least cost. However it's not quite fair to compare what San Francisco did with the High Line. New York's project is in a much denser area with scarce available land for on-the-ground parks, while the rail line is already there. It offered a creative solution for open space. Retrofitting streets like the one in San Francisco is not a one-size-fits-all formula either. Each has to be calibrated for its context. Not only that, but the per capita cost for the High Line may end up being lower if you take into account how many use it and benefit from it. It attracts thousands of tourists and dollars to the neighborhood — and that's not counting the regular locals. I doubt the San Francisco street would bring tourists in, although the benefit to locals is great. Also the area around the High Line has been revitalized since it was completed.

The High Line is not just a retrofit green project, I think it is an excellent exercise in urban place-making.

Doug Kelbaugh

I had the opportunity to walk the High Line for the first time this past, rainy, weekend. It's a delightful reprieve from the hustle and bustle of the street, although I hear it can be crowded in good weather. I don't see it as a particularly replicable idea. It's very expensive, like many things in Manhattan, and the setting is extraordinary. It would be just a raised linear platform in less dramatically dense settings. Nonetheless it's a well-designed and landscaped promenade.

Aaron Parker

You say the High Line is not replicable. What *is* replicable is people of vision finding sublime or even ordinary unused, underutilized or abandoned physical resources in areas of every single city in this nation, and then to leverage generations of previous investment. This means integrating them through thoughtful design and execution, into the neighborhood and the city to the social, economic, and physical benefit of its citizenry. Making them beautiful is not something I should have to argue on this list, is it?

Philip Langdon

I wrote a blog this week about Witold's *NY Times* op-ed piece on the High Line and about my skepticism about public spaces above the streets.

Nicolai Ouroussoff interviewed Liz Diller of Diller Scofidio & Renfro about their High Line project at a seminar for journalists held at the Lincoln Institute of Land Policy in April. Ouroussoff was concerned about architecture as a "generator of gentrification," or words to that effect. He said there has been a deliberate effort to prevent cafes from opening onto the High Line and to prevent gyms from facing it. Diller said the idea of bringing bookstores and other enterprises [up to its] level was rejected. She said the High Line is "about the backs of things, the toughness." It is "not a promenade."

But what is the High Line if not a contemporary promenade?

What I took away from the discussion is that the designers and Ouroussoff have a deathly fear of letting the High Line become bourgeois. They seem almost desperate to prevent it from developing into a mainstream retail and entertainment zone. But isn't it almost impossible in this country to prevent the middle class — and businesses that cater to them — from becoming a big part of any urban setting that attracts lots of people?

The designers and Ouroussoff want to preserve an atmosphere that's evanescent, even though the economic energy that the High Line has unleashed is ultimately unstoppable. That is, unless its removal from street level makes it prey to crime.

Sandy Sorlien

Then Ouroussoff would love the Race Street Pier, Corner's answer for Philadelphia. It sticks out into the water so no buildings could possibly open onto it.

Actually, I agree with both Doug and Ouroussoff about the High Line, and am glad the Pier will not have shops. The High Line was a bracing outdoor experience on a cold winter day when only a few people were on it. I liked that you could still tell it was once a railway behind the back of buildings, dead grasses and all. I would hate it with crowds and flowers. I am not anti middle class; rather, I'm pro industrial heritage. Which explains why I liked the High Line better through Joel Sternfeld's photographs[2] before the Landscape Urbanism got hold of it. It would have been a lot cheaper if they'd just cleaned it up a bit and let people walk along the tracks, and the view would have been the same.

That said, the High Line is more than just a spectacular view. It's another way to experience urban space. There was an effort made to support a series of "prospect and refuge" environments, whether they existed already or were created.

Elizabeth Dowdle

Setting up false dichotomies does not serve our New Urbanist movement: Streets vs. Linear Park. Cities vs. Nature. New Urbanism vs. Parks. New Urbanism vs. Nature. On the contrary, New Urbanism helps achieve conservation of nature and parks.

Sandy Sorlien

Right, attack the general problem of park-making vs. place-making and the people who teach park-making as an ecological solution to development patterns. Don't attack the High Line itself. That's because the High Line is, in fact, place-making.

Karja Hansen

I too love the High Line. I have been frustrated seeing it attacked and picked apart, but I still think it is important to analyze its cost and benefits. We understand that it works only in context, and that it is supportable only there. It also provides an incredibly graspable concept (both in content and in topic) to discuss the ability to finance and build good streets. It is a lightning rod. The best analyses and comparisons [would] show how expensive overly wide streets that 'serve' sprawling development are compared to the cost of what we know to be good, but it is hard to get a wider basis of people to pick up on that.

Paul Crabtree

Mine is a pragmatic comparison of differing scenarios. It is not that New Urbanism is anti-park; that's *reductio ad absurdum*. I'm just pointing out that you could convert 40 miles of bad streets to very good (and green) public realm for every mile of High Line. That's 10 complete neighbor-hoods, about 1200 acres of urban fabric. An investment of that magnitude in green streets would reduce the combined sewer overflows by several billions of gallons. (NYC CSOs average 27 billion gallons per year).

Steve Coyle

Give the High Line a break. The cost-to-benefit ratio for a well-loved stretch of functional art should not be compared with street improvements — even complete streets in a city that spends around 2.4B/mile for a subway extension. The High Line physically and emotionally elevates walking to a sublime experience. It is not meant to compete with streets — complete or incomplete.

Bruce Donnelly

But Steve, a cost-benefit analysis comparing other rails-to-trails projects would certainly be appropriate. I'm *not* saying it isn't successful as an experience. I like it. I'm just saying that in a city that's shutting down amenities in the outer boroughs it's *absolutely* appropriate to check the costs.

Andrés Duany

Actually, the real trick is to achieve the satisfactions of the High Line and the increase in real estate value without the hideous expenditure. Some of us know how to do that. And, by the way, Manhattan doesn't need another spike in real estate value, does it?

Daniel Solomon

Andrés, et al., amongst the many brilliant altogether laudable aspects of High Line was the way in which the fundraising galvanized such a major investment in public place-making and the way in which its endowment provides first-rate maintenance. Taking shots at such a masterpiece is simply foolish, as is claiming that "we" know how to achieve its quality of material, detailing, horticulture, etc. on the cheap. There are times when the right and gracious thing to say is — BRAVO.

Andrés Duany

Dan, is the High Line worth the infrastructure of 10 neighborhoods? Did Manhattan need it? It is the usual designer self-indulgence, except horizontal this time. It is so twentieth century! I would have called for a version at $5,000 / LF. It might have worked even better: more sittable grass, less prissy rusticated landscaping, hundreds of Adirondack chairs, and fewer of those emasculating benchoids. Think about it, you terminal vanguardista. Pity the people.

As an alternative to the star-eyed pandering recommended to me by some, why don't we run a real critique: a Peter Singer-type ethical analysis based on alternative scenarios:

1. What would be the effect of the investment if a "high line" had been located in, say, a) Queens b) Rochester?
2. What would be the effect of a similar investment if applied to another type of infrastructure, in Manhattan, or elsewhere in New York City?
3. What would be the effect of the High Line if it had been designed differently — by, let us say, an "everyday urbanist" or Partners for Livable Communities?

Let us show how a real critique is run.

Ellen Dunham-Jones

I'm all for a rigorous critique. However, [there's] a significant problem with comparing alternative uses for funding like this — and it gets at the heart of Landscape Urbanism's funding — is that patron-based funding is far less likely to be interested in low-profile projects. For example, while it's hard to raise money for new campus buildings, it's *much* harder to raise funds for renovating existing buildings, even if the total cost is *much* less and the impact arguably greater. Starchitect projects with high visibility, let alone lots of "green," give donors more visibility and cachet.

It seems to me that a rigorous critique would:

1. Separate the public and private sources of money and make comparisons only on that basis,
2. Compare the economic development impact of each public dollar invested (i.e., property value increases on adjacent properties, amount of private sector money invested on adjacent properties, the environmental performance, etc.), and,
3. Get creative and formulate a serious alternative means of attracting patron funding to more "everyday" street improvements.

Michael Mehaffy

The definition of "design" must be broadened to mean seeking to transform the conditions too: not taking them as immutable reality. (As I see it, this is a chief aspiration of New Urbanism — in contrast to the artistic/magical approach of so much "architectural culture.") That means taking on the conditions that lead to the wrong kinds of projects getting funded. We design incentives and disincentives too. That follows Herbert Simon's great definition of design, that it's "the transformation from existing states to preferred ones."

Ellen Dunham-Jones

Yes, that's a *great* definition.

I lived one block from the High Line in the '80s (on 17th between 8th and 9th avenues, when the drug dealers were the primary source of protection). I do think one has to grant it credit for assisting the neighborhood's significant transformation/gentrification. The "porthole" building on my block went from being a single room occupancy building for destitute merchant marines to an ultra-expensive hotel. The entire "meat market" district at the lower end of the High Line was already going upscale in the '90s, because Chelsea was rapidly becoming the chic arts district. The High Line certainly didn't cause these changes, but it helped spread them west.

Michael Mehaffy

What do you think of the argument that things have gone too far in the other direction, i.e., gentrified? I have been thinking of this because I have been using Jacobs' *The Death and Life of Great American Cities* in my classes. She did *not* (contrary to Campanella's recent suggestion) ignore gentrification. See, e.g., Chapter 13, "The self-destruction of diversity," which is all about gentrification, or as she described it, a runaway form of growth that is initially beneficial in promoting diversity and "unslumming," but that beyond a certain point fails to respond to feedback forces. It becomes destructive. Her prescription was to clone the positive conditions in other locations, and draw healthy growth away to other areas, where it is likely very much needed. In a sense, it's a supply-and-demand argument.

So in that light, isn't the High Line adding to this unhelpful feedback phenomenon at this point — one that is making Manhattan a kind of overgrown gated community?

Andrés Duany

Landscape Urbanism may yet contribute to the urban planning of the 21st Century. But the application of metaphorical rather than operational environmental systems salves nature not nearly as much as it serves to sucker environmentalists into believing that something effective is being accomplished — and paying for the extravaganza.

Visual biophilia is cynically deployed as camouflage for what is actually the prolongation of some rather tired *avant-garde* tropes. This is not a cost-effective response to the coming age of austerity.

Michael Mehaffy

Great. Let us detail the "rather tired avant-garde tropes." Once again, Jacobs pretty well gave the best exposition fifty years ago:

1. "Open plan urbanism" (an oxymoron), which she called "project land oozes." In contrast, we argue for a street-based public-realm, figure-ground urbanism, and a functional syntax.
2. Following from this, the utter failure to understand the syntax of public to private space — and the need for users to be able to modulate that transition in order to manage their interactions and their quality of life.
3. The confusion of visual order with intrinsic order. If it looks ordered, it is ordered. If it looks green, it is green.
4. The confusion of the city with a work of art. The city *contains* works of art, which at their best will clarify and elucidate its meanings, and the intensity of life.

> "Project land oozes"
> American cities today, under the illusion that open land is an automatic good and that quantity is equivalent to quality, are instead frittering away money on parks, playgrounds and project land-oozes too large, too frequent, too perfunctory, too ill-located, and hence too dull or too inconvenient to be used.
> — Jane Jacobs, from *The Death and Life of Great American Cities*,
> 1961, page 110

Now, one more item can be added to the list above: the rejection of all visually recognizable precedent, in favor of novel aesthetic experiences. From an evolutionary standpoint, it's reverse-Darwinism, rejecting what has worked in favor of what has never been seen — what has never been tried. Again, it's the confusion between art and life. And as Jacobs also noted, it's inconsistent with modern complexity science, evolutionary problem-solving, and collective intelligence. Let me also suggest that it's ultimately inconsistent with ecological human settlement.

But why does the cultural project have to be inconsistent with pattern and precedent? Who says we can't work with fugues, recapitulations, genetic DNA, syntheses? Where did we get the idea for this inconsistency? It is the modernist canard that is still lingering in many forms (and to be fair, Landscape Urbanism is far from alone). Talk about being mired in the past!

I thought what [Charles] Waldheim said at CNU 19 was very constructive, whether or not he intended it as such. He got down to brass tacks about the fundamental point of disagreement: urbanism as a series of public spaces framed by buildings. He thinks this is dispensable. I think without it you don't have urbanism, but those "project land oozes."

He conceded three points of agreement, and one point of disagreement. The three were:

1. The fundamental concept of the neighborhood.
2. The fundamental concept of walkability.
3. Networks of thoroughfares, not a "dendritic" hierarchical system.

So far so good, but there is the area of disagreement:

4. Public spaces framed by buildings.

This goes to [Waldheim's] notion that we can be ecological *and* have "architectural culture" (e.g., be avant-garde) too. We *really* need to understand this point, or else we talk past them.

Waldheim said he parts company with us over the idea that the thoroughfare generates a street wall, and this becomes the fundamental generator of urban form. He thinks an "open plan urbanism" is hunky-dory.

However, we frame urban rooms as public space using tune-able street walls to enclose space. That's how to create a coherent, functional public realm that integrates architecture with urbanism. It is essential to the syntax of public and private realms, as well as their complex network of connections and their modulations.

What about ecology? If Landscape Urbanists mean cleaner water run-off, lower pollutants, and so on, then we agree. Only don't forget that the biggest issue of ecology is how humans live.

Andrés Duany

Michael, the Landscape Urbanists do not think of space. They think of surface, thickened: a functional plane, not a spatial one.

James Howard Kunstler

Michael, they're not serious about ecology. It's just an excuse to shove dirt around and execute costly commissions, with overtones of art and fashion. Y'all take it way more seriously than they really do.

Doug Kelbaugh

Michael's is a very helpful summary of Landscape Urbanism. Pretty much everyone, including most *avant-garde* designers, embrace mixed-use, walkable urbanism, as well as transit. (It's hard to be against these things or their underlying logic.) What they *don't* agree about is the street, especially the room-like plaza or street wall of buildings, which is bedrock to New Urbanism. It's always amazed me that designers who have been to (or live in) European cities, prefer the open plan and super-bock/podium urbanism. My first European trips were permanent game changers for me.

Emily Talen

Doug, I think you are missing what to me is the fundamental difference: As are most movements in the design academy, Landscape Urbanism is allergic to ascribing social purpose to design. They hide behind a fear of determinism, but what they really fear are constraints on design parameters.

Interest in the street as a public room is about prioritizing social diversity.

Doug Kelbaugh

Emily, yes, the street is about social diversity, but it's also a key spatial device. Streets, plazas and squares, etc. with well-defined street walls and comfortable cross-sections are a sine qua non of good urbanism. There are streets and public spaces in Los Angeles that are spatially loose, dismal, and inhumanly scaled, but that are socially diverse. Likewise, some inhumanly wide, empty and bleak streets and squares in Beijing are more crowded and socially diverse.

Hadid, Eisenman, Koolhaas, et al., don't acknowledge the timeless *spatial* value of the traditional street. Hence, I commented that the street remains the big and critical difference between New Urbanism and Landscape Urbanism and other modernist/avant-gardists. They are dead wrong on this design conceit, as all of us agree. It's a non-negotiable, watershed issue and one worth defending to the end.

Ann Daigle

Landscape architecture has historically used many of the principles we use in urban design: primarily that landscape is best understood as a series of spatially framed outdoor rooms. Each has a perceived volume and with specific sensory qualities, connected in diverse ways to generate a progression of delight. The profession of landscape architecture has always focused on human interaction with the natural world, yet this seems to be disappearing in the Landscape Urbanists' reverence for fish territory.

What I notice is that many LU projects ignore these landscape architecture principles altogether.

Michael Mehaffy

It seems to me we're really getting somewhere. Emily, yes, the rationales to write oneself an artistic blank check abound (determinism, reactionary politics, foundationalism, etc.).

Doug, teaching Jacobs again, I am impressed by how she links the urban room to "intricate pools of city cross-use" and thence to social diversity (and thence to "unslumming", etc.). It's all connected. The urban rooms are all about establishing connections. All this is of course tied empirically to what is working and what is not working, as she has observed it. Within that empirical and evidence-based framework, art has an honored place.

Imagine if we could re-establish a Venturi-like relation of art to background buildings — better and more urban this time — and thereby reestablish a leadership role for a new avant-garde. Could it be fully engaged in promoting a healthier and more ecological urbanism?

What if New Urbanists could reclaim the avant-garde for this more genuinely urban agenda? That would require us to step up and do much more adventurous work, while at the same time, confining ourselves within a much more coherent discipline of social and ecological problem-solving than the avant-garde does now. I think this is entirely possible. It would be a new cycle, revisiting the previous period of around 1975–80, which missed the mark. We've learned a lot, and maybe the time has come (will soon come) again?

Doug Kelbaugh

Rereading *Collage City*, per Dan Solomon's suggestion, I'd forgotten about cities and buildings as Theaters of Prophecy and Theaters of Memory, suggesting we live simultaneously in the past and in the future. We do need an avant-garde/vanguard to explore, experiment, and test new ideas. The problem is that the Ivy League avant-gardists, including the Landscape Urbanists, are more interested in preserving their status and increasing their hegemony than in the unglamorous search for hard new truths and practices: cutting edge organic farming in Vermont, making art out of trash, rightsizing Detroit, bike sharing in Portland, tactical urbanism, etc. In the end, other than fractal weaving, folded planes and hefty hydrology, there's not that much *avant-garde* about Landscape Urbanism.

Michael Dennis

"He's all hat and no cattle." (Cowboy wisdom regarding pretenders.) "They're all landscape and no urbanism."

I have not seen, or heard of, any urbanism from so-called Landscape Urbanists. Nor have I read, or heard, any urban principles from them. I have seen some (occasionally) good urban landscape designs, but mostly they are on the edge of urban contexts — waterfronts, etc. But many are completely rural, like Freshkills.

Civic space — the defined space of streets, squares, etc. — is the medium of urbanism, and this requires a certain density (an FAR of 1-2 minimum). They seem completely unaware of this.

Sandy Sorlien

Landscape Urbanists attack Seaside because they perceive that it threatens what they do and they don't recognize its value to civilization. Do the High Line and projects like it (i.e., in urban places) threaten what New Urbanists do? I don't think so. It is civic space no less than what we all love: Central Park or Rittenhouse Square or the San Antonio Riverwalk. It's just a different kind of civic space. Instead of criticizing the High Line for cost, let's assimilate it!

Bruce Donnelly

How about this?

1. In the most skilled hands, Landscape Urbanism can provide an excellent occasional experience.
2. Landscape Urbanism's parks are too often expensive, poorly integrated into the daily life of the city, and wear ecology a little too much on their sleeves.
3. New Urbanism can offer Landscape Urbanism tools to control costs.
4. New Urbanism can offer Landscape Urbanism tools to knit its parks better into surrounding urbanism so they're not such occasional destinations.
5. New Urbanism can offer Landscape Urbanism tools to smooth its ecological performance into livable places.
6. Finally, New Urbanism can thus offer Landscape Urbanism the tools it needs to succeed in a time of limited budgets and concern for liability.

James Howard Kunstler

What's missing from this Landscape Urbanism / High Line chat is a recognition of how Landscape Urbanism grows out of Olmsted-ism — America's first instance of bringing big chunks of "nature" into the heart of the city to mitigate the "illness" of industrial urbanism. In the case of Landscape Urbanism, it has a techno-narcissistic overlay.

Olmsted was great, of course — though his big parks and greenways are such a specific product of a certain time and place — and the fear inspired by the hypertrophic urban growth. Inasmuch as he was creating artificial landscape vignettes of the very landscapes being destroyed by massive urbanization, the character of places like Central Park attempted to mimic the apparent randomness of "nature." Olmsted's work had literary overtones in its evocation of familiar storybook settings. Landscape Urbanism's work has literary overtones in all the competitive pretentious critical horseshit emanating from the need of graduate students to perpetually come up with new theses (that will outdo others in novelty).

The remnants of Olmsted are visible in things like Corner's Hudson Yards master plan—an uninteresting pseudo-forest at the base of half a dozen glass shards. As far as I can tell, the Toronto Lake Ontario Park amounts to little more than an overbuilt boat launch attached to a remnant of restored forest / wetland — the main purpose of which is to demonstrate our moral goodness — kind of an earnest apology for having built Toronto.

Endnotes

1. Mouzon, Steve. 2011. Original Green: Common-Sense, Plain-Spoken Sustainability. Retrieved February 29, 2012, from originalgreen.org/.
2. Sternfeld, Joel. 2001. Joel Sternfeld. Retrieved February 29, 2012, from High Line: thehighline.org/galleries/images/joel-sternfeld.

Additional Works Cited

Appelbaum, A. 2011. The Opinion Pages: New York's Green Grid. Retrieved from *The New York Times:* nytimes.com/2011/04/17/opinion/17Appelbaum.html

Congress for the New Urbanism. 2011. Closing Plenary: Charles Waldheim and Andres Duany Discuss Landscape Urbanism. Retrieved from CNU: cnu.org/19/webcast/1.

Friends of the High Line. 2008. New York City Department of Parks & Recreation. *The High Line Design Video.* Retrieved from High Line: thehighline.org/design/high-line-design.

Jacobs, J. 1961. *The Death and Life of Great American Cities.* New York: Random House.

Jose, T. 2010. Playgrounds for Plutocrats: Who pays for Parks? Retrieved from Capital: capitalnewyork.com/article/politics/2010/12/1015139/playgrounds-plutocrats-who-pays-parks.

Langdon, P. and A. Bruce. 2011. Eight HOPE VI Projects Get $153 million from HUD. Retrieved from *Better! Cities and Towns:* bettercities.net/article/eight-hope-vi-projects-get-153-million-hud-14766.

Next Generation of New Urbanists. 2012. The Next Generation of New Urbanists. Retrieved February 29, 2012, from Nextgen: cnunextgen.org/.

Piepenburg, E. 2012. Arts: Under the High Line, a Gay Past. Retrieved from *The New York Times*: artsbeat.blogs.nytimes.com/2012/02/03/under-the-high-line-a-gay-past/.

Syrkett, A. 2011. In NYC, A Grand Opening for High Line Phase II. Retrieved from Architectural Record: archrecord.construction.com/news/2011/06/110607-High-Line.asp.

An Album of Images

Andrés Duany

Fig.c-1: *Charleston, SC, under the two theories. Left: The actual urbanism of Charleston, with the urban network trumping the natural, thereby achieving the highest density: New Urbanist model. Right: Charleston according to Landscape Urbanism, with the natural network cauterizing the urban network. The population density would be reduced by three quarters — presumably sprawling in Landscape Urbanism elsewhere.* SOURCE: DPZ

Fig. c-2: *Among the opening acts of Landscape Urbanism was Ann Whiston Spirn's The Granite Garden, of 1984. Despite her professorial presence at Penn and Cambridge—the early and later incubators of Landscape Urbanism —she is not now acknowledged by the younger generation as a predecessor. Her contemporaries, the New Urbanists, ignored her propositions based on a perception of anti-urbanism, a claim they later retracted.*
SOURCE: ANNE WHISTON SPIRN

Fig. c-3: *Villa Lante and Bagnaia: The gardens of the Villa Lante are a clear expression of Peterson's idea of the garden as mediator between sacred nature and profane urbanism.*

Source: Google Earth

Fig. c-4: *Chungcheongnam-do Province, South Korea, is a late example of Landscape Urbanist programming as a surrogate for successional protocols such as codes. The little graphic symbols describing activity to be expected are animistic tropes reminisent of cave paintings — when drawing an antelope would assure the morrow's hunt.*

Source: SWA Landscape Infrastructure

Fig. c-5: *Justified Landscape Urbanism. A girls school in Malawi by Markus Dochantschi.*
SOURCE: STUDIOMDA

Fig. c-6: *The raingarden of the Sidwell Friends School in Washington, DC. The urban school could have better used its courtyard as playground rather than as an inaccessible demonstration of technically-assisted natural drainage. (Demolished and replaced by a playing field ca. 2022.)*
SOURCE: KIERAN TIMBERLAKE ASSOCIATES

Fig. c-7: *Mission Bay, San Francisco. A brownfield retrofitted with coastal landscape. Pedestrians remain on the walkways to avoid damaging the grasses (note the children gazing rather than playing). The perennial problem with native planting was that the humans must be contained. But human activity on turf was not originally, conceptually, within the Landscape Urbanist discourse, although it eventually imposed itself in the later stages of the High Line and the New Urbanist Hybrids.* SOURCE: URBANLAND, SEPT 2009

Fig. c-8 : *Freshkills Landill Remediation, Staten Island, NY. This was the appropriate application of highly skillful Landscape Urbanist technique, though it was not known whether a large park unsupported by enfronting buildings could encourage human activity and whether it could ever be made safe enough. This could not be verified as the project was not completed for lack of funds.* SOURCE: JAMES CORNER FIELDS OPERATIONS

Fig. c.-9: *With captivating graphics, never had environmental analysis been so privileged by design attention. Mutual support was thus established between environmental consultants and Landscape Urbanists.* SOURCE: SWA, LANDSCAPE INFRASTRUCTURE

Fig. c-10: *Milton Street Park, Los Angeles, CA. As many photoshopped humans as trees provided superb propaganda. Nature could be induced with sufficient skill and budget, but not the presence of actual humans — their behavior patterns being even less compliant to Landsape Urbanist theory than nature herself.*

SOURCE: SWA, LANDSCAPE INFRASTRUCTURE

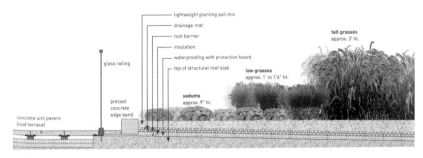

Fig. c-11: *Landscape Urbanist presentations were incomparably superior to New Urbanist ones. Compare with those of the following page.*

SOURCE: SASAKI & ASSOCIATES, INTERSECTION & CONVERGENCE

Fig. c-12: *The Achilles Heel of New Urbanism was not the effective and cost-effective technology, but the mundane graphics and design. Shown: three options for handling rainwater in Transect-based contexts: T5, T4, and T3. Three contextually calibrated deployments of pervious paving, gutters leading to "rainways" providing bio retention, and planting strips. At their best, the performance of such green streets could result in no further requirement for rainwater management outside of the public infrastructure (and maintenance) strata. There would be no requirement for private property to contribute to the mitigation. Private building configurations could retain urban discipline as a consequence, contributing to walkability and reducing VMT. New Urbanists had developed similar design techniques for dealing with hydrology, but Landscape Urbanists had superior techniques of representation.*
SOURCE: CRABTREE GROUP, AND DREILING TERRONES ARCHITECTURE

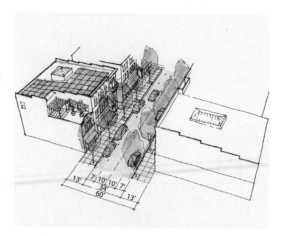

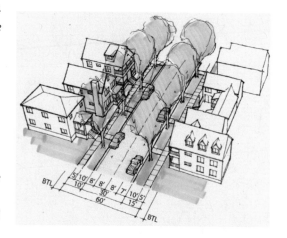

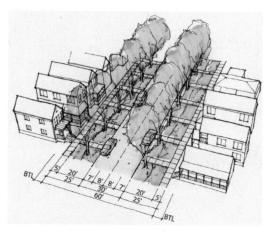

Four tropes for dealing with the implantation of "nature," careful to differentiate itself from Olmstedian precedent.

Fig. c-13: *The National Aquarium, Baltimore, MD. Failing ecological justification, the design of pavement pattern became the surrogate for the flow of nature. Within the critical discourse of Landscape Urbanism, metaphor and mere intention — verbal and visual — enjoyed a very high credibility quotient.* SOURCE: RHODESIDE & HARWELL, LANDSCAPE ARCHITECTURE, AUG 2009

Fig. c-14: *Planting in geometric layouts (the plant nursery).* SOURCE: PAGE SOUTHERLAND PAGE LLP,

Fig. c-15: *Naturalistic landscaping in "quotation marks" by the literal framing of planters.* SOURCE: SASAKI & ASSOCIATES, INTERSECTION & CONVERGENCE

Fig. c-16: *Pathways and mounding that is not consistent with erosion by wind or water, nor with human trajectory.* SOURCE: JAMES CORNER FIELDS OPERATIONS

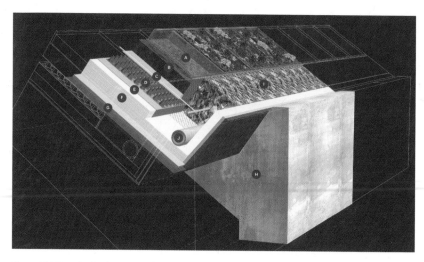

Fig. c-17: *Detail of a Green Roof System. Superb graphics polemicized what was usually mundane technical know-how. The high building cost of such installations was the consequence of the audacious technology necessary to induce plants to grow where they do not naturally do so. Maintenance is not factored into the equation. Belief systems were not then subject to standards of cost-effectiveness.* SOURCE: SWA, LANDSCAPE INFRASTRUCTURE

Fig. c-18: *A typical advertisement for building screens growing plants. The unpopularity of the modernist aesthetics was finally overcome by means presented as ecologically mandated visual biophilia. It was a brilliant strategic/technical solution of lasting value for the evolution of architecture.* SOURCE: ARCHITECTURAL RECORD, NOV 2009

Fig. c-19: *Hongxin Community, Dalian, China, 2009, by Sasaki. The buildings flow in the streamform valley ecology that they replaced. The mythopoetics of Landscape Urbanism are literal, hence its popular success. Compelling graphics and superb design skill support the narrative. As always, humans, fascinated by the plantings, are photoshopped on to walkways and roofs.* SOURCE: SASAKI & ASSOCIATES, INTERSECTION & CONVERGENCE

Fig. c-20: *This housing is for one of the "Carbon-Challenge" towns of Great Britain. Solar-oriented housing is strewn amongst naturalistic landscaping — at low suburban densities. Note the hapless photoshopped pedestrians communing with the brush.* SOURCE: ZED FACTORY, URBANLAND JUNE 2008

Fig. c-21: *Camouflage for an intrinsically unecological development. This one is an office park on an arterial road. One of the more valued roles of Landscape Urbanism is diguising auto-dependent suburban typologies for public acceptance. The design is superb, but the ecological consequences are indistinguishable from those of conventional sprawl.*
SOURCE: URBAN SPACES NO. 6

Fig. c-22: *Civic Center Park, Seoul, South Korea. The artificiality of the walks and mounds is designed to differentiate from the nature replicants of Frederick Law Olmsted. The walkways — always as long radius curves, like rivers or highways — are not determined by the human ability to maneuver, but to acheive syntactic distance from the romantic landscapes of the prior generation, which were too sucessful to grant adequate space to the subsequent avant-garde. In Seoul,*

freestanding, sculpted towers with few streets supply the density without the urbanism. Landscape Urbanist designs were usually accomplished works of landscape architecture but fell short of being a comprehensive urban theory. SOURCE: JAMES CORNER FIELDS OPERATIONS

Fig. c-23: *Diana Balmori, Sejong, South Korea. This was an accomplished example of the refusal of a primary ground plane. The "mat" is one of the more interesting tropes of Landscape Urbanism, especially as promoted by Stan Allen: the roof, the ground, and the semi-basement of buildings were considered interchangeable as planes of movement, like the natural topography that prior Landscape Architects conventionally worked with. This project revealed one of the flaws intrinsic to Landscape Urbanism: as the infrastructure and the building structures could not be disentangled, the entire "urbanism" had to be designed and built in one campaign. Thus, despite claims of "process," Landscape Urbanism was unable to deploy the successional protocols and the subsidiary decision-making that is the essence of urbanism — no less than scale and complexity.*
SOURCE: DIANA BALMORI, A LANDSCAPE MANIFESTO

Fig. c-24: *Sculpture Park, Seattle. This early icon of Landscape Urbanism was a hybrid project combining public art, a cafe and artificial topography, assembled for the purpose of overcrossing a highway. The high cost of such projects was long obscured*

by the enormous budgets of the underlying highway infrastructure. The Sculpture Park was usually depopulated, except when attendance was induced by a festival. Note the straight line geometries: not to be confused with the Olmstedianism of New Urbanism. SOURCE: WEISS/MANFREDI, THE ARCHITECTURAL REVIEW, FEB 2008

Fig. c-25: *The New Town of Sénart, France by OMA/Rem Koolhaas was a lightly acknowledged precedent to Landscape Urbanism. The diagrams illustrate what Koolhaas refers to as the "irrigation of possibilities" — the loosely parametric, sequential process that the Landscape Urbanism aspired to, but for which there were no protocols, having eschewed codes, which were associated with New Urbanism.*
SOURCE: OMA

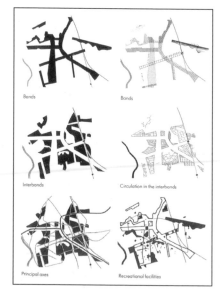

Bands   Bands

Interbands   Circulation in the interbands

Principal axes   Recreational facilities

Fig. c-26: *In the winning competition for Liberty Island by James Corner, the landscape is designed. But on the grey areas, the then-current method of subsidiarity was the selection of sympathetic architects for the buildings. This elite protocol constrained Landscape Urbanism to competitions and high-profile civic work, as it was unable to permeate the operating system of the 27,000 planning departments that — through codes — administered development in the United States. This protocol could not be responsive to Gideon's modernist definition of the "problem of large numbers."*
SOURCE: JAMES CORNER FIELDS OPERATIONS

Fig. c-27: *Premier City, Almaty, Kazakhstan. While kitsch is difficult to achieve by means of natural plant material, it could be done. This version entailed green on the ground, the walls, the roof, and the indoors. Reduction was the fate of most design ideas exposed to modern culture. Landscape Urbanism was unusual in having been for a time resistant to this phenomenon. But the process was accelerated by contact with the wealth and insecurities of Asia.* SOURCE: KEN YEANG, ECOMASTERPLANNING

Fig. c-28: *San Francisco Trans-bay Transit Center. Projects like these predicted the course of decay for Landscape Urbanism: Nature becomes kitsch...at enormous expense.* SOURCE: URBANLAND, SEPT 2009.

Fig. c-29: *Lewis Avenue Corridor, Las Vegas, NV, was a typical retrofitting of a street with porous landscape, at substantial cost. Instead of re-using the existing pipes, there was the "daylighting" of streams where they previously did not run. Nature and the ground plane were the protagonists; buildings and spatial definition were incidental. This toolbox was exactly the opposite of New Urbanism's. It was possible to reconcile them at sub-urban Transect Zones, but not at the urban cores.* SOURCE: SWA, LANDSCAPE INFRASTRUCTURE

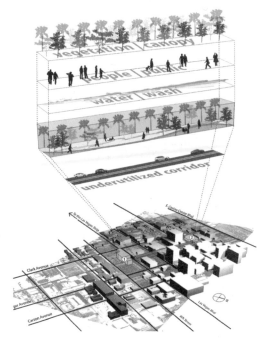

Fig. c-30: *Brooklyn Bridge Park of 2005. Highly skilled in the restoration of nature for urban parks, Valkenberg did not claim to possess a full urban theory. He was an old-line Landscape Architect — and thereby marginalized by the Landscape Urbanist discourse.* SOURCE: MICHAEL VAN VALKENBURG AND ASSOCIATES, SOURCE BOOKS IN LANDSCAPE ARCHITECTURE 1

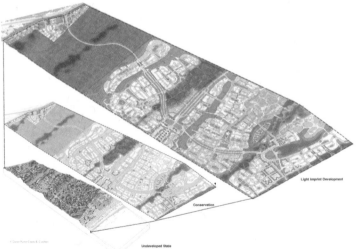

Fig. c-31 and c-32: *Costa Verbena, Brazilian Coast, 2012. The design of a new community respects and clarifies the site's topography of dunes, drainage patterns and sensitive ecosystems. There was urbanism where appropriate at the town centers (upper image). This was an early example of beneficial Landscape Urbanist influence on New Urbanism.*
SOURCE: DPZ

Fig. c-33: *Harvard's New and Old
Testaments: The "Red Book" of
Landscape Urbanism (2010) and
Rem Koolhaas' "Silver Book" (1995).
These joined the bibliography of New
Urbanism, where "Delirious New York"
(Koolhaas et. al.) and "Learning from
Las Vegas" (Venturi et. al.) already
resided.*

Fig. c-34: *East Fraserlands, Vancouver,
Canada, 2005. Urban design is not
tightly determinstic. There is always a
range of possibilities to be studied, not
just as a matter of aesthetics, but as an
exploration of performance. After the
absorption of Landscape Urbanism,
alternatives were considered as a
matter of course. Alternative A was
determined primarily by social issues.
B and C were responses to view and
breeze orientation. D had agricultural
potential. E had an enhanced
hydrology. The first three schemes
are New Urbanist, the latter two are
Landscape Urbanist.* Source: DPZ

Fig. bw-1: *Vallingby, Sweden, 1957: In crude terms, Landscape Urbanism was a revival of 1950's planning, updated by a very superior theoretical apparatus, based this time on natural rather than human prerogatives. Discussion of the human interface was judiciously avoided in the academic discourse at the turn of the century, as it had not performed "according to plan."* SOURCE: HARVARD DESIGN MAGAZINE, SPRING 2006

Fig. bw-2: *Late in the evolution of Landscape Urbanism, Charles Waldheim acknowledged three precedents: Wright's Usonia, Branzi's Weak Metropolis, and Hilberheimer's New Regional Planning. All were ideal for the purpose: formally neutral and intellectually problematizing. Other predecessors were denied acknowledgment: Team 10, Ann Whiston Spirn, Frederick Law Olmsted and Ian McHarg among them.* SOURCE: THE NEW CITY BY L. HILBERSEIMER

Figs. bw-3 and bw-4:
Team 10 precedent: Bochum
University by Candilis, Jossic &
Woods, and the Smithson's plan
for Berlin 1958, both equipped
with walkways as surrogate
ground-planes and indeterminate
geometries. Team 10 came up
for its turn in the chronological
sequence of revivals coincident
with (and perhaps consequent
to) Landscape Urbanism's
ascendancy.

SOURCE: TEAM 10 PRIMER, ALISON SMITHSON

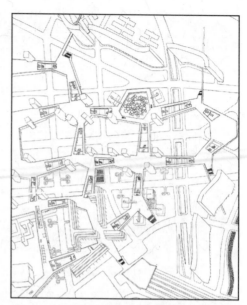

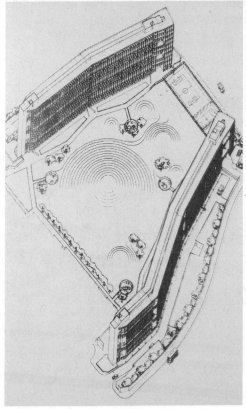

Figs. bw-5 and bw-6:
The principal Team 10
precedent for Landscape
Urbanism was Robin Hood
Gardens, one of the world's
most admired projects of
1962, 50 years later subject
to a debate for demolition.
It predicted four Landscape
Urbanist tropes: 1. Artificially
shaped topography (not to be
confused with nature, 2. Thin,
flowing, streamform buildings
(with the characteristic
skew), 3. "Streets in the air"
dissipating the primacy of
the ground plane, and 4. The
carefully random composition
of the façade, as visual
surrogate for the absence of
programmatic complexity.
SOURCE: OPPOSITIONS, KURT FORSTER

Fig. bw-7: Robin Hood Gardens by the Smithsons of Team 10, in its heyday of 1962. By 2012 it was subject to a demolition order for its comprehensive social failure. The design could be mitigated only by repopulating it with high-income Londoners. The social housing reverted to the traditional urban typologies that the New Urbanists had vetted first in the United States with H.U.D.'s Hope IV program.

Source: Oppositions by Kurt Forster

Fig. bw-8: The High Line in its early days, exactly 50 years after Robin Hood Gardens. This was designed for a high-income demographic from the outset.

Source: Friends of the Highline

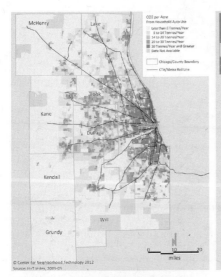

Fig. bw-9: Absolute and per capita greenhouse gas (GHG) production in greater Chicago. The suburbs produce less GHG per acre but more per capita, which is the crux of the excellent environmental performance of cities. New Urbanism kept score by reducing carbon, Landscape Urbanism by hydrological performance. Two theologies in contention on the end of civilization: by drought or by flood.
SOURCE: CENTER FOR NEIGHBORHOOD TECHNOLOGY

Fig. bw-10: The Big Dig, Boston. The cover of this highway burial ended up being landscaped—an early instance of the emerging alliance between NIMBYism, environmentalism and biophilia, which came to be brokered by Landscape Urbanism. The replacement of the covered highway by additional buildings would have been much more effective environmentally than the token greening, as it would have reduced VMT (vehicle miles traveled), but the calculation of carbon was outside the discourse of Landscape Urbanism.
SOURCE: LANDSCAPE ARCHITECTURE, MARCH 2010

Fig. bw-11: The Town of Brambleton was designed in 1989 by Sasaki, at the time when New Urbanism was at the high point of acceptance by the academy — even Harvard's.

The critical edge was subsequently to be lost by New Urbanism upon achieving hegemony in the middle-class market. The academy (and Sasaki) moved on to Landscape Urbanism. This was a common trajectory among design firms.

SOURCE: SASAKI & ASSOCIATES, INTEGRATED ENVIRONMENTS

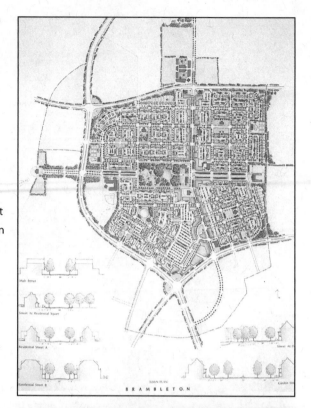

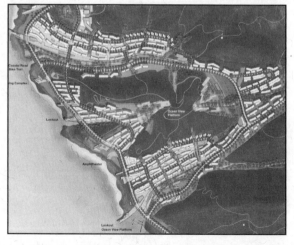

Fig. bw-12: Hongxin Community, Dalian China, 2009. Twenty years after Brambleton, Sasaki had mastered Landscape Urbanism. For this firm it was a particularly fortuitous evolution, as it had been founded by a Harvard Landscape Architect of the Gropius/Sert generation.

SOURCE: SASAKI & ASSOCIATES, INTERSECTION & CONVERGENCE

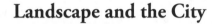

2

Landscape and the City

Michael Dennis and Alistair McIntosh

THERE IS GREAT CONFUSION TODAY about the relationship between architecture, landscape and urbanism. The interrelationship of landscape[1] and the city has undergone a formal and philosophical transformation over more than five hundred years: from landscape and the city during the Renaissance, to landscape in the city during the nineteenth century, to the city in the landscape in the twentieth century, and, finally, to landscape as the city in our time. This transformation, from an urbanism conceived as physically distinct from its surrounding agricultural and wild natures, to one of a boundless horizontal spread, has weakened the cultural idea of the city as the center of community life and turned nature into a pictorial setting. In the last several decades this enervated notion of the natural environment has been reinvigorated by the insights of ecological analysis and its incorporation into landscape planning and design. However, in much contemporary, ecologically based planning and design, architecture has been divorced from any concept of compact urbanity, reduced to the trivial by most contemporary architects and by "Landscape Urbanists."

Steven Peterson has observed that, traditionally, the city was considered sacred and the country profane, and the designed landscape of the garden was the mediator between the two.[2] Gradually, however, the "natural landscape" became sacred and the city profane. Dense, compact cities were replaced by "towers-in-the-park" and suburbia, and the

intentionally designed landscape disappeared as mediator between ideas
of city and country. The role of landscape architecture became the provision of what became thought of as a non-rhetorical, authentic natural
setting for a new dispersed (sub)urban life. Thus, the end of the long-
standing, fruitful relationship between deeply held cultural concepts of
the nature of nature, as well as a rejection of nature's instrumentality
and expression in landscape planning and design, means that the city as
a distinct geographic and cultural concept has now been lost within a
continuous geography of development.

This essay outlines the long transformation from the Garden and the
City during the Renaissance, to the Garden as the City in our time. Cities
require density of urban buildings and people. Thus, there can be cities
without landscape, but landscape without density of urban buildings and
people cannot be a city. Moreover, dense, compact cities are more culturally effective and resource efficient on a per capita basis. The urban design
of cities should comprise both urban buildings and designed landscapes
of streets, squares, gardens and parks. The integration of architecture,
landscape and urban design in the mid-nineteenth-century Paris of
Adolphe Alphand and Georges Haussmann provides a suggestive model
for the contemporary city.

1. The Garden and the City
Renaissance gardens

Renaissance and baroque gardens had a clear and unequivocal relationship to town planning. They could at once be more immediate and more
fanciful than cities. Often they were associated with country villas such
as the Villa d'Este at Tivoli (begun in 1560), but others enjoyed a more
direct relationship with a town or city, such as the Boboli Garden in
Florence (begun in 1549) and the Villa Lante at Bagnaia (begun in 1568
see Figure bw-9).[3]

The plan of the gardens of the Villa d'Este, for example, could easily be imagined as the plan of an ideal Renaissance town. The plan of
the Boboli Gardens in Florence, like that of the Villa d'Este, could also
be imagined to be an urban town plan, but slightly more baroque with
larger blocks and more flamboyant shapes.

The gardens of the Villa Lante at Bagnaia are generally regarded as
among the most beautiful in Italy. It is the villa's relationship with the

town, however, that is most compelling — a clear expression of Peterson's idea of the garden as mediator between sacred and profane. The villa consists not only of the famous walled garden, but also the adjacent "wild" wooded area. The parterre of the garden relates directly to the town square, cementing the connection of city:garden:nature.

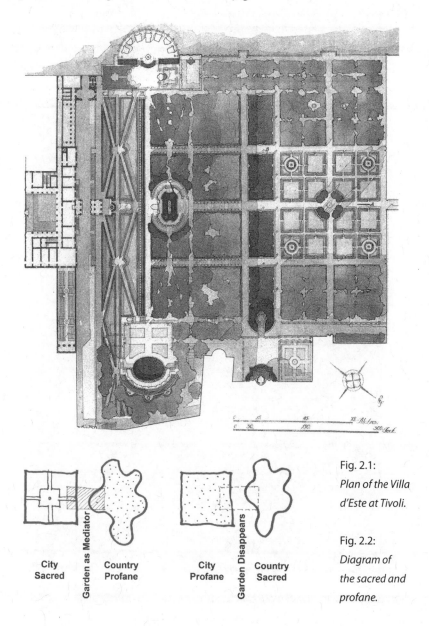

Fig. 2.1:
Plan of the Villa d'Este at Tivoli.

Fig. 2.2:
Diagram of the sacred and profane.

Baroque gardens and cities

If walled Italian Renaissance gardens like the Villa Lante and the Boboli gardens could be seen as urban models, and as mediating between the city and the country, French Baroque parks and gardens might be seen as more direct models for the city. Indeed, the Bois de Boulogne was bigger than the city of Paris, and twice as big as the city of London.

Free of the actual constraints of cities, French Baroque parks and gardens could be designed more freely. They were composed of long, straight streets and allées arranged orthogonally and diagonally through woods and parterres. Curves were rarely used except for intersections,

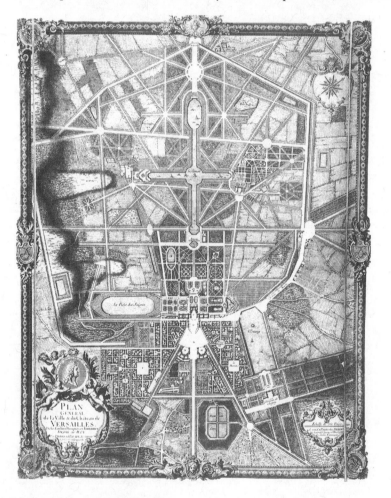

Fig. 2.3: *Plan of the gardens at Versailles.*

which were often *ronds-points*, but unlike Sixtus V's plan for Rome, the "streets" did not terminate in objects but in spaces. Le Nôtre's design for the gardens of Versailles, for example, may be seen as a dry run for mid-nineteenth-century Paris.[4]

The plan of Versailles is also an obvious ancestor of the plan for Washington, DC. The original author of the Washington plan, Major Pierre Charles L'Enfant, grew up at Versailles, where his father was a court painter for Louis XIV. The relationship between the plans can be overstated, however, for three major reasons. The first and perhaps most obvious reason is that Washington is (finally) a city, not a park. The interstitial areas defined by the *allées* are not transparent woods or parterres but a dense urban fabric of blocks and streets. The second is that Versailles is composed primarily of diagonals but Washington is primarily an orthogonal grid plan. L'Enfant himself described the plan: "I made the distribution regular, with every street at right angles ... and afterwards, opened ... avenues to and from every principal place...."[5] The third is that at Versailles, the diagonals connect spaces, but in the original plan for Washington they connect monuments, and this is more neoclassical than Baroque. In other words, it is a late eighteenth-century, neoclassical plan that articulates an enlightenment society's institutions as detached civic monuments.

2. The Garden in the City

In the mid-nineteenth century, the garden entered the city for the first time as a public amenity for the expanding city of the bourgeoisie. In Paris it was as an aggressive and integrated medium of urbanism; in New York it was as an antidote to the city. Each was the product of a major landscape figure: Adolphe Alphand (1817–91) in Paris, and Frederick Law Olmsted (1822–1903) in New York. Although Alphand and Olmsted

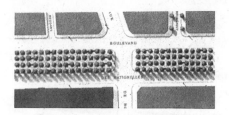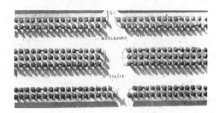

Fig. 2.4: *Typical street plans, Alphand.*

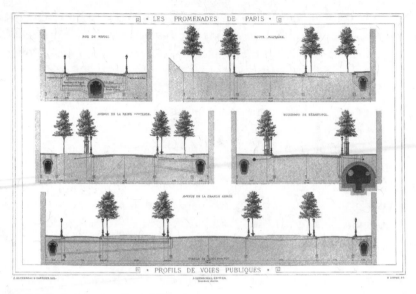

Fig. 2.5: *Typical street sections, Alphand.*

were contemporaries, and although there is some formal overlap in their work, their philosophies regarding the relationship of landscape and urbanism could not be more different. For Alphand, landscape was an equal partner with urban and architectural form in the making of an enhanced but compact city. For Olmsted, the city was a problem; the solution was to provide a natural substitute. These two opposite attitudes towards landscape and the city produced two distinct lineages that only converged in the modernist city of the twentieth century.

Paris

With the beginning of the renovation of Paris in 1853 by Napoleon III, Georges Haussmann and Adolphe Alphand, landscape became an essential component of urban design. Alphand's Promenades de Paris illustrate a continuous landscape of boulevards, squares and parks — a completely new type of city. The spaces of nineteenth-century Paris provided a robust framework for the city that has endured until today. Within this framework architecture, landscape, urban design and infra-structure were interrelated.[6]

Alphand's Paris landscape is a fortuitous blend of two landscape tradi-tions: the formal tradition of the *allée*, the *cours*, and the promenade; and the Romantic tradition of the picturesque landscape. Napoleon III was particularly fond of Hyde Park and the English Romantic landscape, and one of his first initiatives after 1848 was to have Alphand transform the Bois de Boulogne from a geometric hunting wood into a Romantic park for the bourgeoisie. Later, the same was done with the Bois de Vincennes. Notably, at the time, both of these were outside the city proper. Within the city, the formal — more urban — tradition prevailed, although some medium-sized Romantic parks, like the Parc des Buttes Chaumont, Parc Monceau and Parc Montsouris were created.

Historically, urban streets were relatively narrow and without landscape. Movement within the city was limited. To accommodate increased population and movement, however, Paris and other cities "loosened" in response. As streets became wider, landscape became an important design component.

The boulevards were wide, monumental, often multi-lane thoroughfares, with generous amounts of trees and other vegetation, combined with street lighting and underground drainage facilities. Trees were an effective way of articulating various modes of traffic and pedestrians within the same system. The boulevards were crucial to facilitate and separate traffic flow, but also to bring in air and light. They also formed

Fig. 2.6: *Alphand's plan of the Bois de Boulogne.*

the backbone of the promenades of Paris. The promenade, originally a rural walk that was conceived as an alternative to the motion of city life, was built into the city fabric itself by Alphand.

The various landscape designs — from small squares to urban forests — worked as the climaxes of Alphand's promenades. Within their quarters, the squares filled a need for accessible neighborhood parks. The squares often resulted from a pattern of diagonal streets forming an irregular open space. These leftover spaces were resolved by the landscape design, which might be either formal or picturesque. The number of spatial conditions required an almost endless variety of solutions.

The city structure was enriched by several large parks, the most significant being the Buttes Chaumont.[7] A 62-acre (25-hectare) area that had been a quarry was transformed into a curvilinear landscape, with a mountain crowned by a temple of Sibyl at its highest point. Another attraction was a large grotto with a 105-foot (32-meter) cascade. The park was a reserve of an exaggerated and artificial nature that was more natural than nature itself. It was dedicated to recreation, pleasure and entertainment of the citizens. It cost more than all the other Parisian parks combined.

The Bois de Boulogne had been a hunting reserve for France's kings until it was transferred from the national government to the city of Paris. Since Napoleon III was in favor of contemporary English landscape architecture, especially Hyde Park, Alphand transformed its geometry of linear axes into labyrinthine promenades composed in curves and sinuous lines. He introduced large water features, including cascades and grottos, and nested pavilions and building ensembles, a hippodrome and smaller gardens within the park, forming various attractions. The choice and layout of new vegetation gave the area an informal character. These transformations served for the entertainment and recreation of the bourgeoisie. Later, the design of the Bois de Vincennes followed the example of the Bois de Boulogne, though it was located away from the wealthy districts of the city.

The Paris of Napoleon III was constricted within its fortification walls, and though its population had roughly doubled since 1740, he saw it as a compact city that he wanted to make healthy, monumental and beautiful. Indeed, Haussmann, Alphand and others demonstrated that an industrial city with old roots could be functional, economical, more social, and more beautiful. They also showed that urbanism could be conceived on a large scale, and that the relationship of buildings to space should be at least as important as the design of individual structures. Moreover, a new attitude about the architect's duty towards the community was born. It was a conception that was fundamentally different from that of the École des Beaux Arts, whose teaching was blind to social conditions and site. Most important was the introduction of landscape as a fundamental component of urban design. Not only could the city be conceived holistically, but this could only be done by including landscape — both formal and Romantic types.

Haussman and Alphand's Paris served as a model for successive late nineteenth-century planners, including especially the City Beautiful movement. It might even be argued that the interest in rationalizing movement led fairly directly to Le Corbusier and the Ville Contemporaine. It seems to have had a limited effect on Frederick Law Olmsted, however. Olmsted went to visit Alphand in 1859, so he was aware of what was happening in Paris.[8] But if he was influenced, it was only by the Romantic tradition, not the formal one. Thus, if Alphand may be seen as the father of modern urban landscape, Olmsted went on to become the father of suburban landscape.

New York

The Commissioners Plan for the expansion of New York in 1811 was a rigidly functional real estate plan for an extensive new town — one of unknown scope. All natural features would be erased, and there were few allowances for recreation or open space. New York was a commercial enterprise and the grid plan was intended to facilitate rapid expansion.[9]

In the mid-1800s, half a million people were living in New York City, most in crowded, cramped quarters below 38th Street. To escape the din of city life, they sought refuge in pastoral spaces such as Green-Wood Cemetery in Brooklyn.

In 1844, poet and newspaper editor William C. Bryant called for the creation of a large public park. Landscape designer and writer Andrew J. Downing and Bryant pressed officials to set aside land before it was swallowed up by the fast-developing city. Between 1853 and 1856, the independent board of commissioners paid more than $5 million for land from 59th Street to 106th Street, between Fifth and Eighth Avenues.[10]

Fig. 2.7: *View of the Long Meadow, Prospect Park, Olmsted and Vaux.*

In 1857, the commissioners sponsored a public competition to design the new Central Park. They chose the Greensward plan by Frederick Law Olmsted, superintendent of the Park work crews, and British architect Calvert Vaux.[11]

Central Park was the first purpose-designed public park in the United States, and Olmsted's first landscape commission. In 1872 Olmsted also did the conceptual design for Riverside Park and Drive in Manhattan, and with Vaux, designed Prospect Park in Brooklyn.

The Romantic naturalism of Central Park was an antidote to the psychological intensity of daily work life in the commercial city. Even though the park was completely fabricated — completely man-made, in the manner of the Buttes Chaumont — it seemed natural, and was big enough to wall off the city outside. In fact, formally and philosophically, the park contained the seeds of the disintegration of the American city. At this point in time, i.e., well before the worst of the industrial era — an era of filth, congestion, crime and disease — the idea of a less dense, less integrated city had emerged in America.

The Birth of Suburbia

The idea of separating the place of work from the place of living had been around since the early nineteenth century, and by mid-century mechanized transport enabled longer commuting distances. Paris experienced a similar articulation between work and living, but in Paris, Napoleon III, Haussmann and Alphand built wider streets to accommodate increased vehicular circulation and a different kind of urban life. In contrast, America, lacking a more refined urban tradition, implemented suburbia and mono-functional zoning in lieu of a revised, compact city. Schuyler points out that Olmsted felt that "a large part of the ideas of a city, which have been transmitted to us from the period when cities were walled about and necessarily compact and crowded, must be put away."[12] Olmsted believed the new city should have a compact business district, but that housing should spread out into the natural landscape on a less dense basis.

For Olmsted the need for landscape in the city as a counter-force to the stress of the built urban experience created the need for a large urban park. It was a form of psychological recreation. He saw the Parkway as a means of extending the influence of the park into the surrounding expanding city, and that the interconnected park system — many parks connected by parkways — could be used to structure the growth of the city. Finally, he was one of the first urbanists to conceive of landscape as natural infrastructure — urban drainage, the preservation and incorporation of natural landscape units into the development strategies of the expanding city. All of the above, in addition to advocacy for the separation of commercial and residential life and an insistence that the latter had to be within a landscape setting, gave birth to the suburb, and the ecological landscape movement along with it. This vision influenced all three of the late nineteenth- and early twentieth-century urban visions: the Garden City, the City Beautiful and the Modernist City.

3. The City in the Garden

The two opposite mid-nineteenth-century attitudes towards landscape and the city — that of Alphand and that of Olmsted — each produced distinct lineages that only converged in the modernist city of the twentieth century. The tradition of Haussmann and Alphand led to the dominance of circulation — the rationalized street — in the work of late nineteenth-century planners such as Joseph Stübben and Eugène Hénard. The tradition of Olmsted led to the dominance of nature in the Garden City movement.

All of the ills of the dense, unhealthy, industrial city were the impetus for the low-density Garden (non) City and its cousin, the (non) City of Modern Architecture.[13] In both cases, sun, space and greenery, coupled with new non-street-oriented architectural typologies, were considered sufficient to produce a salubrious new environment. Nature became sacred, the traditional city profane. Landscape design became comatose until Ian McHarg and the rise of landscape ecology in the second half of the twentieth century. Despite the power and importance of McHarg's ecological insights, however, landscape, like architecture, had lost its long relationship with the city. The modernist schema of towers-in-the-park was simply not urban, and the idealized continuous landscape was no substitute for a legible public realm. Unfortunately, the landscape legacy of the mid to late twentieth-century urbanism devolved into a disaggregated suburban spread facilitated by highway infrastructure. The economic, social and environmental fallout is now a well-known legacy of "city in the garden" dogma.

4. The Garden as the City

There has been a recent concerted effort to reformulate landscape design out of science and ecology, and to place landscape in the foreground of thinking about the future shape of cities. This effort, often referred to as Landscape Urbanism,[14] proposes a means to creatively intervene in the contemporary urban environment using landscape as the principal organizing force for the future. This effort is based on a strategy of analyzing the complex interactions of human culture, land use and natural systems to plan for an indefinite future. Time and morphological change are central to the conception of these landscapes. For "Landscape Urbanists," the reality of the contemporary geography we have inherited — of suburban dispersal, the abandonment of many urban cores, and restless movement — is the condition of the future. This idea of the environment has been described using words such as surfaces, flows and networks. Theirs is a large-scale, organizational concept of a world ceaselessly becoming. It is an environment of landscape as process and culture as event, both managed by a beneficent ecology that can be used to understand and, one assumes, control the whole messy interaction of human culture, economic development, politics and the environment.

Cities require density, continuous urban fabric, and a legible civic realm of space, however, and the long evolution from landscape and the city to landscape as a substitute for the city, has led to much current confusion. Claims of landscape's hegemony over an impotent architecture are often professed, and with justification. But beyond a clever marketing strategy, this is one slice of pizza posing as the whole pie; the proposals of Landscape Urbanism fall short of the goal of a better integration between city and nature. To paraphrase Gertrude Stein's well-known saying "there's no there there," one has to admit "there's no urbanism there." Landscape as the city is simply not enough; it's an incomplete paradigm. If the ominous urban and environmental issues of the twenty-first century are to be addressed, a more comprehensive strategy involving architecture, landscape and urban design must be used. This means beginning with the city again — but the city as part of a larger ecological construct.

5. The Garden in the City: *Redivivum*

Diminishing natural resources, rapid climate change, and world population growth make a compelling economic argument for denser forms of urban development, with built form and landscape closely intertwined. This is more energy efficient when measured in terms of carbon emissions per capita, and translates into less expenditure on resources per person. Locating more on less would leave more of that other finite resource — land — for ecological uses integral with the creation of a sustainable natural environment that will be the ecologically based foundation for a compact urbanism. This will be an urbanism where designed landscape is an equal partner with urban and architectural form in the making of a city within its specific natural region. In the paragraphs below, we differentiate this approach, which we term "urban landscape," from Landscape Urbanism.

The rediscovery of the city began in the 1970s. One of the earliest and most compelling urban images is the project for La Villette in Paris, 1976, by Leon Krier. Krier's project was a complete reversal of Le Corbusier's Ville Radieuse:[15] a reconstitution of the city as a complex organization of streets, blocks, urban spaces and parks. Fundamental to his plan was a remarkable landscape element that was at once the core of the quarter and a connection to the axis of the water basin and Paris beyond. This project is symbolic of a new exploration of the relationship of architecture, landscape and urban design through the last part of the twentieth century. Despite a continuously developing urban sensibility, however, architecture and landscape have tended to pursue ever more autonomous, narcissistic and anti-urban directions, and this is inadequate for twenty-first century issues.

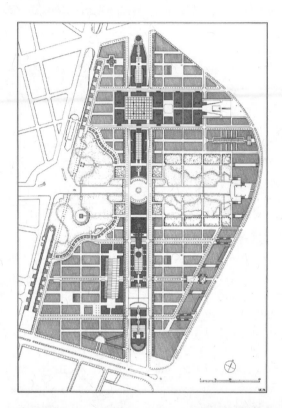

Fig. 2.8: *Plan of La Villette, Leon Krier, 1976.*

Fig. 2.9: *Sketch view of the Ville Radieuse.*

Contemporary Urban Landscape

There is a reinvigorating position within landscape architecture — one that is complementary to urban density. This strain of built urban landscape emerges out of the interaction of specific sites and places — usually over an extended period of time, often at least a decade — and as part of a larger strategy of urban, environmental, economic and social regeneration. It displays a shared elemental language of landscape architecture: earth, rock, water, plants and weather deployed to environmentally situate people in a particular urban place. These are landscapes where the continuity and transformation of the inherited fabric of sites are manipulated to renew and reinvigorate an understanding of the nature of nature in the contemporary world — much as the Buttes Chaumont did in nineteenth-century Paris.

Moreover, these landscapes are integral to an understanding of the city as a compact, historically layered environment where the proximity of people can lead to a more complex and humane city life. This position shares the common ground of ecology as the analytical paradigm for understanding how to shape the land. The application of ecological thinking is different, however. Landscape Urbanism takes the whole messy world in its ceaseless becoming as it is, and seeks to use ecology to manage it. Urban landscape uses ecology to help change, and frame, the pattern of urban development. Urban landscape also does not use "ecology" and "design with nature" as metaphors. The natural world is a biophysical reality, a topographic reality, and an ecological system that must be understood in its depth — as a sectional and temporal reality — and in its geographic manifestation: the region. Mapping and other graphic displays are used to describe and explain the development of a landscape in time, and its current functioning, but they are instruments of understanding, not a deterministic planning prescription or a cool graphic display. They must yield information that can guide the physical reshaping of the landscape within an understanding of natural and cultural processes. The insights of landscape ecology[16] afford a way of understanding and acting on the landscape in productive ways.

Landscape Ecology and the Region

If the current and future urban landscape is to be relevant it must be based on the discipline of landscape ecology. Ecology is a branch of evolutionary biology that investigates the way organisms interact in space and over time. Landscape ecology is a branch of ecology that analyses, understands and predicts the workings of heterogeneous landscape configurations — the sort of landscapes often associated with human modifications of the natural landscape. Simply put, landscape ecology is a horizontal study of a matrix of landscape ecosystems as opposed to the traditional ecological approach of a vertical analysis of the interactions of a single ecosystem. These heterogeneous landscapes have three basic components — structure: spatial relationships of elements, distribution of energy, and materials; function: interaction among spatial elements and energy flows among components; and change in time: alteration of structure and function of the ecological mosaic in time.

These three elements operate within specific climatic, geomorphological and disturbance conditions. The natural environment is never static. There is no balance of nature. Climate has always fluctuated (the contemporary arguments are about the rate of change and the extent of human agency in accelerating the rate of change). At any given moment geological processes are at work, rivers are carrying the hills to the sea, suddenly the earth shakes and a city falls.

Human cultures too have for millennia changed the landscape, for intended and unintended ends. These are some of the disturbance conditions within which heterogeneous landscapes develop. When seen from the window of a plane, heterogeneous landscape structure forms a predominant pattern. For example in rural Lowland Scotland it would be one of farm fields, woodlands and hedgerows. Within this pattern, the woodlands form patches of different sizes and shapes and the hedgerows are corridors often connecting the woodlands. This landscape matrix creates a physical environmental structure that allows species — plants and animals — to migrate in response to changing climate and other environmental pressures. The size, shape, connectivity and distribution of the patches and corridors determine the robustness of the landscape and its ability to function as an environment. Patterns of sustainable urbanism must comprehend and manipulate a landscape's morphology and manage the energy flows that move through it at a regional scale. From this analysis a reasoned understanding of an urban landscape of reality can be conceived, developed and constructed. It will consist of a range of regional landscapes that include urban settlements. These settlements will re-aggregate urban life in compact, vital and human communities. Each city is set within a regional landscape infrastructure that will environmentally sustain them.

This landscape must be constructed and managed in a time of rapid climate fluctuation, and the shape of the landscape will change dramatically. Plants and other organisms have evolved within constantly fluctuating climate regimens, fires, floods and earthquakes, and the disturbance they all induce. Individual organisms, using their species-specific reproductive strategies, have changed their geographic ranges in response to all of these disturbances. One simple example may serve: the natural vegetation of eastern North America has been moving in a fluctuating north/south drift for a very long time. What is different now is that the rate of change may be more rapid than the evolutionary response of many species, and that the movement of species is constrained by the geography of a distributed and disaggregated urbanism. To counter this reality we have to stop thinking of nature as a beneficent balm. Rather, we must conceive of nature and its manifestation in landscapes, of which human civilization is a part, as a spatial, environmental infrastructure that provides the vectors for species movement and survival and also situates a re-aggregated urbanism within a regional, sustainable environmental context.

There is nothing in this description of landscape ecology and its role in the shaping of landscapes that practitioners of Landscape Urbanism or ecological urbanism would disagree with. The difference between Landscape Urbanism and what we are describing — landscape and the city — resides not in the understanding or use of landscape ecology but as to where and how its environmental insights are applied. In our view, using landscape ecological knowledge to manage and plan a dispersed urbanism is at best a rearguard action. Rather, ecologically based planning should also include the re-aggregation of cities. These compact, humane, urban environments of blocks, streets, squares, parks and other open spaces would be situated within an ecologically sustainable natural infrastructure region. This landscape infrastructure would surround cities, and be within and under them. Within the urban fabric, designed landscapes would mediate between the urban architecture and the larger landscape ecological infrastructure. This landscape mediation will be both a sustaining biophysical interaction and an imaginative rejuvenation of the

relationship between urban culture and a contemporary idea of nature —
a transformation of Steven Peterson's thesis of sacred city and profane
country mediated by the garden, to one of an interdependent city/region
with urban landscapes mediating the nature of nature in the twenty-
first-century city. It is this understanding of the designed landscape that
has informed the authors' design practices. Two examples, Texas A&M
University and the Central Indianapolis Waterfront, are described below.

The University Campus as Urban Laboratory

The campus of Texas A&M University is an example of these principles
used to reconnect and improve both natural and urban environments.
During the period of unprecedented expansion that followed World
War II, the campus sprawled west from its compact core with anti-urban
building types and aimless landscape. In the process, water systems, vegetation and habitat environments were seriously eroded and broken.
Lawns replaced native vegetation, and what then-president Robert Gates
called Soviet-style buildings were placed in isolation, ever further from
the historic community of buildings.

The existing civic open space structure of the core and the outly-
ing, but discontinuous, ecological systems served as the basis for the
development of an extended landscape infrastructure that could at once
reconnect the natural systems and provide the spatial structure for a
long-term future building program. This landscape structure provided
for a transition from the well-maintained urban quadrangles and court-
yards of the core to the riparian landscape and native vegetation to the
west — a transition from the formal to the picturesque. In addition, at
least fifty years of building growth could be accommodated and used to
support an extended campus fabric of civic spaces within a sustainable,
walkable campus.

The Central Indianapolis Waterfront and
the Reintegration of Landscape in the City

The Central Indianapolis Waterfront is an example of landscape designed
to help regenerate the urban fabric of a city. For over one hundred years
Indianapolis had not engaged the natural environment of the White
River, which lies to the west of the downtown. The riverbanks were lined
with floodwalls and old industrial buildings. The abandoned dry trench

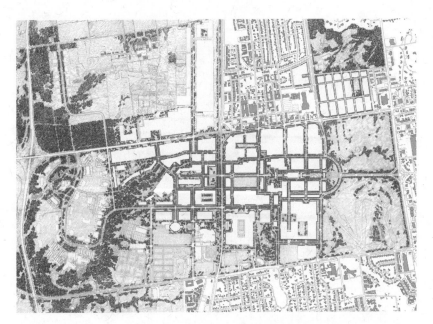

Figs. 2.10 and 2.11: *Michael Dennis and Sasaki: Long range plan for Texas A&M University. Landscape infrastructure reconnects the natural systems and provides a spatial structure for future building. This works exceedingly well with the type known as the American Campus.* SOURCE: ALISTAIR MCINTOSH.

of the Central Canal formed the only tenuous link with the nearby urban fabric. The historic Military Park, the State Capitol grounds, and a previously renovated section of the Central Canal were isolated fragments of landscape within a loosened urban fabric of roads and scattered buildings.

The new landscapes have created a civic structure around which an urban fabric of streets, blocks and architecture have coalesced into a downtown district. The banks of the White River have been transformed into a linear open space sequence linking to regional environmental systems to the north and the south of downtown. Park spaces extend from the river environment into the urban core of the downtown, integrating Military Park, the canal fragment, and the State Capitol grounds into a unified open space sequence. These landscapes relate immediately to their built surroundings and also mediate between the city and the larger environmental context of the White River valley.

Three strategies govern the design and making of this place. First and most important is the deliberate re-aggregation of built urban form around a designed landscape that mediates between a redeveloping, compact city and the larger environmental context. The ecological idea of this project lies in the sequence: urban form, designed landscape and larger environmental context. The civic landscape is part of the re-aggregation strategy and this approach, over time, will free the larger natural context to take on a sustaining ecological role. Second, these landscapes are stages for the daily life of the community. They are specifically designed to accommodate a range of activities and programs. They have "thickness" as opposed to "surface." Changes will inevitably occur; trees will die; uses will change; but all within a resistant physical context. Finally, the landscape design situates these activities in their particular geographic setting. The making of these spaces creatively reconstructs the found physical fabric of the existing city. This is not an essay in historicism, however, but a balancing of the forces of transformation and continuity — the making and remaking of humane cities in place and time.

Towards An Urban Future

Both of these projects are models of landscape and the city. Each is an essay in the creation of a compact urban environment that relates to a larger reconstituted environmental context using the languages of civic design and landscape architecture to shape a legible, useful and expressive public realm. They represent a search for a relevant contemporary urbanity within an environmentally and psychologically sustaining nature using a shared elemental built language to shape landscapes in the city.

The designers of all built landscapes struggle with materials, construction, weather, site particularities and the passage of time. In the end, the continuous becoming of Landscape Urbanism may be more planning and literary trope than a guide to physical design. There are limits to the meanings languages of description confer on particular projects. Locations become meaningful over time because of the way daily life productively interacts with the specifics of physical forms and the way they are made. This process escapes the capacity of language to define it.

"Rationem ex vinculis orationis vindicam esse"[17]

Endnotes

1. From a geographic perspective a landscape is the sum of all human activities that transform the environment. This definition includes the city/suburb and its associated parks, gardens and other open spaces. They are conceived as parts of the sum of all human activities on the land. It is a definition that understands both urban and landscape form as the result of ongoing social, cultural and economic processes. This essay has a narrower focus. Its subject is the role of designed landscapes — urban parks, gardens, tree-lined boulevards — in mediating differing relationships between urbanism and nature. Designed landscapes are places where the materials of the natural world — rock, earth, wood, water and plantings — have been intentionally manipulated to physically embody and express cultural ideas about the nature of nature and its relationship to urbanism. In this essay these ideas of nature and their expression in physical landscapes range from an Italian garden designed to reveal the underlying order of nature (Lazzaro) to the morphological analysis of landscape ecology (Forman and Godron, *Landscape Ecology*, 1986). Our goal is to reestablish the mediating role of the designed landscape between a revitalized, humane, compact and sustainable urbanism and a natural systems understanding of nature.
2. Lecture at Cornell University, and private conversations.
3. See especially, Lazzaro, C. 1990. *The Italian Renaissance Garden: From the Conventions of Planting, Design, and Ornament to the Grand Gardens of Sixteenth-Century Italy.* New Haven and London: Yale University Press; Mosser, M., and G. Teyssot, Eds. 1991. *The Architecture of Western Gardens: A Design History from the Renaissance to the Present Day.* Cambridge: MIT Press; and Shepherd, J. C., and G. A. Jellicoe. 1925. *Italian Gardens of the Renaissance.* Princeton, NJ: Princeton Architectural Press, 1986. First published by Ernest Benn.
4. See, Adams, W. H. 1979. *The French Garden: 1500–1800.* New York: Braziller; Baridon, M. 2008. *A History of the Gardens of Versailles,* trans. Adrienne Mason. Philadelphia, PA: University of Pennsylvania Press; and Mariage, T. 1999. *The World of André Le Nôtre,* trans. Graham Larkin. Philadelphia, PA: University of Pennsylvania Press.
5. Reps, J. W. 1965. *The Making of Urban America: a History of City Planning in the United States.* Princeton, NJ: Princeton University Press, p. 249. See also, Berg, S. W. 2008. *Grand Avenues: The Story of Pierre Charles L'Enfant, the French Visionary Who Designed Washington, D.C.* New York: Vintage Books.
6. See, Alphand, A. 1867–73. *Les Promenades de Paris, histoire — description des embellissements — dépenses de création et d'entretien des Bois de Boulogne et de Vincennes, Champs-Élysées--parcs--squares--boulevards--places plantées, étude sur l'art des jardins et arboretum.* Paris. 1 vol text and atlas; Jordan, D. P.

1995. *Transforming Paris: The Life and Labors of Baron Haussmann*. New York: Free Press; and Pinkney, D. 1958. *Napoleon III and the Rebuilding of Paris,* Princeton, NJ: Princeton University Press.

7. See, Alphand, and Plazy, G. 2000. *Le Parc des Buttes-Chaumont,* Paris: Flammarion.
8. Newton, N. T. *Design on the Land: The Development of Landscape Architecture.* Cambridge MA, 1971, p. 245.
9. See, Schuyler, D. 1986. *The New Urban Landscape: The Redefinition of City Form in Nineteenth-Century America.* Baltimore and London: Johns Hopkins University Press.
10. See, Cohen, P. E., and R. T. Augustyn. 1997. *Manhattan in Maps: 1527–1995.* New York: Rizzoli.
11. Ibid.
12. Schuyler, op cit., p. 5.
13. See, Le Corbusier. 1967. *The Radiant City: Elements of a Doctrine of Urbanism to be Used as the Basis of our Machine-Age Civilization.* New York: Orion Press; Le Corbusier. 1928. "The city of tomorrow and its planning," translated from the 8th French edition of *Urbanisme.* New York: Payson.
14. See, Waldheim, C., Ed. 2006. *The Landscape Urbanism Reader.* New York: Princeton Architectural Press.
15. Le Corbusier, op cit.
16. Forman, R., and M. Godron. *Landscape Ecology,* 1986.
17. "Reason must be released from the chains of speech." Dedication to Ludwig Wittgenstein on the wall of Trinity College Chapel, Cambridge.

Additional Works Cited

Beveridge, C. E. and C. F. Hoffman, Eds. 1997. *The Papers of Fredrick Law Olmsted.* Supplementary Series Volume 1, *Writings on Public Parks, Parkways and Park Systems.* Baltimore, MA: Johns Hopkins.
Blanning, T. 2010. *The Romantic Revolution: A History.* New York: Modern Library.
Carmona, M. 2002. *Haussmann: His Life and Times, and the Making of Modern Paris.* Chicago: Ivan R. Dee.
Creese, W. L. 1992. *The Search for Environment: The Garden City: Before and After.* Expanded edition. Baltimore: Johns Hopkins.
Du Cerceau, J.-A. 1559, 1561, 1582. *Livre d'architecture.* Paris. Facsimile reprint, New Jersey, 1965.
Fein, A. 1972. *Frederick Law Olmsted and the American Environmental Tradition.* New York: Braziller.
Geddes, P. 1915. *Cities in Evolution: An Introduction to the Town Planning Movement and to the Study of Civics.* London: Williams and Norgate.
Hazlehurst, F. H. 1980. *Gardens of Illusion.* Nashville: Vanderbilt University Press.
Krier, L. 1981. *Drawings: 1967–1990.* Brussels: Archives d'Architecture Moderne.
Lablaude, P-A. 1995. *The Gardens of Versailles.* London: Zwemmer Publishers Ltd.
Martin, J. 2011. *Genius of Place: The Life of Frederick Law Olmsted.* Cambridge, MA: Da Capo Press.
Masson, G. 1961. *Italian Gardens.* New York: Abrams.
McHarg, I. 1969. *Design With Nature.* Garden City: Natural History Press.
Meller, H. 1990. *Patrick Geddes: Social Evolutionist and City Planner.* New York: Routledge.
Moore, C. W., W. J. Mitchell, and W. Turnbull, Jr. 1988. *The Poetics of Gardens.* Cambridge and London: MIT Press.
Mukerji, C. 1997. *Territorial Ambitions and the Gardens of Versailles.* Cambridge: Cambridge University Press.
Papayanis, N. 2004. *Planning Paris Before Haussmann.* Baltimore: Johns Hopkins University Press.
Rogers, E. B. 2010. Genius of the Place: The Romantic Landscape, 1700–1900. In Elizabeth Rogers, Elizabeth Eustis and John Bidwell, Eds., *Romantic Gardens, Nature Art and Landscape Design.* New York: David R. Godine.
Rybczynski, W. 1999. *A Clearing in the Distance: Frederick Law Olmsted and America in the 19th Century.* New York: Scribner.
Saalman, H. 1971. *Haussmann: Paris Transformed.* New York: Braziller.
Van der Ree, P., G. Smienk & C. Steenbergen. 1992. *Italian Villas and Gardens.* Amsterdam: Thoth.
Wharton, E. 2008. *Italian Villas and Their Gardens.* New York: Rizzoli. First published by the Century Company, 1904.
Wiebenson, D. 1978. *The Picturesque Garden in France.* Princeton, NJ: Princeton University Press.

3

Landscape Urbanism, New Urbanism and the Environmental Paradox of Cities

Doug Kelbaugh

"The City Council, as you can well imagine, swallowed this line whole. Who wouldn't? Landscape is good; (the) building is landscape; therefore (the) building is good. One hears this three-car train of logic constantly in architectural discourse today....Nothing sells like landscape. It's our sex."

— David Heymann, *Places*, 11/28/11

"It is more than being about 'two movements'. It is about the primacy of the 'street' as opposed to the primacy of the 'park' as the primary setting for a civil society. The distinction is stark and nothing is more fundamental in urbanism."

— Paul Murrain, email, 1/9/11

"What we call natural and what we call human are inseparable. We live one life."

— Stewart Brand, *Whole Earth Discipline*, 2010

I. Density and Mixed Use Matter

A NY DISCUSSION OF LANDSCAPE URBANISM AND NEW URBANISM will benefit from first recapitulating the major deficits and benefits of cities. The environmental pros and cons of urbanism are especially important and relevant when comparing cities to other patterns of development, such as suburbs.

Cities perform better environmentally than sprawling suburbs. It is obvious that cities consume colossal amounts of resources and produce prodigious amounts of pollution and waste. Yet, they are surprisingly — shockingly in some ways — greener environmentally. Arguably, they also perform better economically and socially. They are, in short, more sustainable.

This advantage can be expressed in a number of ways to different audiences. For the *urban planner* it is no surprise that dense urban space that is mixed use, walkable, bikeable and transit-served impacts global climate change less than low-density sprawl that is oriented to motorized vehicles. More surprising is that it has less impact than urbanism of *equal density* that does not have a fine-grained network for physical accessibility. However, dense urbanism of *any* pattern typically has greater impact than sprawl on *local* climate, because of the "urban heat island effect" caused by the more spatially concentrated absorption and retention of solar energy, as well as by the waste heat generated from energy usage. Despite being hotter than surrounding suburban and rural areas (more so at night than in the morning), cities decrease their impact on *global* climate change more than they *increase* their impact on the *local* climate, with a considerably positive net effect.

For the *environmental scientist:* the darker albedo/lower solar reflectivity of urban surfaces and materials, greater water and air pollution, lower level of evapotranspiration from vegetation, and higher ambient air temperatures of the typical city are higher *per acre* than low-density sprawl, but its average ecological footprint *per capita* of greenhouse gases (GHGs), carbon, water and solid waste is smaller.

For the *economist*: Measuring all of these factors per person is the most significant and equitable metric in a growing global populace with widely varying levels of land, wealth and population. Cities are more efficient per person in terms of land consumption, the construction and maintenance of infrastructure, and the mechanical heating and cooling of buildings, as well as transportation and communication. Cities also have been shown to deliver higher personal and collective productivity and creativity with fewer negative externalities than less dense settlement patterns.

Last, for the *average citizen*, the paradox can be expressed simply: suburbs may look greener and perform greener per acre, but not per capita. Leafy neighborhoods are usually not as environmentally benevolent as cities or as they appear.

In short, the ecological footprint and environmental impacts of cities are larger than suburban sprawl per acre but smaller per capita; and the benefits of cities with a grid/network are even greater than non-gridded, fragmented ones.

This environmental paradox is very welcome news for a rapidly urbanizing humanity that is simultaneously facing some of the severest and most unprecedented challenges in its history. In addition, there are other, better-known benefits and advantages of urbanism that favor our species. Many of the positive consequences of urbanism help compensate for the heavy human load on the planet. By mitigating and adapting to environmental impacts, on top of all their other social, economic, and cultural merits, cities are an essential part of addressing the multi-faceted crisis of climate change. This is not to say that cities are the only solution, or even that there is *any* single comprehensive solution to the cumulative and compound pressures of humanity on the planet.

Before discussing Landscape Urbanism (LU) and New Urbanism (NU) in light of these and other issues, it would be helpful to be reminded of some of the *downsides* of cities.

"Cities are acts of violence."[1] They are growing in size, number and type, with their extensive ecological footprints made by intensive, entropic resource consumption and the need for vast amounts of land, water and air to absorb their voluminous wastes. (Full consideration of the entropic, aka negentropic, roles and effects of cities, indeed of humans, is beyond the scope of this chapter). Cities are also stressful for the human species, with their concentrated crime, disease, pollution, noise, psychological stress, social friction and political dissent. In spite of these real perils, urban dwellers currently live longer on average than non-urbanites. Cities have become an inevitable and unavoidable part of nature, as the primary habitat of, by, and for the human species.

Human life has always been dangerous and fraught with difficult challenges and surprises, as well as full of impressive successes and staggering achievements. In light of the gravity and magnitude of the current crises, especially climate change, how can cities help mitigate, adapt to, and ameliorate our pending problems? Will they contribute to the ongoing and overwhelming success of our thriving species without unduly compromising millions of other species and fouling ecological systems? Or will our best efforts end up in the too-little, too-late category, as they did for so many earlier civilizations? Will the near-perfect conditions for human beings over the last ten thousand years since the end of the most recent ice age soon give way to inhospitable climatic conditions that will diminish or even eclipse our species' reign?

II. The Benefits of Urbanization

There are many human benefits of urbanization, five of which are relevant here: smaller ecological footprints, greater creativity and productivity, self-correction of self-inflicted problems, social resiliency through diversity, and the city's ability to transform itself as required by internal and external forces.

A. *The lower environmental impact per capita of cities is the first, most important, and most paradoxical of the five benefits.* As violent interventions in the landscape, not to mention in the greater biosphere, cities pollute the atmosphere, deplete the lithosphere (through mining and other extractive industries), and foul the hydrosphere, from groundwater to ocean. They could even be called ecological sacrifice zones (were this term not so politically incorrect and environmentally inflammatory) because they inflict local environmental wounds and scars that nature must either tolerate or heal, and accumulate deficits for which nature must compensate with benefits of other coinage. This contradiction is vividly illustrated by Venice, Italy, or the historic section of Charleston, South Carolina — two beloved examples of compact, traditional urbanism at its best. Both were built in swampy coastal areas where development would not be permitted with today's environmental regulations and ethic.

   The environmental paradox of cities is prompting a reevaluation of the *net* damage of these and other delicately located cities. Any historian, resident or visitor can attest to the many ways these and other cities compensate for their violence to nature. (Of course there are imperatives and ways to shrink the ecological footprints of cities, including these two examples, and if cities like these can be built in less-sensitive natural areas, all the better.) In this way, cities can be seen as anti-entropic, as complex and dynamic as ecological systems. Both examples are arguably as physically rich, intriguing and complex per acre as the ecology of the lagoons that surround them. And when their human culture is included, they are profoundly richer and more operatic in their complexity, order and intelligence.

Cities are on the right side of the energy and carbon equation. Physicist Geoffrey West and his Santa Fe Institute team[2] have concluded that cities' metabolism increases in a sub-linear manner — that is, their metabolic rate increases at a slower rate than their increase in density. Doubling the density, for instance, has been shown to increase energy consumption by only 75% to 85% — not 100% as might be first expected — due to the efficiencies and economies of scale.

Until recently, metropolitan maps of greenhouse gas production depicted central cities as the hotspot, with their cores brighter red than the pink inner city neighborhoods and green outer suburbs and blue rural hinterlands. When several New Urbanists looked at the metric as a per capita (rather than per land area) measurement, urbanism was suddenly revealed to be part of the solution rather than part of the problem. It redeemed the city, despite its hard streets and buildings, as "greener" in terms of CO_2 production, than the lush open space and leafy foliage of the suburbs. The urban environment achieves this superiority because of much higher transit ridership, more compact buildings that are more efficient to mechanically heat and cool (although more difficult to naturally light and ventilate), and greater walkability/bikeability. This per capita footprint takes into account the extensive agricultural and logistical region needed to support both urban and suburban dwellers (see Figure bw-9).

A counterintuitive aspect of the environmental paradox of cities is the frequent lack of the obvious and conventional markers of "natural" ecology, such as plentiful plant and animal life. Indeed, our conception of nature is more and more couched in how ecological systems and processes *function* than how they *look*. Vegetation and animals may or may not be abundant to the eye, ear and nose in a healthy human ecology, and vice versa. We now know that the beautifully manicured and natural landscape of suburbia typically masks an unsustainable human habitat (and unsustainable ecology of grass and ornamental shrubs in the over-fertilized and often irrigated lawns). In fact, the apparently gritty and gruesome can be ecologically healthy. As Marcus Aurelius forcefully pointed out two millennia ago in *Meditations*, "...the foam flowing from the boar's mouth, and many other phenomena that are far from beautiful if we look at them in isolation, do nevertheless ... follow from Nature's processes...."[3] Two thousand years of observation and science have shown how unimaginably complex, unified and dynamically interconnected natural systems can be. We need to beware ecological cosmetics and the sprinkling of perfume on toxic dumps.[4] This ecological dimension of urbanism will prove significant in later parts of this chapter that deal directly with LU and NU.

B. *Cities are, on average, more productive, creative and economically prosperous per capita than towns, suburbs or countryside.* (There are obvious exceptions, e.g., metro Detroit and other Rust Belt cities.) Many authors, most notably Jane Jacobs (1961) and more recently Edward Glaeser (2011), have lauded this tendency, which is more intuitively obvious than the environmental paradox. Creativity is the hardest of these proclivities to measure, both in available data and statistical handles, but patents per capita per year have been used by Glaeser and others as a respectable stand-in metric, with consistently positive results. Literary, musical and visual arts productivity are generally also thought to bloom, but their quality is more subjective to measure; needless to say cultural creativity is widely thought to be positively connected to large cities (with the exception of rural arts colonies, communities and camps, which thrive in "natural" settings). Richard Florida (2004) and others have written on the arts spillover effect, which is economic as well as cultural.

Of course, this creative output must be weighed against the fact that excessive production, wealth and consumption can be counterproductive environmentally. The richest seven percent of the world's population are estimated to consume at such prodigious rates that they produce half its anthropogenic GHGs.[5] Nor does concentrated private wealth necessarily increase economic growth. A recent IMF study[6] indicates that increasing wealth at the top of the pyramid does not spur (and may decrease) economic growth, suggesting that the trickle-down theory is flawed and, in fact, a trickle-up effect may sometimes be in play. Wealth may well beget environmental poverty.

C. *Cities produce many problems but tend to self-correct them with new laws, norms, technologies and institutions.* Most communities and societies have the capacity to address their problems, but cities appear to be especially effective at dealing with seemingly insurmountable challenges. For instance, we know many cities prior to the twentieth century were plagued by pestilence and disease, with frequent outbreaks of cholera, malaria and influenza and high incidence rates of dysentery, tuberculosis, syphilis, etc. However, as Jane Jacobs pointed out a half-century ago, cities were particularly adept at overcoming these afflictions, inventing and implementing more and better infrastructure, codes, hospitals, public education and, not incidentally, ambulance service. Frequent and widespread fire was corrected by urban advances in fire codes and firefighting; social ire quieted with housing reforms; racial inequality was reduced; crime dropped with organized police departments to enforce the laws and keep the peace. More recent technologies, like the mobile phone and its proliferating "killer apps," make understanding and negotiating the city easier and communication faster, as well as simultaneously augmenting physical reality with instant information. (Paradoxically, many digital technologies that shrink or erase distance do not encourage the geographic dispersion of people, but instead support compact, urban lifestyles.)

D. *Cities also present a social paradox: they can absorb and maintain difference while sponsoring social unity and a sense of community for diverse demographics.* Healthy cities tolerate and mitigate sharp differences while simultaneously imbuing neighborhoods and individual inhabitants with self-identities. Paradoxically, these identities are both sharpened and blended by offering many role models and behaviors to observe and experience. Their public realms bring and bond people closer together — but not too closely — much like a dining or conference table connects while separating them, as Hannah Arendt once observed:[7] if the table is removed, the people are no longer separated, but they are no longer connected either. Despite today's highly wired population, city squares remain popular public outdoor living rooms, accommodating and celebrating the incredible diversity of the human condition, serving as sites for public events from civic ceremonies and festivals to demonstrations and protests, from flea and farmers markets to horse and foot races, from people-watching and carousing to sleeping. It is also true that the public realms in some societies are too contested, legally or socially off-limits for open mixing of different people, or that there is little, if any, public gathering space, as in some Islamic cities and totalitarian cultures. Despite these challenges, many subaltern and forgotten groups find alternate places to congregate or do commerce in the "Everyday Urbanism" that cities provide.[8]

E. *Cities have the ability to evolve and transform themselves over time.* With new technologies, institutions, cultures, energy sources and other innovations, they can reconfigure and rehabilitate themselves, tearing down and rebuilding continuously and in spurts. Occasionally they even reboot their particular functions if not their original *raison d'être.* Some cities have not been able to correct or recover from their particular problems for a host of reasons: their structure was too outdated or rigid, the depletion of a local natural resource, a natural or wartime disaster, or a lack of leadership, capital or luck (e.g., Chernobyl, Detroit and Butte, Montana, in no particular order). These declines and collapses are characterized by the British-Canadian historian Ronald Wright falling into as three types — runaway train, house of cards and dinosaur.[9] However, in general, cities are resilient; many have lasted millennia, full of the palimpsests and barnacles of time. Like ecosystems, they alternate between longer, slower periods of accumulation and consolidation followed by shorter periods of fast, abrupt change, responding to new opportunities and challenges (which they may have themselves precipitated). They slough off and bury outdated building stock and infrastructure, and rebuild on top of themselves, sometimes amassing many strata of rubble, like Rome or most any ancient city that has endured.

III. Landscape Urbanism and New Urbanism

The paradoxes and benefits of cities provide a productive lens to compare two major, competing theories and practices of urbanism and the two that are the focus of this book: LU and NU.

The two movements share many common values, beliefs and goals. Both movements claim to be committed to and expert in environmental sustainability and urbanism, which each considers to be a very high priority and consequential issue for humanity. (For purposes of this essay, the more inclusive *Ecological Urbanism* [EU] is considered aligned with Landscape Urbanism, despite some differences in their credos and agendas, as outlined in Ecological Urbanism, edited by Mohsen Mostafavi.) Both have academicians, professionals and academician-professionals in their group. Each group originated in the US but has attracted or joined with colleagues internationally. And both are covered in the media, including newspapers, websites, blogs and listservs, and professional and scholarly journals.

LU and NU also embrace aspirations, principles and theories that share many mutual values and ideals (despite the inevitable challenges of living up to and implementing them). Both movements purport to be empirical and pragmatic, as they claim to be scientifically informed and outcome-based. Each is design-based and form-oriented, believing design has an essential (and typically underappreciated) role to play in addressing society's environmental, social and economic problems.

To a varying degree, each eschews post-structuralism, although LU touts the flux, flow and indeterminacy of natural systems as much or more than their stability. Both reject in different ways the "Critical Project" in favor of more "projective" and proactive theory and practice, developing promising or proven solutions rather than focusing on critiques of society's many shortcomings. However, neither group has gone back to the pure empiricism of positivism or to the mixture of the empiricism and rationality of logical positivism.

Each rejects the mechanistic, reductionist paradigms and the one-variable-at-a-time engineering syndrome of modernism (but the pragmatism of engineering is still welcome). Both repudiate the human-nature dichotomy — whether it be the Cartesian split between mind and body, "the machine and garden," or Emerson's "rural strength and religion" and "city facility and polish." They address these too-often-separated categories as inter-related, overlapping magisteria, to use Stephen Jay Gould's terms for domains of discourse and teaching.[10] Essentially, they both believe cities are as natural as beehives, anthills, schools of fish, and buffalo herds, but with more elaborate technological systems and props. They'd agree with Jane Jacobs, who wrote that the economic law of supply and demand, law of diminishing returns, are as much a part of the universe as the laws of gravity and of thermodynamics. People-watching in cities is as natural an activity as bird-watching in the wilderness, or, for that matter, birds watching people in cities.

Both focus on public space, LU almost exclusively. LU seems to embrace the neighborhood and walkability that is basic to NU, although their ideal neighborhood is typically more open and campus-like, and their walk is through the park rather than along the street. It's not clear if LU accepts the gridded, as opposed to the dendritic, network of streets and roads that is foundational to NU. Each embraces a more regional approach to urban planning than has become the political, academic and professional norm. (NU also believes in regionalist architecture, including climate-specific passive solar systems and natural building techniques.) Both look or claim to look for the underlying structure beneath these and other types of form, rejecting a superficial or arbitrary application of form to the designed environment.

It is because of these overlaps and congruities that LU and NU can engage and debate with each other, however heatedly or one-sidedly. And there's George Baird's[11] suggestion that Peter Calthorpe, because of his radical regionalism, is arguably more *critical* (in a positive sense) of the status quo than Peter Eisenman, the arch-champion of "critical design," that is, architecture that challenges convention (in his case sticks to disciplinary rigor, while leaving interdisciplinary issues like sustainability to others). Despite its all-too-frequent architectural mediocrity and historicism, NU is in some senses more radical than avant-garde architects-turned-urban-designers, whose morphological inventiveness is often socially conventional. In any case, here the similarities between the two movements end.

IV. Differences

NU is a larger and more organized movement, with the Congress for the New Urbanism (CNU), a charter, a national office with staff, and a growing number of state chapters. It has developed, sponsored and co-sponsored codes, policies and programs, and its staff and members engage in legislative and regulatory reform. It is fair to say that over a generation the movement has reshaped the contours of the conversation about suburbia, and relentlessly enlightened it. As well as design professionals, its membership includes developers, builders, elected and appointed officials, and interested citizens, and it regularly attracts as many as 1,500 members and non-members to its annual congress, now in its twenty-first year. Less connected to the academy than LU, NU still enjoys some scholarly attention, and is even central at several schools of architecture, as well as being endorsed passively by many if not most urban planning programs.[12]

LU is more academically ensconced and intellectually positioned, with strongholds in Ivy League institutions (which generally consider NU a third rail). At least one leader of LU associates himself with Habermas,[13] and claims to disassociate the movement from post-structuralism and the Critical Project that has dominated the academy for a generation, especially in architecture programs. Nonetheless, it still embraces and defends forms that are arguably post-structuralist, despite their new and different rhetoric. The fractal geometries, in particular the flowing, interwoven stream forms, may be ecologically based, but this vocabulary often seems more stylistic than derived from ecological patterns, especially when applied to buildings and urban complexes instead of the landscape. LU's preoccupation with surface, especially folded green planes and sinuous terrain, may seem to be *site-adjusted, site specific,* or even *site conditioned/ determined,* but they often tend to be site dominant, on the lowest rung of artist Robert Irvin's taxonomy.[14]

LU's leading designs have been more celebrated in the media than those of NU, and are typically more media- and photogenic. Although no LU designer has reached the "starchitecture" level of status or publicity, there are a few that could be called landscape starchitects. They tend to lead collaborative teams more frequently than landscape architects have in the past. Indeed, there are some LU detractors, including NUists, who consider the movement *primarily* a power play to assert a more central role for landscape architects in planning and designing the built environment, particularly after years of playing a subordinate role to architects. While this is an understandable motive, it is not sufficient when the full panoply of urbanism is in play. It is also too disruptive and inefficient to engage in tussles over leadership for its own sake. What is needed are more team collaborations, public-private partnerships, and multi-disciplinary design charrettes, with talented designers that can lead without dominating. To their credit, landscape architects and urban planners generally have a better record of collaboration than architects (but LUists do not have as much experience as NUists have with private developers and builders).

According to its major proponents, LU arises directly from an interest in landscape ecology and infrastructure, with roots in Ian McHarg (however much his influence has since been downplayed as too homeostatic). It has further developed his and related ecological theories and practices, with greater emphasis on ever-evolving, unstable ecosystems and their rapid changes and dynamic oscillations that overturn or rattle longer periods of static equilibrium (within overall limits of carrying capacities). The most vivid example of this natural flux is the positive feedback of current climate change, which is shuffling the meteorological deck in ways not seen in the last ten thousand years, a period of remarkably stable climatic conditions that were very well suited to the ever-accelerating growth of *Homo sapiens* and the flourishing of their civilizations.

NU is much less fluid and continuous in its forms, with its roots more in traditional architectural vocabulary and urban syntax. It is not embarrassed, as LU would be, to use conventional or traditional urbanism if this is sensible and desired. Nor is it against fresh ideas and new form if these are practical, appropriate and promising. NU is more committed to evidence-based design and the physical determinism of design and planning, although it realizes the inherent limits. The original East Coast contingent grew out of a European formalism, while the original West Coast contingent had been previously involved to varying degrees in the environmental/passive solar and regionalism movements. The six founders came together a quarter century ago, having *independently* come to stunningly similar conclusions about the deficits and antidotes to suburban sprawl, including a similar shared vision for neighborhoods, cities and regions. The early proponents coalesced around more compact, traditional urbanism that is mixed-use, street-oriented, human-scaled, small-blocked and transit-oriented. They were all sympathetic to and influenced by the early counterproposals to the industrialist/capitalist city, like Ebenezer Howard and the dragon slayers of Corbusian/CIAM urbanism, such as Jane Jacobs and Leon Krier.

The East Coast founders, with European urban sensibilities, have promoted traditional neighborhood development (TND) and more traditional design language, while the West Coast proponents, with their environmental backgrounds, have been more interested in transit-oriented development (TOD, originally named "pedestrian pockets") and have typically been less insistent on low-rise traditional architecture (though NU's early period overlapped with postmodernist architecture, so initially both contingents were relatively conservative and historicist). Although there is nothing in the CNU charter that prescribes style, the resultant work of the unified movement was, with a few exceptions, more conservative and less contemporary than LU. However, NU has room[15] for contemporary architecture if it is not expected to congeal around the modernist superblock, superhighway, or superhighrise. In any case, the ongoing creative rivalry between these two NU strains, and between other contingents, has proved healthy and productive. West Coast founder Calthorpe describes the ongoing tensions:

> New Urbanism struggles between two identities, one a lofty set of principles that many criticize as too utopian and the other a style that is stereotyped as retro and simplistic. In fact, it is many other things as well; a coalition meant to unify a broad range of disciplines and interest groups; a rebirth of urban design over planning; and a powerful counterpoint to the norm of sprawl.
>
> — Baird, 2007, p. 15

Although they clearly differ in aesthetic sensibilities, the most salient difference between LU and NU boils down to how they define and embody *urbanism*. The first difference is structural, measurable and subject to rational discourse (i.e., reasonable people could disagree, but the positions can be clearly stated). NU, as its name would suggest, is first and foremost about urbanism. Architecture per se has been less important from the outset. It has come to more fully embrace the environmental and infrastructural dimension of sustainability later in its trajectory than LU. *NU believes the first obligation and role of towns and cities is to provide livable, resilient human habitat that is compact enough to simultaneously reap the paradoxical, inherent benefits of urbanity and leave as much of a region's natural habitat intact for other animal and plant species.* It does not believe in maximizing the amount of "nature" per se in the city proper, but in optimizing and balancing it with the hinterland. Accordingly, in the city it usually opts for less open space, wildlife, streams and forest or grasslands than LU, which has criticized NU for promoting a "parks desert." NU, particularly its regional advocates, would rather concentrate development in the city and build compact, complete communities on the periphery than continue the agonizing compromise of suburban development.

NU is also for greening cities, but would prefer to *civilize* rather than *naturalize* its infrastructure. The *street* is seen as the most important infrastructure, as well as the public vascular system of the city. Although NU welcomes and celebrates bodies of water, vegetation, food production (especially with its recent Agrarian Urbanism), and animal life in the city, these are more for the psychological, aesthetic and health benefits to humans than for the other species *per se* (though clearly beneficial to them). To repeat, NU believes the *optimal* ecological strategy is to favor the human species in these concentrated zones of habitation, *saving as much unspoiled space and habitat as possible elsewhere for other species.* This figure-ground or host-guest reversal is arguably an ironic switch back to a type of Euclidean zoning and land-use specialization at the regional scale that CNU abhors at the local scale. It's zoning land use by *species* — human (and domesticated, compatible and symbiotic animals) away from wildlife — rather than by *function*. Indeed, this traditional spatial congregation of humans for purposes of living and working, although never total, is the nexus of the environmental paradox of cities. And *NU takes better advantage of both its local and global benefits.*

In his seminal LU essay "Terra Fluxus," James Corner describes the more traditional way of seeing landscape and cities as looking through a "nineteenth century lens of difference and opposition ... landscape in the form of parks, greenways, street trees, esplanades and gardens, is generally seen to provide both the salve and the respite from the deleterious effects of urbanization."[16] He goes on to describe New York's Central Park as a paragon of this model, as well as a catalyst of surrounding real estate development: "... for Olmsted and even Le Corbusier in his Plan Voisin, this green complex comes in the form of parks and open spaces, accompanied by the belief that such environments will bring civility, health, social equity and economic diversity to the city."

NU sees deeper and more enduring human and ecological merits in Central Park, which are better understood a century and a half after its nineteenth-century conception. Moreover, it believes that the park is fundamentally different from the Plan Voisin or CIAM urbanism, because it is more *urbanistically spatial.* Its overall containment by the high, straight street wall of buildings that "enfront" the park, craning their elegant necks to see into it, and the picturesque places within the man-made landscape, are more spatially enclosed and humane than the open-ended expanse of Le Corbusier's Paris plan. Both LU and NU appreciate how much Central Park serves ecological functions in detaining and retaining storm water, providing food and natural habitat for animals from earthworms to bees to deer, converting sunlight into vegetation, absorbing CO_2, producing oxygen and compost, cooling the ambient temperature by evapotranspiration, etc. From a NU perspective, Central Park's human-centric design can claim an even greater ecological purpose, because the park helps a very high concentration of humans to live more symbiotically on the crowded island of Manhattan.

Fig. 3.1: *Manhattan's Central Park may, as James Corner writes, look at nature "through a nineteenth century lens of difference and opposition," but NU contends that the park continues to successfully serve urbanistic as well as ecological purposes, as it eases and lubricates the dense human habitat that spatially defines and emphatically contains it. (The Upper East Side has the city's highest residential density.)*

Jane Jacobs argued in ways we are only beginning to fully appreciate that human culture and commerce are integral parts of the same seamless natural system, and that typically the needs of *Homo sapiens,* the most complex and highly evolved species, trump those of less-evolved species. This *subsidiarity* distinction, in which some species and systems are below or less consequential than others, may be one of the primary discursive differences between LU and NU. Both agree that natural systems are needed in cities to feed, hydrate, oxygenate and cleanse life, but perhaps do not agree about the extent and degree to which the ultimate role of cities is to accommodate and advance humankind more than other species, always respectful of the essential and miraculous roles other species play in reversing entropy and sustaining physical and ecological resilience and order. Despite the innate rights of animals, it should be remembered that only humans build self-conscious cultural and metaphysical order in the face of the universe's ceaseless dissipation and dilution of energy and information in its cosmic cooling and diffusion.

This difference has many implications. Perhaps the most representative and important is the attitude toward the *street.* As NU's Michael Mehaffy states, "Waldheim said he parts company with us over the idea that the thoroughfare generates a street wall, and this becomes the fundamental generator of urban form."[17] It's the apex of a long list of differences: the open campus plan of free-standing buildings vs. street-based, street-fronting buildings; dendritic road/street hierarchy vs. highly connected networks; superblocks vs. small blocks; freestanding, object buildings vs. background, fabric buildings; limited vs. substantial sense of enclosure and framing of space in public places; high-rise vs. low-rise buildings; artistic license vs. norms and codes; abstract vs. articulated architectural detailing; fine art vs. artisan model; invisible vs. visible contexts; void-dominated vs. solid-dominated urban fabric; limited vs. full declension of architectural and building types; polycentric/hybrid density patterns vs. the Transect; surface vs. mass; and abstract vs. figurative form and composition. This relentless list reveals among other things that LU has left neither orthodox modernism nor post-structuralism as far behind as claimed.

On the other hand, it also suggests that NU has not been as open to or accepting of contemporary form as much as its charter — which claims that its design principles are "beyond" architectural style — allows, or as much as is defensible. It is easy for the defenders of neo-traditional architecture to blame the often mediocre and banal architecture on middle class, bourgeois taste and the market economics of speculative development (where one market-rejected project can bankrupt a company). However, its leaders *could* fight for better design with the same fervor they've shown in other aspects of NU's mission. As this author and some other members of the Congress for the New Urbanism (CNU) have been pushing since its birth, this means *more contemporary architectural design.* The standard NU response would be that you can only move public taste and the market so far so fast, and that *urban* reform was and is more important and impactful than *architectural excellence* — a tactical argument to use familiar style as a Trojan horse in which to hide or obscure otherwise unacceptable social, cultural and environmental design. That tactic may have been compelling ten to twenty years ago, but is no longer persuasive. NU needs to embrace the successful and popular aspects of modernist design.

The second basic difference follows on from this style issue, moving further from the discursive logic of ecological science and urbanism to the emotive, non-rational realm of visual form. This realm includes aesthetic sensibilities, artistic taste, and even group dynamics. These subjective feelings tend to run deeper and to change slower than an individual's or group's rational constructs; they are more difficult to express in words and to discuss. (A sound argument can change someone's mind, even an opponent's, but it takes a long time to change his or her taste or feelings about something.) About feeling more than *logos* or logic, the second difference is more subjective and less conducive to rational analysis and discourse. Nonetheless, it bears scrutiny.

In matters of architectural style and culture "wars," group dynamics and partisanship can play a deciding role, as often "people choose one or the other according to the cohort espousing it, and only secondarily for hedonic reasons."[18] In this case, the academic design world is quick to dismiss NU aesthetics as nostalgic and trite (which is sometimes true, especially with its speculative housing for the conservative middle class). Indeed, NU is unpopular or ignored in many schools of architecture and rarely, if ever, present in the faculty conversation, lecture series, curriculum or culture. To their credit, these same schools are now jettisoning the hybrid legacies of modernism, post-structuralism and deconstructionism, and beginning to embrace parametric/digital design, infrastructure design, environmental sustainability and social justice — the "projective project."

However, Eisenman calls our era a period and condition of "lateness".[19] Is it a late-modernist cul-de-sac of rococo or mannerist excess or dying capitalist exuberance and indulgence? Or is it the continuing, semiconscious complicity with big and powerful institutional and corporate patrons, implicitly to make the impersonalized world of global culture and industrial production more elegant, exciting and salable? Is it as market-and profit-driven as middle-class "developer" NU, but just driven by a wealthier and more sophisticated clientele who are better patrons of design? Is LU still caught in avant-garde sensibilities and moods? Even as the academic agenda changes to LU and ecological urbanism, the forms and aesthetics still seem unable or unwilling to escape the former design style. Like many avant-garde and academic movements, does LU simply assume that any design based on traditional typologies or form *has* to be outdated and wrong?

As mentioned earlier, forms often speak louder than words, and the difference between LU and NU form per se is highly relevant to the environmental paradox of urbanism. Sustainable, resilient urbanism is a natural part of ecology. It doesn't mimic nature; it *is* nature. Like passive solar buildings, it may not *look* naturalistic. As habitat, it has to function in a way that is sympathetic and beneficial to its dominant species. Bio*morphic* shapes and patterns may appear to be more natural than a rectilinear built environment, but may nonetheless be less bio*philic* and ecological. Built environments that make humans feel alive, comfortable and secure often are not as biomorphic or literally green in color, but they are more sustainable if they resonate with humans, as well as meet the density, mix and scale of the environmental paradox. Bio*mimetic* design *learns* from nature; it may *appear* no more like nature than Velcro strips look like the natural thorns they mimic. Paradoxically, NU's more conventional rectilinear forms typically constitute a more resilient urbanism than the flowing, fecund forms of LU. The latter may have a high *net* density in places — with high-rise building clusters or towers in the park — but when all the open space is included, it too often lacks the gross density, mix and scale of NU. A dense, geometric grid can be more aligned to the paradox of cities than lush serpentine parks.

Even though reading these forms is often more ambiguous than reading texts, the more salient differences between LU and NU design are visually obvious. For instance, LU is more enthralled with surface and "thick," continuous horizontal form, especially folded ground planes or interweaving, curvilinear landscapes and wetland-scapes. Folded plates may help urbanize landscapes, and sinuous form may be a vivifying counterpoint to the straight lines of existing cities, as well as a sympathetic way to embody and express important ecological flows, loops and rhythms, but this palette can be as formulaic as NU's formal master plans (an overplayed but often accurate criticism). Nor does it sufficiently define the outdoor rooms and streets — defined by buildings — that people from all cultures seem to find spatially comfortable, pleasant and sociably humane. This brings into question Charles Waldheim's assertion that LU has "the ability to produce urban effects traditionally achieved through the construction of buildings simply through the organization of horizontal surfaces."[20] (See Figures c-16 and c-22).

This is not to say that NU shouldn't take more advantage of contemporary sensibilities. In fact it should pay more attention to twentieth-century breakthroughs and liberations, such as fractal and exponential geometries (beyond NU's ubiquitous circles, squares and the occasional ellipse) and the glazed transparency of contemporary architecture that connects indoors and outdoors so seamlessly. On another axis, both groups need to better recognize the diversity of today's urban demographics, and how they not only represent different values, histories and aspirations, but also different architectural iconographies, sensibilities and tastes that should not be ignored or teased into a one-size-fits-all design and planning template.

On the other hand, LU must recognize that urban form naturally evolves into the traditional urban patterns of any given culture. The informal squatter settlements of the developing world, given sufficient time and resources, almost always develop into a dense, street-oriented network of mixed-use urbanism, with paratransit. When left to their own devices and resourcefulness, without top-down interference (other than the provision of minimal infrastructure and municipal services), these eventually morph to look like medieval European or Asian villages and towns. From the air they become almost indistinguishable, which is not surprising given that cities are essentially expressions of their occupants' culture.

LU's form is as indebted to post-structuralist flux and fractals as NU's form is to Beaux Arts, City Beautiful, and neoclassical symmetry and monumentality. (Architects like Zaha Hadid and Leon Krier have respectively represented these sensibilities at their extremes.) If LU's form usually maps onto ecological systems and their fractal geometries, it already seems as stereotypical as they claim NU forms to be. And at the large scale, it falls into the intoxicating trap to which architects have long been prey: *treating the city as a work of art.* Again citing Jacobs, art has a very important and unique role to play in cities, namely conveying, interpreting, and bringing deeper meaning and richer understanding to our individual and collective lives, as well as humanizing the cacophony of our cities. But art should not be confused with city design and city building.

Cities, like ecosystems, are beyond humans' ability to successfully mastermind and intentionally shape into gigantic, coherent works of visual art (with the possible exception of small cities in autocratic or totalitarian regimes). Not only are cities too operationally and sensorially complex and managerially intractable, but today's urban demographics are too diverse to coalesce around universally shared values and aspirations. This is why NU resorts to more traditional, universal typologies and codes, especially form-based, typological, and generative codes, which allow variation within a consistent system that makes change not only more manageable but also more predictable. In the end, humans can aspire and work to harmonize and even unify their cities, and to incorporate art within them, but they are fooling themselves if they think they can orchestrate them like a conductor or shape them like a sculptor.

Last, both movements should realize that they are provisional and transitional to a world that needs to be denser, more equitable, more sustainable, and less carbon-based. As Jeremy Rifkin points out in *The Third Industrial Revolution,* the emerging confluence of distributed but connected renewable energy systems in conjunction with a new, lateral communication systems is a shift on the same order as the first two industrial revolutions.[21] These changes will require that urbanism adapt to new conceptual, economic, legal and business models and norms, to help provide for humans without endless economic growth that depletes the plane.[22] LU and NU may both be good steps in many ways — perhaps as big as our culture can currently countenance and absorb — but ultimately they are not transformative enough to mitigate, adapt or geo-engineer our way out of the many pressing problems we face, none bigger or longer term than the many impacts of climate change.

V. Learning From and Moving Beyond the Differences

Although the environmental paradox of cities is a timely and welcome realization, like LU and NU, it is not sufficient assurance. We will have to learn from each other and other parties to determine what the next steps need to be. There has been progress, to be sure. Both schools of thought have moved beyond the over-simplified reductionism and over-mechanized model of nature in modernism. Both have rejected conventional suburban sprawl, although LU is softer on the use of the automobile and the incredibly broad right-of-way accorded to motorized vehicles in motion — and space devoted to them at rest — since World War Two. In this light, Charles Waldheim's embrace of Lafayette Park in downtown Detroit, the classic modernist housing project by Mies/Hilberseimer, is a harbinger of a problematic route LU might take. As elegant as its pristine architecture set among now-mature landscape is, it is a superblock/campus that makes for an overwhelmingly single-use urbanism that is too fragmented, diffuse and auto-dependent. It is a poor precedent for a time and place that needs more compact, mixed-use, street-oriented, walkable, bikeable and transit-friendly urbanism that is more tightly gridded than LU projects to date. (Detroit *does* have a congestion problem: a *lack* of it).

To LU's credit, James Corner describes his work as "the tactical work of choreography" rather than "formal object-making".[23] Years earlier, landscape architecture professor Elizabeth Meyer wrote that the *site* and designer are collaborators, and "that the double-voiced discourse is predicated on a systems aesthetic, not an object aesthetic; it's about the relationship between things and not the things alone".[24] She also poignantly writes, "The landscape does not sit silent awaiting the arrival of an architectural subject. The site — the land — speaks prior to an act of design". NU would quickly amend this to say that the city and its designers are also collaborators. In Meyer's terms, LU is a correction to "the marginal role landscape architecture has been assigned in the histories of modernity ... [the] silent female or irrational feminine role". Is LU the needed manifestation of feminization of landscape architecture after centuries of "a masculine discourse focusing primarily on the works of great landscape architects — mostly men"?. It is a good question ... for both movements.

The recent assertiveness and rise of LU is understandable and perhaps inevitable, given the background role landscape architecture has historically been asked to play since Olmsted and his student John Nolen launched it as a professional endeavor over a century ago. NU can no doubt learn from landscape architects, most importantly about sustainable site design and landscape ecology. While architects know more about structure, and NU knows more about urban structure, landscape architects are usually more expert and experienced in sustainable infrastructure (and deserve credit for popularizing it). LU could help NU on the rural end of its Transect.

The Transect is basic to NU, with the gradient in density, use and height going from wilderness to rural to suburban zones to the three zones of urbanism, plus a special sector for uses that don't fit in easily, like warehouse districts, industry, airports and so on. (This gradient works at the rural to urban scale, but most neighborhoods consist of only two or three Transect zones.) In general, sociocultural diversity increases as density increases, while natural/ecological diversity decreases. A more mature and sustainable urbanism would attempt to keep sociocultural diversity AND natural/ecological diversity as high as possible in all zones, as illustrated in Fig. 6.3 (see Andrés Duany's chapter) by DPZ, the firm of CNU founders Andrés Duany and Elizabeth Plater-Zyberk.

LU could learn a great deal about urbanism from NU, which has put considerable effort into the empirical study of what works and what doesn't work in cities (at least in North America, Europe and Australia). It has actively explored and cultivated these aspects with more than twenty years of conferences, writings and community engagement, testing them in the field in both the public and private sectors. LU needs to better master *urbanism per se* if it's to justify its name and if its practitioners want to continue to assume professional leadership on large-scale projects and to work more with real-estate developers. This includes increasing their understanding of and emphasis on urban social, economic and political dynamics and processes, which are as open-ended and indeterminate as ecology.

There are other areas where cross-fertilization is needed. NU can learn more about hydrology, below-grade infrastructure, toxic industrial sites, fractal form and parametric/digital design and fabrication from LU, which in turn could profit from NU's detailed and time-tested knowledge of urban streets and sidewalks, codes and the public/private continuum of urban space, especially at the urban end of the Transect. It could also learn from design methodology like form-based and generative codes, bricolage (per Colin Rowe), and pattern language (per Christopher Alexander). LU would benefit from a deeper appreciation that the *city*, like the landscape, has a voice that is equally site-specific and unique, and that often speaks louder and more urgently than landscape in the design and planning of human habitat. A big question to co-explore is whether all systems can be indeterminate or whether some need to be more determinate.

In short, there's not enough urbanism in LU, and not enough ecology in NU. To be more specific, there's not enough human habitat and human culture in LU and not enough habitat for other species and design audacity in NU — a battle with one axis that might be crudely simplified to "mixed use vs. mixed species." On another axis, A. O. Scott wisely writes, "The alternative is an uncritical embrace of the new for its own sake, a shallow contempt for tradition and a blindness to its beauties. But there is an equal risk of being blinded by those beauties to the energies that surround us, and to mistake affection for a standard of judgment."[25] Indeed, nostalgia for either a beloved past or for a coveted future is dangerous when the survival of the human species and its incredibly impressive civilization are at stake. *Lastly, there's not enough sustainability and resilience across the whole of the built and natural environment in either school of thought or professional practice.* Both are too often bent on promoting their specific agendas and conceits rather than tapping more deeply and radically into resilient patterns that have served humanity and the planet well for millennia, as well as new ones that have promise to do so in the future.

VI. The Global Challenge

There are hurdles to any reconciliation or collaboration, to be sure. Some are likely insurmountable. Corner wrote, "…landscape urbanism is first and foremost an imaginative project, a speculative thickening of possibilities."[26] NU would quickly counter that it is first and foremost a pragmatic, time-tested, empirical-, and outcome-based project, thick with possibilities. It too cares about the creative, the imaginative, and the poetic, but not as the primary drivers or characteristics. NU believes that the world can no longer afford the time or the resources for the near-endless speculation and insatiable quest for novelty upon which the avant-garde professional and academic design world thrives. Unlike scientific research (which should continue full speed), design novelty and extravagance is now a luxury, sometimes an orgy. We Westerners thought the excessive consumption was affordable before peak oil, peak capital, peak hegemonic power, and peak growth — call it peak BIGness — conspired to give us the biggest economic "haircut" since the Depression. There is already a surfeit of new ideas and discoveries, as well as a backlog of recent and enduring old ideas, that need to be better understood, leveraged and integrated to design and build better environments.

Love of the new — neophilia — is not sustainable if pursued for its own sake, or for its value as commodity, entertainment or spectacle.[27] Sustainability and resilience, the purported mandate of LU, have sometimes made neophilia an irresponsible indulgence or a slavish need. We have neither the time nor the money nor the resources to test a continuous torrent of raw, wild or undercooked ideas on the ground at full scale. Nor do we have the time or wealth to address problems one at a time; we need to synergistically and collaboratively address and solve multiple problems at the same time — or mitigate ones without full solutions. Change and creativity will come in any case — sometimes slowly and sometimes suddenly, like shifts in ecological systems that episodically leap forward and loop back. With maturity, they can emerge from a deeper, quieter and more grown up understanding of nature than from being enslaved to obligatory invention or beguiled and bedeviled by our own human cleverness and hubris.

Stewart Brand said, "We have become Gods. We might as well get good at it".[28] We may have become divine in our spectacular technological prowess and scientific knowledge, but we should remember that we are mortals. It would behoove us to cultivate the longest temporal view that we can sustain in our memories and minds, and to learn the discipline and foresight this requires. Climate change is arguably the first, biggest and most threatening problem primarily caused by humans that cannot be mitigated or adapted to in a single lifetime, even in the best of circumstances — even if we ceased all GHG production tomorrow.[29]

We are hardwired by evolution to respond to more pressing problems and immediate threats, as well as to immediate pleasures. It will take everything the global WE can individually and collectively muster to rise to the long-term challenges of climate change; it will be genetically easier to focus on more immediate and palpable crises, such as diminishing reserves of resources and the extreme weather events caused by positive feedback of climate on itself (which is anything but positive for humans and their built environment). Positive tipping points, which have always accelerated human progress, are giving way to more and more negative tipping points. This is a time for bold initiatives and even transformative rebooting in the built environment, not for indulgent experimentation and frivolous or open-ended speculation, however artistically sophisticated, titillating or poetic it may be.

It's also a time to boldly revisit past successes, relevant traditions, and time-tested patterns for adaptation to today's conditions. As Bill McKibben, Tim Jackson and New Urbanist James Howard Kunstler advise, we would be better served by backing off from the old model of endless growth and changing to mature, creative and graceful downsizing.[30] Global climate change may not be as in-our-face or urgent as poverty, corruption, terrorism, gender oppression, pandemic disease, nuclear weaponry, water scarcity or polluted air. Nor does it represent the most immediate risk or worst odds. But it does have the highest stakes and potentially the most far-reaching and devastating impacts on more aspects of civilization and more species than anything since the last ice age (when humans were far, far fewer in number and lesser in dominion).

Climate change gravely threatens our interwoven social, political, institutional and economic systems that are more fragile than our planet, which has survived many, far larger changes. There is widespread evidence that this crisis is already accelerating. The African poor are now having to choose more and more between acquiring food or fuel; insurance companies are dealing more and more often with the aftermath of increasingly extreme weather events; government, banking and public education are more financially challenged; and scientists reported a much higher than normal jump in the global rate of increase in GHGs in 2011: 6 percent.[31] In any case, the great climatic unraveling has begun and the great reset is now needed to avoid "climax climate" or "peak environment" in what can now justifiably be named the Anthropocene Age.

The built environment is a very large, if not *the* largest consumer of energy and emitter of the gases that drive global climate change. It also has nasty impacts on *local* climate change, as noted earlier. Carbon, in short, is both the solid, liquid and gaseous fuel, as well as the byproduct, of the ceaseless and often profligate combustion that has enabled civilization to grow and thrive since its beginnings. Billions of tiny fossil fires, fueled by concentrated carbon taken from the Earth's crust, have the planet glowing in the night sky, a gossamer veil of lights woven by and for humans. Visible from outer space, this beautiful twinkling is our greatest if least intended and least seen work of art, an ironic testimony to how much energy we consume and how urbanized we have become.

Polar ice is melting faster and glaciers are shrinking and calving more icebergs into rising seas. Much of this is caused by combustion to keep us comfortable in our buildings — to light, heat, cool and connect over seven billion of us, as well to build, maintain, renovate and rebuild our buildings, or to raze and build them anew, which is done far more than necessary. LU and NU are both positioned to play a valuable, unique role in mitigating, adapting to, and ameliorating climate change and its consequences in a rapidly urbanizing world.

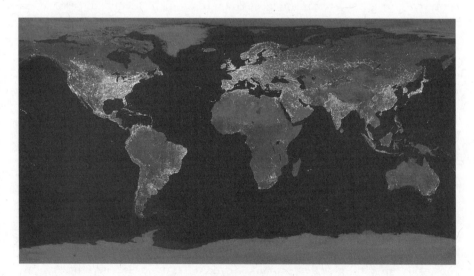

Fig. 3.2: *Set ablaze against a dark sky by the burning of fossil fuel, the planet is now half urban in human population and is soon expected to have 3 out of every 4 humans living in cities.*
Credit: Photo by NASA

The environmental paradox of cities is a big and welcome part of any mitigation/adaptation strategy for slowing climate change and blunting a decline or even collapse of population, not to mention physical standard of living, cultural health, and general well-being and happiness. More green technologies and important breakthroughs are sure to emerge, thanks to the imagination and resourcefulness of our ingenious, adaptive species,[32] but they will bring, as always, unintended consequences with their benefits. The *planet itself* and many of its hardiest and most adaptive species will survive swimmingly; the big question is whether the most advanced and successful of its species — human beings with their astonishingly diverse and vibrant culture — will endure and live fulfilling lives in similar numbers. The sooner LU, NU, and the million plus other environmental/social justice groups and organizations in the world[33] act, the less painful and costly will be the mitigation, adaptation and amelioration required,[34] and the more likely there will be more positive tipping points and fewer negative ones ahead.

Postscript

Prompted by David Heymann's provocative essay "Landscape Is Our Sex: Observations on Buildings and Landscapes"[35] I more recently and more stridently wrote:

> David Heymann has intelligently and convincingly shown that the emperor has few if any clothes on. It's a disarming as well as disrobing essay. The conceit and deceit of convoluted rationales and theories used to promote and defend an architect's design with clients and the public — something all of us designers have engaged in to greater and lesser degrees and with more and less transparency — range from the unctuous and saccharine to the cunning and unscrupulous. Even the hi-tech rational architects of Britain indulge in it, when they sell their wares as pure engineering and economic rationality. (I remember when my small firm was Richard Rogers' Architect of Record and doing all the drawings for his first building in the US three decades ago: if the preferred engineering solution from brilliant structural engineer Peter Rice didn't look as good as Roger's personal

preference, the latter usually won out — in what was nonetheless an elegant, rational building and a creatively productive collaboration.)

In many cases intentional obfuscation and self-righteous veiling HAS facilitated good, even great, buildings. But the naked use and abuse of allusions to "nature" and natural landscape in the design "mapping" of Hadid, Libeskind and others tend to the slippery and disingenuous. The way starchitects use site mapping and other ecotropes to justify their buildings and landscapes is a shell game, and will no doubt change as needed to suit well-intended but often capricious clientele and to tilt to prevailing public sentiment. (Much less in the conscientious and sometimes sublime projects of designers like Peter Zumthor, Glenn Murcutt, Herzog & de Meuron, and perhaps younger artist/architects like SHoP, Brooks + Scarpa, and Adam Kalkin). The starchitects' rationales still ricochet in a post-structuralist hall of mirrors and subjective narratives, despite their claimed or imputed rootedness in unique landscape, place and ecology. It can verge on patronizing purity and convenient virtue.

And the Landscape Urbanists aren't far behind when they promote their tilted planes, sinuous stream forms, and abstracted landscapes as ecologically derived. They ARE more genuinely concerned about environmental footprint, but too little about the carbon tire prints of the automobile in their schemes of relatively high net density but low gross density. And they are correct to drop earlier conceptions of "nature" that divide and contrast the "man-made" and "natural" as romantic and outdated, but the post-structuralist form-making persists in spite of the rhetoric to the contrary. It's always a matter of degree (there has to be some room for fun, ego and conceit, just to get the human juices going), but, again, the question drags and nags about whether they will truly let ecology get in the way of designing form they favor.

A final, more personal note: NU has been publically critical of LU, but it has nonetheless included LU in its public discourse, including acknowledging and crediting some of LU's strengths and accomplishments. For those of us who continue to think there's much to be learned from each other, it's discouraging that the public exchange is not more two-way. I have seen very little acknowledgement or even mention of NU in LU literature, internet blogs, or posts. This relative silence could be interpreted as arrogant and close-minded or as an expression of denial or jealousy, or as a dismissal of NU as either not in their best interest to acknowledge and lend legitimacy to, or unworthy to be a sparring partner. Whatever this reluctance — and whether it's genuine or tactical — it seems ironic if not hypocritical for a group that so strongly professes to believe in the public realm. It is my hope that, despite any hard comments on LU, this essay will encourage more debate and cross-fertilization.

In the end, it's better to collaborate than compete. Competition for design commissions — a zero sum game — is one thing, but competing in the realm of on-the-ground urban systems and infrastructure is not productive. We can not afford to build competing sewer or street systems, any more than to duplicate street lamps or waterfront promenades. Public works within a city, urbanity itself, are not competitive, zero sum enterprises; they are common, civic monopolies whose commonwealth is meant to exceed the sum of the parts. Designers of the urban environment and public realm need to collaborate, and to be free enough and wise enough to know when to reclaim forgotten traditions and when to be audacious.

Endnotes

1   Krier, L. 2011. *Seaside at 30*. South Bend, IN: University of Notre Dame.

2   West, Geoffrey. 2011. *The Surprising Math of Cities and Corporations*. TEDGlobal www.ted.com. Filmed July 2011

3   Berry, Luc. 2011. *A Brief History of History*. New York: Harper Perennial.

4   I first heard this memorable phrase from the distinguished professor and practitioner of landscape architecture Richard Haag, a close colleague at the University of Washington from 1985–98.

5   Stephen Pacala, Director, Princeton Environment Institute, Princeton, NJ, 2011.

6   Berg, A. & J. Ostry, 2011. *Inequality and Unsustainable Growth: Two Sides of the Same Coin?* SDN 11/08. Washington: International Monetary Fund. Retrieved from www.imf.org/external/pubs/ft/sdn/2011/sdn1108.pdf, April, 2011.

7   Arendt, H. 1958. *The Human Condition*. Chicago: University of Chicago Press.

8   Crawford, M. 2005. Everyday Urbanism. *The Michigan Debates on Urbanism*. Ann Arbor, MI: Taubman College of Architecture and Urban Planning, University of Michigan.

9   Wright, R. 2004. *A Short History of Progress*. New York: Da Capo Press.

10 Gould, S. J. 1999. *Rock of Ages, Science and Religion in the Fullness of Life*. New York: Ballantine Books.

11 Baird, G. 2005. Foreword. In R. Fishman, Ed., *New Urbanism*. Ann Arbor, MI: Taubman College of Architecture and Urbanism Planning.

12 Architecture programs at Notre Dame, U. of Miami, Andrews University, and to a lesser extent at U. of Maryland, plus Urban Design program at U. of Michigan, including the author, who is a CNU board member and has attended almost all the CNU annual conferences.

13 Michael Mehaffy, in an email, June 10, 2011, based on his conversation with Charles Waldheim after his "debate" with Andrés Duany at CNU19, Madision, WI, May 2011.

14 Heymann, D. 2011. Landscape is Our Sex. *Places.* Retrieved from *places.designobserver.com/feature/landscape-is-our-sex/31228/*

15 A number of NU activists, most notably the author and CNU founder Dan Solomon, have long argued for both higher quality and more contemporary architectural design.

16 Corner, J. 2006. Terra Fluxus. In Charles Waldheim, Ed., *The Landscape Urbanism Reader.* New York: Princeton Architectural Press, pp. 21–33.

17 Michael Mehaffy, in an email, June 10, 2011, based on his conversation with Charles Waldheim after his "debate" with Andrés Duany at CNU19, Madision, WI, May 2011.

18 B. Donnelly, email, October 31, 2011.

19 Eisenman, P. 2011. Representation/Lateness. Ann Arbor, MI: Taubman College of Architecture and Urban Planning, University of Michigan.

20 Waldheim, C. 2006. *The Landscape Urbanism Reader.* New York: Princeton Architectural Press.

21 Rifkin, J. 2011. *The Third Industrial Revolution.* New York: Palgrave MacMillan.

22 Jackson, T. 2009. *Prosperity without Growth.* London: Earthscan.

23 Corner, op cit., pp. 21–33.

24 Meyer, E. K. 1994. Landscape Architecture as Modern Other and Post-Modern Ground. In H. Edquist and V. Bird, Eds., *The Culture of Landscape Architecture.* Melbourne: Edge Publishing, pp. 12–34.

25 Scott, A.O. 2011. Film is Dead? What Else is New? *New York Times,* November 20: 1, 18–19.

26 Corner, op cit., pp. 21–33.

27 I admit to becoming addicted to following the world news on TV, often for its sheer excitement; indeed, electronic media have never been more titillating and habit-forming.

28 Brand. S. 2009. *Whole Earth Discipline.* New York: Viking Press.

29 For instance, the ozone hole and selected species decline and loss have been sufficiently mitigated or reversed in less than a lifetime; theoretically problems as big as global poverty, many diseases and the universal provision of clean water could be solved in a lifetime with sufficient political will. (For instance clean water for all may possibly cost less than the money we spend on items like plastic water bottles every year.)

30 Wright, op cit.

31 Gillis, J. 2011. Carbon Emissions Show Biggest Jump Ever Recorded. *New York Times, December 5.* Retrieved from *nytimes.com/2011/12/05/science/earth/record-jump-in-emissions-in-2010-study-finds.html.*

32 Benyus, J. 2002. *Biomimicry: Innovation Inspired by Nature.* New York: Harper Perennial.

33 Hawken, P. 2007. *Blessed Unrest.* New York: Penguin Press.

34 Stewart Brand uses "amelioration" in lieu of "geo-engineering."

35 Posted on the Web in *Places: Design Observer's* on November, 2011.

Additional Works Cited

Bettencourt, L. M. A., J. Lobo, D. Helbing, C. Kuhnert, and G. West. 2007. Growth, Innovation, Scaling, and the Pace of Life in Cities. *PNAS* 104 17: 7301-7306.

Florida, R. 2004. *Cities and the Creative Class.* New York: Routledge.

Glaeser, E. 2011. *Triumph of the City.* New York: Penguin Press.

Jacobs, J. 1961. *The Death and Life of Great American Cities.* New York: Random House.

McKibben, W. 2010. *Earth.* New York: Times Books.

4

The Metropolis versus the City

NEAL I. PAYTON

The case for the Metropolis:

> *"Over the past decade landscape has emerged as a model for contemporary urbanism, one uniquely capable of describing the conditions for radically decentralized urbanization, especially in the context of complex natural environments."* [1]
>
> — Charles Waldheim, 2006, *The Landscape Urbanism Reader*

The case for the City:

> *"We live today in cities and suburbs whose form and character we did not choose. They were imposed upon us, by federal policy, local zoning laws and the demands of the automobile. If these are reversed — and they can be — an environment designed around the true needs of individuals, conducive to the formation of community and preservation of landscape, becomes possible. Unsurprisingly, this environment would not look so different from our old American neighborhoods before they were ravaged by sprawl."* [2]
>
> — Duany, Plater-Zyberk and Speck, 2000, *Suburban Nation*

BOTH LANDSCAPE URBANISM AND NEW URBANISM represent radical critiques of contemporary suburban development. They both acknowledge the environmental and cultural destruction wrought by sixty years of planning that treats urban land as a commodity, resulting in placeless real estate spread across the North American continent. However, these movements view the origin and legacy of postwar suburban planning from differing perspectives. The implication of this is that, as the quotes above suggest, they argue for different responses.

Framed as a debate between opposing scales and speeds of urbanity, this essay will characterize these two models of urbanism in terms of the cultural and social imperatives that underlie their respective formulations and the spatial experiences that result. As competing proposals for repairing and creating settlement patterns, the arguments for both Landscape Urbanism and New Urbanism will be considered as distinctly different, but equally viable alternatives. Whereas Landscape Urbanism prioritizes the spatial ambiguity resulting from a conceptual merging of city and country (the Metropolis), and correspondingly, a speed of experience that Waldheim refers to as *automobility,* New Urbanism finds its muse and its moral imperative in the most traditional of urban types, the street, where a slower pace of movement commonly termed *walkability* is dominant (the City).

As in any debate there is an opportunity for rebuttal, where each of the urbanisms is viewed and critiqued through the lens of the other. The Landscape Urbanists view the New Urbanism's concern with street types and "place-making" as hopelessly naïve and passé, whereas the New Urbanists view the Landscape Urbanist project as a sophisticated form of sprawl.

The schism identified in this point/counterpoint leads to the conclusion that there is little space for overlap. True, there are examples of projects designed by Landscape Urbanists that sit within the kind of traditional urban environments favored by the New Urbanists, for example the "High Line" in Lower Manhattan. However, such parks are not full manifestations of Landscape Urbanism theory. They are framed by buildings and, ironically, the kind of civic spaces supported by the Charter of the New Urbanism. In such examples, Landscape Urbanism is manifested as an aesthetic theory, not a prescription for settlement. As alternatives for the contemporary and destructive pattern of suburban development, i.e., as recipes for city-making or regional planning, these two prescriptions for urbanism are irreconcilable as they do not originate from nor share the same ethical imperative.

Urbanisms at Differing Speeds of Habitation

Proponents of Landscape Urbanism view planning after World War II as a product of the forces of technological and economic modernity — characterized by mass communication, personalized and autonomous transport, and decentralized manufacturing, which necessitate vast logistical networks for warehousing, distribution and sales. In their eyes, the evolution of postwar planning parallels a timeline in which the corner store is supplanted by the supermarket and the latter by the warehouse club. As a result, Landscape Urbanists propose new, and one might say more open-ended, urban paradigms, including those that "challenge architectural conventions of closure and control...."[3] In other words, as will be shown below, they tend to promote urban or metropolitan morphologies that, among other characteristics, lack spatial definition and even celebrate *automobility*.

Charles Waldheim, James Corner, Alan Berger, and others make the case for a "Landscape Urbanism" that is vehicular in its scale yet fundamentally guided by a commitment to environmental restoration. These founding theorists aim at "expanding the scope and efficacy of the landscape project"[4] beyond any given site or program, beyond even such normative urban spatial typologies as parks and streets. In both an homage to the decentralizing forces of natural systems and a recognition of (some might say, fascination with) more than a century of industrial production and contemporary transport modalities as well as sixty years of postwar sprawl, Landscape Urbanism seems intent on diluting the fundamental distinction between city and country. In other words, from a human settlement point of view, it embraces the Metropolis with its boundlessness and corresponding speed of movement, rather than the City with its spatial limits and diversity of pace.

New Urbanists consider the past two generations of planning as an aberration, representing something of a self-imposed collective amnesia rather than a permanent change to the cultural episteme. Rather than representing the forces of modernity, they view the past half-century of planning in terms of the dominating influence of Euclidean zoning and traffic engineering, nothing more culturally significant than that. In fact, they would argue, traditional, pre-war urbanism has proven to be far more resilient in the marketplace than any other model precisely because of its continued cultural relevance. In contrast to Landscape

Urbanism, they argue for an urbanism that is spatially and temporally defined.

Andrés Duany, Elizabeth Plater-Zyberk, Peter Calthorpe, and other advocates of New Urbanism make the case that pedestrian-scaled urbanism can help restore a sense of community. In both its opposition to the decentralizing forces of postwar sprawl and its recognition of the problems emanating from contemporary real estate development practices, New Urbanism aims to restore the fundamental distinction between city and country. This translates to an explicit embrace of a distinct typology that recognizes the neighborhood, the town, and, most significantly, the City.

Viewed according to this dichotomy, the words "metropolis" and "city" are not used here simply as terms denoting different scales of urban habitation. The term "metropolis" is not meant merely to connote an excessively large and sprawling urban mass, nor even a collection of cities and suburbs. Rather the Metropolis and the City represent different *speeds* of habitation, where different sizes and scales of the building blocks of urban construction are utilized. While the City is composed of neighborhoods defined in size by the pace of a pedestrian, bound together by corridors — e.g., vehicular thoroughfares, rivers, railway lines and the like — the Metropolis is characterized as much by the corridors themselves, i.e., the green, grey or brown swaths of land that connect neighborhoods and districts to one another, defined more by the pace of the automobile.

At the scale of the City, the highway may have a role only in linking city to city. The New Urbanists would eschew their necessity in linking neighborhoods to one another. A highway-less city is necessarily slower, more navigable by means other than an automobile. The ligaments connecting neighborhood to neighborhood will, of necessity, be experienced at a greater diversity of speeds. The City's form is often described in terms of its "walkability."

On the other hand, at the scale of the Metropolis, the highway becomes as much a place to "inhabit" as any other physical component of the urban milieu. Geographic scale is important, but mostly for the experience of place it necessitates, the miles and miles of in-between landscapes or "drosscapes," as Berger calls them," places that are mediated by the frame of a car windshield. And true to form, Waldheim describes the experience of the Metropolis in terms of its "automobility.[5]

Fast Urbanism: Spatial Experience at the Scale of the Metropolis and the Highway

Because Landscape Urbanism does not have an originating manifesto or defining charter (as New Urbanism does), it is challenging to characterize it succinctly. *The Landscape Urbanism Reader,* an anthology edited by Waldheim, is composed of a series of manifestos proposing a future in which the profession of landscape architecture emerges as the definer and shaper of the new metropolis. It is a collection of strategies aimed at ending the real or imagined marginalization of landscape architecture in the field of urbanism, to make landscape architecture as a profession the dominant player in the resurgent field of urbanism.[6] To accomplish this, Waldheim aims at promoting a "disciplinary realignment, in which landscape supplants architecture's historical role as the basic building block of urban design." Yet by oversimplifying the formal language of urban design rather than acknowledging that such design requires a language of buildings, blocks, streets, corridors, parks, landscapes, rivers, regions and more, Waldheim perpetuates an ahistorical and anti-empirical argument for the sake of advancing a highly speculative, theoretical position.

It is a ploy in which most of the contributors to *The Landscape Urbanism Reader* are happy to participate.[7] Allen Berger, for example, laments that "Landscape architects in academia give little attention to urbanization, often dwelling instead on the traditional areas of landscape history — site engineering, construction detailing, and project based design studio education."[8] He goes on to write that as a result, landscape architects tend to overlook the inevitable "waste landscapes," or "drosscapes,"[9] those "in-between" sites that simply appear as a result of the normative process of real estate development. By expressing an urgent need for a particular breed of landscape architect to take the lead in the field of urban planning, Berger adroitly sidesteps the evidence that landscape architects are indeed actively engaged as designers, repairers and critical thinkers within the traditional urban milieu. This is because in the end, for the Landscape Urbanist, this is not a turf war but rather an ideological battle over the language of urbanism itself.

Aware that such ideological positioning needs some justification by way of its cultural relevance, if not inevitability, Landscape Urbanism offers circumspect evidence of its connection to American cultural and settlement traditions. In distinguishing Frank Lloyd Wright's Broadacre

City or Ludwig Hilberseimer's New Regional Pattern from eighteenth-
and nineteenth-century urban parks, Waldheim asserts that they are
"uniquely American typologies in which the fundamental distinctions
between city and countryside, village and farmland, 'urbanism' and
'landscape' are dissolved in favor of a third term: a 'landscape urbanism,'
for industrialized American modernity." [10]

However, this lineage ignores another set of American settlement
traditions, from early New England villages to the French settlements
around the Gulf of Mexico to the Spanish settlements of the Southwest,
all of which incorporated spatially delimited public realms within defined
villages and towns. These traditions continued throughout the eigh-
teenth, nineteenth and early twentieth centuries as hundreds of North
American towns developed as compact spatial units. Under the Roosevelt
administration, the US Resettlement Administration established the
"greenbelt" new towns, loosely based on Ebenezer Howard's Garden
City, using topography and a protective edge of forestland both to contain growth and as a didactic hieroglyph of community. [11] Even as late as
1957, Colin Rowe and John Hejduk were able to describe such western
villages as Leadville, CO, Carson City, NV, and Globe, AZ, as "potent
symbols of urbanity by reason of the emptiness through which they are
approached." [12] While a case can be made that a "split personality" of sorts
has always infused the American psyche when it comes to urbanism,
this relegates the debate as merely a case of conflicting theories without
acknowledging the well-known and longstanding urban traditions.

Landscape Urbanism correctly argues that the analysis of landscape
should play a fundamental role in the making of urbanism, but this is
hardly the first time this theoretical ground has been traversed. In *The
Reader*, Christophe Girot characterizes Landscape Urbanism's principal
goal: to "decipher what happened in city landscapes of the last decades
and to consequently act upon them." While Landscape Urbanists are
quick to align with mid-century American and European planning traditions, missing is the proper crediting of Patrick Geddes who, almost
a century earlier, posited a theory of city planning that forged a relationship between the social and cultural structure of a community as
synergistically integrated with its corresponding physical environment. Geddes was confident in his ability to map this relationship and
to act upon it as it existed in situ. Urban form, architecture, and all

human settlement and cultural activity, he argued, derive from a region's resources and geography. For Geddes, the "regional survey" method he deployed "gave understanding of an 'active experienced environment,' ... the motor force of human development [and] ... the mainspring of cultural evolution."[13] This can be contrasted with the views of fellow Scotsman Ian McHarg, whose mapping techniques seemed to relegate human settlement to the leftover bits unfit for other use. Geddes' goal was a merging of human settlement activity with the natural landscape and geology of a place. This statement from *The Reader*, which provides no Geddes attribution, is nevertheless pure Geddes logic: "The promise of landscape urbanism is the development of a space–time ecology that treats all forces and agents working in the urban field and considers them as continuous networks of inter-relationships."[14]

In comparison to Geddes, however, the Landscape Urbanists observe their terrain with a considerably more jaundiced eye. They selectively identify the bits that seem the most interesting; that pique their muse. Eschewing nostalgic definitions of community, they prioritize both the post-industrial landscape, or "drosscape," and the suburban miasma of the metropolis, embodied in such iconic American locales as Houston.

Emphasizing its break from tradition, Waldheim distinguishes Landscape Urbanism from nineteenth-century urban landscape architecture, influenced as it was by the American landscape painters of the Hudson River School and as best observed in the work of Frederick Law Olmsted. He notes that contemporary Landscape Urbanists do not camouflage ecological and infrastructural systems with pastoral imagery. Instead their subjects are the infrastructural systems necessary for modern life (whether currently in use or as relics of a site's industrial past) and "the public landscapes" that result, "the very ordering mechanisms of the urban field itself."[15] Landscape Urbanists find "meaning" in these "enchanted" landscapes as organic and natural manifestations of industrial growth. They are the canvases upon which the Landscape Urbanists act.

Not only do the Landscape Urbanists reject the romantic subject matter of the nineteenth-century landscape painters and designers, they also eschew these artists' techniques for composing spatial experience. Waldheim and his colleagues reject the picturesque, or its cinematic equivalent, *mise-en-scène*, literally "putting in the scene." They view the idea of attempting to frame a set of experiences as one might find in

Central Park, for example, or in one of Frederick Church's expansive canvases, as an invalid technique for place-making. Instead, theirs is a concern for the spaces *in between* the places, what they might call the "black holes" or the New Urbanist might call the background. In his discussion of landscape design as sequence, Christophe Girot expresses his fascination with digital photography as it easily allows for evolving narratives, represented in motion as a characteristic that prioritizes experience over plan. Here we once again encounter the primacy of *dross*. The ability of the camera to frame, record and therefore focus one's perception on the leftover spaces of the metropolis, the "dross," is presented as an important analytical tool that allows the consideration of continuous landscapes. Once again it is the experience of riding in a car that is prioritized.

At first blush, this perspective does not seem to contradict the values of New Urbanism. One of the key analytical tools championed by New Urbanists is the "synoptic survey," a method for rigorous documentation of the particular characteristics of any specific locale.[16] But while the New Urbanists tend to employ in their urban analyses a ground floor vantage point at the speed of the pedestrian, the Landscape Urbanists seem to prefer the "windshield survey" and a detached, birds-eye perspective that only a high-rise tower or aerial photograph can provide.[17] The resulting differences in strategy are profound.

For example, bewildered by the Houston landscape that he observes from the twenty-eighth floor of an office building, Lars Lerup finds that he must rename such conventional concepts as foreground and background, which suppose a compositional strategy, into "stim and dross," i.e., areas of stimulation (shopping malls, high-rise buildings, iconic landscapes) and areas of, well, everything else, seemingly more arbitrary, and less the product of will (dross). In describing this landscape of stim and dross — the metropolis — Lerup warns that, "Urban threats prevail in this huge ecological envelope." Then in describing the dross, "Largely hiding out in the spaces between [the dross]," he contends that "the threats are kept away from the stims." By "threats" he means anything unscripted or circumstantial. In authoring one of the "most interesting manifestos about the urban landscape of the last two decades," according to Berger,[18] Lerup is more interested in the dross than the stim, and who wouldn't be, given such an intriguing characterization?

Lerup continues, noting that a nighttime view from his high-up vantage point may yield few visible patterns, "but the individual points [of light] and their various qualities and constellations are many …. the moving lights easily match the intensity of the far more numerous immobile ones, suggesting the monstrous possibility that none are definitely fixed. All is labile, transient, as if it were only a question of time before all these lit particles would move — billiard balls on a vast table." [19] For Lerup, the city is a place of movement, fast movement, the kind that occurs in a car or a high-speed elevator, a place to be filmed, not photographed. Lest there be any doubt about this, in a footnote, he clarifies, "The hegemony of the pedestrian, the plaza, the street and the perimeter block must be challenged not because the values they embody are no longer valid, but because they are suffused with a set of fundamental misconceptions about the nature of contemporary civilization and its outside, leading to a false understanding of the whole." [20]

Slow Urbanism: Spatial Experience at the Scale of the City and the Street

Others, however, have come to different conclusions about Houston. Writing about the city a decade earlier, Jaquelin Robertson is not so much bewildered as dismayed. Viewing the same iconic, figural structures and vast swaths of urban wasteland, Robertson argues for a relearning of urban ordering systems that had been normative only forty years earlier. Robertson's city is to be experienced at many speeds — walking, driving, by train, by bus. Cognizant of urban design's status as a meta-language of sorts, a language of languages encompassing architecture, building typology, landscape architecture, hydrology, traffic engineering, and other collaborative disciplines, he argues for "replicable urban design devices, made up of some limited number of generic building types, or urban parts, which when aggregated will create a larger and more cohesive system than we now encounter on the road to the airport…. What we need today is a reasonably simple language of city building that is free of malignancy, is easy to use and has symbolic and ethical value." [21] It is a call for a normative design language that can be coded and institutionalized to create a predictable result.

These two manifestos by Lerup and Robertson, both deans of architecture schools, serve as prologues for the narratives of Landscape

Urbanism and New Urbanism respectively. While Lerup concludes that we must "close the book on the city and open the book on the metropolis," Robertson sees the promise for an "American 'order of things,'" an urbanism that is not at odds with its continent but is somehow inextricably tied to its landscape, an urbanism that embraces virtue and beauty. Both arguments posit a new way of looking at the city. One views traditional urbanism as a social and ecological anachronism, a longing for the return of the "bourgeois pedestrian," in some misguided hope that he/she will bring us a sense of community, while the other sees the city as an essential tool in reformulating humankind's relationship with the planet, arguing for an experience that is both abstract and representational; at rest yet dynamic, both old and new.

While it is important to avoid ascribing too much importance to singular authors, Lerup and Robertson do provide a window into fundamentally different perspectives on urbanism. Indeed, it is at the scale of the street where the most profound difference between the "isms" makes itself felt. In Houston, it is the lack of spatial definition that Robertson finds so distressing, what he refers to as the "Nagasaki Syndrome." Street design is not a simple matter. It begins by considering where the street falls within a cross-section of urbanism. Once context is established, the street is considered not only in terms of its capacity but also its character, including: the height-to-width ratio of building face to building face; the relationship of street trees to those proportions; and whether trees are necessary to further reproportion the space or the street; and the completion of this ensemble with private frontages that mediate between the public realm and the building façade. This composition of the street space must also be considered systematically as part of a larger typology of streets applied to an entire neighborhood or city.

The Metropolis Rebuts the City: Fast Beats Slow

The Landscape Urbanist would argue against such a typological methodology. Controlling the heights of buildings and maintaining the continuity of the street wall are viewed as tropes that come out of an idea about urbanism that overstates the social and environmental benefits of density and spatial definition. They would argue that urban form in North America has been and will continue to be driven by mass automobility, decentralized industrial networks, and private land ownership rights. To consider reconstituting a "Great Street" would be to ponder the irrelevant, as fruitless as Don Quixote battling windmills. [22]

It follows that the Landscape Urbanists' characterization of New Urbanism as "nostalgic" derives less from the latter's predilection for traditional architectural styles and more from its faith in the city — in traditional urban spatial ordering devices such as the street and the square, which it uses as conveyors of cultural meaning and as the containers within which community structures form. Because New Urbanism fails to properly engage the "dross," it is slow (both temporally and intellectually) and hopelessly sentimental, ignoring vast swaths of the urban landscape while attempting to impose a "dead spatiality ... to rule over history and process." Lacking this engagement, New Urbanism is also naïvely at the mercy of the processes "imposed by finance capital." [23]

So, while the manifestos of Landscape Urbanism openly criticize the inherent spatial formalism of New Urbanism, these same manifestos propose, ironically, an equally prescriptive formality. The difference is that dross formality privileges the horizontality of landscape architecture. And, despite Landscape Urbanism's rhetoric about the need for a multidisciplinary approach to urban design, it is a view of urbanism that would not likely emerge out of a more inclusive engagement with stakeholders: neighborhood residents, along with architects, landscape architects, planners, traffic engineers, civil engineers, politicians, lawyers, real estate developers, and even firefighters.

Because Landscape Urbanists are motivated by their ambition to work at the metropolitan scale, i.e., to make very big moves, the highway might be a more important constituent than a neighborhood resident. There are payoffs for this. The opportunity for any designer to create iconic gestures — figures or landscapes, observed at 60 mph — is seductive, if not powerful. Here the assertion that New Urbanists and Smart Growth advocates reject cars fits the narrative position that Landscape Urbanism provides a better, more realistic approach. As Tatom writes, incorrectly, New Urbanists have "demonized cars and the highways that serve them as the primary culprits in a perceived urban malaise and impending ecological disaster." [24]

Landscape Urbanists view the decentralized metropolis epitomized by Houston and reproduced across the continent as "natural," the inevitable result of industrialization and contemporary real estate development norms. In this context, Landscape Urbanism aims to mediate complex natural and man-made environments and celebrate public infrastructure (highways) in a search for meaningful order in the metropolitan miasma.[25] While not necessarily accepting the status quo, their work is meant to find meaning within an existing template of suburban/urban form, devoid of any call for the transformation of regulatory regimes. There is no need to be concerned with the technical minutiae of built form (from curb–return radii to building heights). While the individual projects of Landscape Urbanism may require significant code variances, no alternative regulatory order is offered. Free from technical and regulatory requirements, the proposed order comes from a reading of place — its history, its ecology, its culture — but it is highly personalized. The City and the Metropolis are scenic stage sets upon which dramatic action takes place. Landscape can thus be viewed as a tool to "reproduce urban effects traditionally achieved through the construction of buildings simply through the organization of low and roughly horizontal surfaces." [26] This creates a significant, if rhetorical, advantage: it is a cheaper, quicker and more flexible way of making a human environment than filling in land with buildings.

This plays itself out in grand public works gestures, such as Barcelona's Cinturon, in which an ambitious circulation system, complete with its own set of decked parks and hyper-turning circles, is conceived as being autonomous from its adjacent urban structure. One is left wondering how such interventions become anything more than glamorized highways, the "black holes" reconceptualized as green holes, and the landowners along the route left to do whatever they please, given the futility of spatial enclosure.

This is not to say that large-scale, individual projects cannot have a transformational or restorative effect on a given place. The High Line in New York, for example, catalyzed an estimated two billion dollars in economic development along its path.[27] But such projects require an erudite and willing client, one who is able to control a sufficient quantity of real estate, with pockets deep enough to transcend the "decorative practices" of New Urbanism, and who can thus elude concern for formal order to focus only on the "systems that condition the distribution and density of urban form." [28] And in the end, such a project is only possible within the frame provided by over a century and a half of city-making. As an urban pleasure park, built literally within the frame of historic artifact on which it is built, the High Line is, quintessentially, a civic space that sits comfortably within the transect of urbanism that New Urbanism uses as its yardstick. In other words, it does not supplant the basic urban typologies of parks and streets. Rather it fills in the details.

The City Rebuts the Metropolis: Slow Beats Fast

The New Urbanists believe that the urban form still possesses the capacity to provide the framework within which communities can evolve. Therefore, they seem less interested in the metropolitan-scale systems that prioritize *automobility*, focusing instead on the tactics of city-making, including an understanding and deployment of desired typologies that prioritize *walkability*. Their goal is to reconstitute a formal order because, they believe, formal orders are not arbitrary, nor are they the exclusive domain of a bourgeois social order, as the Landscape Urbanists have alleged, but are recurrent across cultures, continents and economic milieus. The New Urbanist argument in support of civic space — including the need for a hierarchy of articulated street spaces — stems from this recognition. These formal, culturally relevant orders are derived from fundamental principles about human scale and time-honored requirements for building civic capacity, defined by sociologist Robert Bellah as the willingness and ability of a populace to utilize the shared resource of cooperation to affect the common good. Civic capacity, he argues, blends civic habits and networks of trust, a recipe in which public space is an essential ingredient.[29]

Thus New Urbanists view metropolises like Houston as aberrations, the result of controls — via financing and deed restrictions (in the case of Houston) or zoning and subdivision ordinances (in other cities) — which actually abdicate control of the city's physical form. New Urbanism aims to upend the existing regulatory structures that have codified suburban sprawl and established the primacy of the automobile. They aim to transform the suburban environment through a context-sensitive urbanism of streets, squares and public transportation, and to repair the urban landscape by filling in under-utilized and abandoned sites, inverting suburban-style back-front relationships while reprogramming streets and neighborhoods from mono-cultural to diverse environments. To accomplish these tasks, New Urbanists concede the need to form working relationships with those in power, i.e., the development community, regulators, and capital markets. This renders New Urbanism not only compositional, but technical and political.

Their concern for walkability and urban scale notwithstanding, the New Urbanists have not ignored the larger regional planning issues that contemporary settlement patterns require. Calthorpe and Fulton's *The Regional City* elegantly connects the dots between the "emerging region, the maturing suburb, and the renewed city" as interrelated phenomenon.[30] "Designing the region IS designing the neighborhood" [emphasis mine].[31]

Irreconcilable Differences

The emerging differences between Landscape Urbanism and New Urbanism goes beyond matters of aesthetics, theoretical propositions, or proclamations about lineage. These differences point to a struggle to define an urban ethos for the twenty-first century. Landscape Urbanists see the "site," which may be at the scale of the city or the region, as having inherent characteristics, where the role of the urbanist is to make visible those characteristics. But their implementation of this ideal is inexplicit. They offer only limited ideas for fixing the vast array of urban and ecological problems brought on by postwar physical planning, preferring to use drossscape as a palimpsest upon which poetry may be composed. It is telling that Landscape Urbanists eschew direct empirical observation of, for example, the day-to-day interactions of people, which they dismiss as "leading to a false understanding of the whole." Ignoring empirically based social effects, they respond to the ecological ramifications of sprawl by relying on technological solutions. As Waldheim suggests, hopefully, "There may be a form of *automobility* that is carbon-neutral or in which the consequential effects of *automobility* are mitigated."[32]

Most of us can acknowledge, at least, that Landscape Urbanism has brought to the forefront a discussion of the leftover landscapes — the "dross" — that don't easily fit within the New Urbanist frame. New Urbanists sometimes relegate these spaces to "special districts," which can include anything from a designated area for big box retailers to mono-functional industrial areas or airports and highway rights-of-way (the "dross," on steroids). This is particularly fertile ground for the Landscape Urbanism.

At the same time, the Landscape Urbanists' research may have brought them to acknowledge many of the conditions that the New Urbanists have been at the forefront of resolving. For example, Waldheim asserts that "we might imagine suburban communities in the US being retrofitted, reorganized, to accommodate pedestrian activities, bikes, smart cars and car-shares and then converting the suburban lawns into productive landscapes. Taken as a whole it's a fairly radical vision, but stated in more incremental terms." When viewed within a context of New Urbanist agendas, as advanced by Dunham-Jones and Williamson in *Retrofitting Suburbia*, Tachieva in the *Sprawl Repair Manual*, and DPZ and Low in the *Light Imprint Handbook*, this hardly seems like a breakthrough idea.[33]

The differences between New Urbanism and Landscape Urbanism cannot be characterized by the firmness of the terrain (hardscape versus softscape) — by urbanism versus naturalism — since both lament the absence of "urban form and process from any ecological analysis."[34] Instead, the difference lies in the pitting of the Metropolis against the City, of metropolitan scale formulations versus human-scale priorities. Landscape Urbanism celebrates design for the vision it brings and the set of experiences it can conjure up within the imagination of a mobile culture, but it rejects the reality of city-making. Where this reality is engaged, it is viewed as a condition beyond the designer's control, not something that can be creatively acted upon.

Landscape Urbanism arose out of dissatisfaction over the marginalization of landscape architecture, bound as it was to the leftover spaces that remained after the planners, architects and transportation engineers had finished. It evolved out of an astute reading of utopian proposals for decentralized urbanism as well as a reframing of decentralized settlements embodied in places like Houston. The sprawling metropolis came to be viewed as a place to analyze, reframe and even celebrate for its inherent modernity, automobility and metropolitan scale.

New Urbanism originated not from any particular utopian fascination or celebration of the flotsam and jetsam of contemporary urbanism. Rather, it grew from a critical appraisal of Main and Elm Streets, not for nostalgic purpose, but for the contemporary lessons of human settlement they embody. It continues to evolve as an interdisciplinary movement destined to catalogue, through experience and pedestrian-level analysis, what works and what doesn't — at every scale and every context of human settlement, placing that acquired catalogue of experience at the service of city-making.

Landscape Urbanism argues that the Metropolis is our destiny, because we are driven to it by the inevitable advance of human culture. The only ethical imperative here is how artful we are with the landscape we are given. By contrast, New Urbanism argues that the City, and more importantly the public spaces contained within it, are important to our society because these places of urbanity are necessary in building civic capacity. In other words, an urbanism of streets, spaces and buildings continues to be relevant.

Endnotes

1   Waldheim, Charles. 2006. *Landscape as Urbanism.* In Waldheim, Charles, Ed., The Landscape Urbanism Reader. New York: Princeton Architectural Press, p. 37.

2   Duany, Andrés, Elizabeth Plater-Zyberk, and Jeff Speck. 2000. *Suburban Nation.* New York: North Point Press, p. xiii.

3   Pollak, Linda. 2006. Constructed Ground: Questions of Scale, In Waldheim, Charles, Ed., *The Landscape Urbanism Reader.* New York: Princeton Architectural Press, 127.

4   Corner, James. 1999. *Recovering Landscape.* New York: Princeton Architectural Press, p. 12.

5   Waldheim, Charles. 2008. Urban Design after Oil: Charles Waldheim on Automobility, youtube.com/watch?v=6Jaq9FFDOXw

6   Of course New Urbanism counts landscape architects as significant theoretical and professional contributors in its ranks, so the profession was already a player.

7   Among them, Julia Czerniak acknowledges the landscape designers' conventional analysis of site ecology and terrain, but laments the small number who would "draw from a site's specific organizational systems, performative agendas, formal languages, material palettes and signifying content for use when generating landscape design work," in Looking Back at Landscape Urbanism: Speculations on Site, p. 107. And Linda Pollak writes about the possibility of widening landscape architecture's purview to focus on cultural and historical processes as well as its more traditional considerations of nature and ecology in Constructed Ground: Questions of Scale, p. 127.

8   Berger, Allan. 2006. Drosscape. In Waldheim, Charles, Ed., *The Landscape Urbanism Reader.* New York: Princeton Architectural Press, p. 199.

9   Berger's term "drosscape" comes from a reading of Lars Lerup's article Stim and Dross. 1994. *Assemblage 25.* Cambridge, MA: MIT.

10 Charles Waldheim, Precedents for a North America Landscape Urbanism. 2008. *Center 14: On Landscape Urbanism.* Austin, TX: Center for American Architecture and Design, p. 293.

11 See Stein, Clarence. 1957. *Towards New Towns for America.* New York: Reinhold. Greenbelt, MD, was to be "of a size that makes possible a full measure of social life, but no larger." Stein quotes from the "accepted definition of the Garden City" and from the Report of the Senate Subcommittee, written by Senator Paul H. Douglas: "The particular portion of the amendment relating to adequate open land is intended to preserve as far as practicable the original design of having each of these projects protected by green belt of park and forest land surrounding such a community" (p. 136).

12 Rowe, Colin and John Hejduk. 1957. Lockhart, Texas: *Architectural Record,* March, p. 202.

13 Hall, Peter. 1990. *Cities of Tomorrow: An Intellectual History of Urban Planning and Design in the Twentieth Century.* Cambridge: Basil Blackwell, p. 140.

14 Corner, James. 2006. Terra Fluxus. In Waldheim, Charles, Ed., *The Landscape Urbanism Reader*. New York: Princeton Architectural Press, p. 30.

15 Waldheim, op cit., p 39.

16 For a description of the synoptic survey, see Codes Project website, codesproject.asu.edu/php/your_life. php

17 For a discussion of the role of aerial photography in Landscape Urbanism, see Waldheim, Charles. 1999. Aerial Representation and the Recovery of Landscape. In Corner, James. 1999. *Recovering Landscape*. New York: Princeton Architectural Press, pp. 120–39. Among other things, Waldheim highlights the use of aerial "surveillance" as a tool for identifying new sites for work, such as transportation corridors, infrastructure easements, and flight patterns of urban airports, among others.

18 Berger, op cit., p. 201.

19 Lerup, Lar. Stim and Dross. 1994. *Assemblage* 25. Cambridge, MA: MIT, pp. 94–107.

20 Lerup, footnote 5, p. 106.

21 Robertson, Jaquelin T. 1983. In Search of an American Urban Order, Part I: The Nagasaki Syndrome. *Modulus 16*. Charlottesville, VA: The University of Virginia Architectural Review, p. 6.

22 Tatom argues that "Allan Jacobs's documentation, Great Streets, fuels the prevailing narrative of lost urbanity that permeates the public discourse by proposing these historic urban forms as models to solve contemporary needs for circulation and public space." She never actually gets around to explaining why these historic forms are not appropriate. She assumes that the reader just understands this as a given. Tatom, Jacqueline. Urban Highways and the Reluctant Public Realm. In Waldheim, Charles, Ed., *The Landscape Urbanism Reader*. New York: Princeton Architectural Press, p. 183.

23 Harvey, David. 1996. *Justice, Nature and the Geography of Difference*. Malden, MA: Wiley-Blackwell, p. 420.

24 Tatom's assertion that the New Urbanists demonize the automobile is unsupportable. It would be more appropriate to state the New Urbanists reject the hegemony of the automobile and its associated infrastructure over other forms and speeds of movement and their related infrastructural requirements, instead favoring an equivalence of circulation technologies and means. Tatom, p. 183.

25 My characterization derives from Waldheim's assertion: "In place of traditional dense urban form, most North Americans spend their time in built environments characterized by decreased density, easy accommodation of the automobile, and public realms characterized by extensive vegetation. In this horizontal field of urbanization, landscape has a newfound relevance, offering a multivalent and manifold medium for the making of urban form, and in particular, in the context of complex natural environments, post-industrial sites, and public infrastructure." Waldheim, Charles. 2006. Introduction. In Waldheim, Charles, Ed., *The Landscape Urbanism Reader*. New York: Princeton Architectural Press, p. 15.

26 Waldheim, Charles. 2008. Precedents for a North America Landscape Urbanism. *Center 14: On Landscape Urbanism*. Austin, TX: Center for American Architecture and Design, p. 292.

27 According to Hawthorne, Christopher. 2011. Critic's Notebook: Shifting Horizons in Santa Monica Parks Design. *Los Angles* Times, July 30. The High Line was designed by James Corner Field Operations with architects Diller, Scofido + Renfro and garden designer Piet Oudolf.

28 Corner, Terra, op cit., p. 28.

29 Bellah, Robert Nelly. 1985. *Habits of the Heart: Individualism and Commitment in American Life*. Berkeley, CA: University of California Press.

30 Calthorpe, Peter and William Fulton. 2001. *The Regional City*. Washington, DC: Island Press.

31 Ibid. p. 49.

32 Waldheim, op cit., 2008.

33 See Dunham-Jones, Ellen and June Williamson. 2009. *Retrofitting Suburbia*. Hoboken, NJ: Wiley; and Low, Thomas E. and DPZ. 2008. *Light Imprint Handbook*, version 1.3. Charlotte, SC: DPZ Charlotte.

34 Corner. 2006, p. 27, and Low and DPZ.

5

The Social Apathy of Landscape Urbanism

EMILY TALEN

IN THE HISTORICAL ACCOUNT OF CITY-MAKING, it is not unusual to judge the worth of an ideal on the basis of its social value. Was the idea better, or worse, for the quality of human life? Were people's lives improved in a just and equitable way?

So it is surprising that the movement known as "Landscape Urbanism," devoted as it is to fashioning a new kind of city, has escaped social evaluation almost entirely. As many of us in urban design have been laboring over the past decades to inject awareness of the social implications of all that we do, the turn toward social indifference seems a step backward. How, and why, did this repositioning of the link between urbanism and social objective happen?

My thesis is as follows. For the purpose of maintaining artistic license and the ability to engage in conceptual experimentation, Landscape Urbanism sidestepped any constraining connection between urban form and social requirement by forming three theoretical alliances: one with post-structuralism, one with ecology, and one — peculiarly — with Marxism (or a pseudo version thereof). Because of the awkward meld involved, these alliances seemed driven not by a deep or coherent conviction, but by contrivance.

The post-structuralist connection is axiomatic. In vogue since the 1960s, post-structuralism summons the ungraspable and the uncertain

105

to support an only-here-and-now, anti-scientific approach that, for the designer, unleashes an irresistible orgy of value-free experimentation. In a world where there are no underlying structures, no objective truths — really no dominant explanations of anything — post-structuralism provides the near-perfect theoretical cover for design immunity. Landscape Urbanism has certainly done its part to help spread the gospel, perpetuating the allure of limitlessness now playing out on the computer screens of architects and landscape architects the world over.

The Marxist and ecological groundings are more tangled and far more interesting, and it is these interconnected strains that I want to try to decrypt in this essay. Because of the political awkwardness of overt allegiance to capital's overthrow (whilst seeking high-profile commissions made possible by neoliberal politics), the Marxist connection is especially intriguing. Adherence to a dual Marxist–ecological apparatus has proved useful for providing evidence of social commitment, while simultaneously undermining the application of ground-level lessons about what a socially informed — and designer-constrained — urbanism might look like.

Construing cities as fleeting, temporary, in constant motion — *indeterminate* is a favorite descriptor — is the single most important narrative undergirding Landscape Urbanism philosophy and practice, and, while straight from the post-structuralist playbook, it also provides the conceptual linkage to both Marxism and ecology. In Landscape Urbanism, as in post-structuralism, it is essential to avoid "the end, the grand scheme" in favor of "cumulative directionality toward further becoming."[1] This has profound consequences for connecting social goal and built environment, as urban form can never be delivered a *priori* on the basis of nature's indeterminacy. In short, it shuts down the possibility of an urbanism that responds to the fixed needs of people as semi-predictable social and economic beings. A theory that rests on the notion that all is in flux is unlikely to adopt normative social content except in the most abstract of terms.

By analogy with the interminable flow of natural processes — erosion, deposition, molting, etc. — cities, too, are deemed unknowable. Translated to urban design, indeterminacy means that facts are separate from values, needs are subjective, there is no human nature, virtues cannot be identified or ranked, and, in general, there is no need to decide between different substantive conceptions of social good. Knowing that the universe is not deterministic but self-renewing and infinitely creative translates — in this case — to an openness to aesthetic experiments, regardless of their social consequences.

Under the hegemony of indeterminacy, the solid/void durability of master planning and architecture is revoked. To maintain the argument that all figural space is irrelevant, this has required the lumping together of master planning with any other kind of human-centric enclosed urban formation, as if all occurrences of it are ultimately a product of top-down, "master" planning. Obscured is the generative, compacted form of traditional cities evolving out of centuries of collective endeavor. Any approximation of figural space, especially New Urbanist attempts at replication, are reduced to an orthodox stylistic preference — old and traditional in the most pejorative of terms.

This is where Marxism enters the narrative. Citing works by Lefebvre, Harvey, Soja, and other critics of global capitalism and neoliberal "spatialities," the judgment is that attempts to replicate form — the solid/void of cities — is little more than an inept desire to control history and process.[2] New Urbanist replication of enclosed cities — what New Urbanists perceive to be the *product* of history and process — is a nostalgic effort to falsify a past that can never be returned to. Precedent has no standing. This is why Landscape Urbanists are fond of quoting Henry Ford, who wrote: "There is no city that would be rebuilt as it is, were it destroyed."[3]

Yet in an incomprehensible twist, and despite Marxist rejection of all of it, Landscape Urbanists trace their roots to the CIAM side of modernist urbanism. While "the modernist project" is rejected abstractly, it is retained in the lineage for its support of both decentralization as an inevitable urban trajectory, and for its view that *landscape* is "the primary medium of urban form."[4] Modernism was an ideology that supported the view that buildings did not have to be subordinated to the urban fabric, that streets and blocks were nuisances. Oscar Newman aside, modernist planners rejected the social difference between visual open space and habitable open space — now an apt description of the urban forms emanating from Landscape Urbanism.

The modernist rejection of figural space was briefly justified — i.e., one can see how access to green legitimately trumped enclosure and street life in the early-twentieth-century slum. CIAM logic was that, to free up more open, green space and let in more light and air, one could build at greater and greater heights and therefore occupy smaller and smaller land area. This could produce the "biologically important advantages" that Le Corbusier thought so important.[5] Consideration of the third dimension was limited to height, since "it is in admitting the element of height that efficacious provisions can be made for traffic needs and for the creation of open spaces for recreation or other purposes."[6] This, as Eric Mumford points out, was a "fateful formulation" used to justify "vast numbers of high-rise slab projects built over the last seventy years around the world,"[7] a development form CIAM's own members came to hate.

How does this exhuming of CIAM modernism reconcile with the ardency for process and indeterminacy? The ecological argument does not present much of a problem here, and in fact, as McHarg demonstrated, is almost perfectly complementary. Current proposals in the ecology-begets-urbanism vein — solar panel clad buildings set in green — are well suited to an ideology that prioritizes the unclipped flows of nature.

The Marxist idea of historical process, however, requires more maneuvering. After all, end-state representations of urbanism amount to a neoconservative "blueprint for placelessness" based on "centralized corporate decision-making."[8] Landscape Urbanists profess a natural affinity to the works of Hilberseimer, Mies van der Rohe, and other icons of modernist urbanism, so it is necessary to find a way to absolve their blueprint-prone impulses.

Enter the egalitarian rhetoric of high modernism. Within it, even Wright's Broadacre City can be held up as a model, wherein hyper-segregation on one-acre parcels is welcomed for its "social critique" of private ownership and "conspicuous consumption."[9] Given that there can be no direct linkage between social goal and built form — one that might involve an understanding of the historically informed implications of spatial pattern, access or figural definition — the social differences between Broadacre City and the streets of solid/void urbanism become imperceptible. Egalitarianism based on equal divisions of things — everyone gets their own equally sized plot! — provides sufficient evidence of social concern in an abstracted, rhetorical world in which costs are extraneous and uncounted.

Despite the absorption of egalitarian pretense, however, Landscape Urbanists still face a fundamental problem in terms of process. Landscape "process" mirroring economic "process" is a hollow sort of idea, and not one done well by way of analogy. In practice, Landscape Urbanism has not been able to distance itself from neoliberal capitalism. Master planning of green solar array spectacle — the new sustainability aesthetic — is sanctioned by a benevolent corporate world now put in charge of managing nature for the human consumer. It is a blunt lesson, well known to New Urbanists, that places derived from "nature" or "ecological process" are not immune from commercial exploitation. Form produced by "landscape" is every bit as susceptible to commodification.

Such displays could never be considered a solution to Harvey's degenerative utopias of global capitalism. Like every other design attempt, whether rooted in ecological process or not, Landscape Urbanists will be turned away. Any ideal put into concrete form and action — from hybrid infrastructure to recycling — is quickly discounted as the "residues of a utopian environmentalism" found in the "landscapes of capitalism."[10] With increasingly high-profile corporate sponsorship (which is in fact the goal), Landscape Urbanism will find it difficult to inoculate itself against the "structural conditions" of global urbanization.

Ever cognizant that some connection to the Marxist critique of capitalist socio-spatial transformation is necessary for academic legitimization, Landscape Urbanism attempts to work around this problem by reducing the notion of "city" to ideological construct, and then positioning itself well outside of it. In Landscape Urbanism, it is possible to start tabula rasa, devising a whole new conception of urbanism that, this time around, will find a way to enjoin ecological and cultural process. The Marxist narrative can now be realigned, since the ecological/cultural merger is seen to counteract the dehumanizing consequences of globalization, homogeneity and standardization.

Rhetorically, both the Marxist and the Landscape Urbanist (and the New Urbanist, for that matter) deplore the alienation, the loss of autonomy, and the seizing of control over cultural expression and self-organization that define the postmodern world. One proposal for rectifying this calamity involves harkening back to a primordial existence, when dwelling and land were one — back to a "mythic, ahistorical and abstract concept of spatial essence." Then, when presumably "built and unbuilt environments worked as an ecosystem," the "pragmatic adjustment" to natural conditions engendered an "indigenous Landscape Urbanism" that "created marvelous civilizations."[11]

Yet human history exposes the unpredictable transformations that eventually broke down this synergy, whereby "landscape," always the primordial condition of urbanism, was extracted from, re-graded, paved over, bought and sold, condemned, and contested for all sorts of human purposes. In this historical metamorphosis, landscape became backdrop because humans required it, for employment, education, culture, finally arriving — until CIAM — at the "formalistic solid/void of older models" that can be seen as the product of several millennia of the "conflating of natural and cultural systems." Dismissive of this history, Landscape Urbanism requires us to accept that now — through technological exploits with untested and often tenuous environmental claims — humans will be that much more adept at respecting nature's ecological flows.

Marxists are unlikely to be happy with this technological solution, since there can be no meaningful change to the urban trajectory without a radical reworking of the existing political economy. Absent that possibility, landscape as "organizing framework" must confine itself to the "holes" of urbanism,[12] where design prescription is limited to wherever the initial condition of urbanism — i.e., open land — can be found. The Landscape Urbanists do not interpret this as a constraint. Instead, they see the depleted, rejected, annihilated city made up of "holes" as a celebration of the remnants of a failed urbanism. Anything else would constrict the possibilities for a new sustainability aesthetic. More to the narrative point, occupied space leaves no room for the creative working out of an alternative urban progression based on cultural/ecological integration.

The vacant sites upon which Landscape Urbanism preys, that "inward vacancy and outward expansion" that is the by-product of post-industrialism and the "Shrinking City," would require, this time around under a landscape-based process, turning a blind eye to the underlying reasons for the vacancy and the outward expansion that created these conditions in the first place. That is, the human frailties of prejudice, greed and neglect — or, more literally, white flight, suburban shopping malls, and slumlords — will have to be tamed. By rallying around "ecology", would these human infractions have been avoided? Does human nature allow us to escape these conflicts? Enter Marxism again, which offers the interpretation that humankind is perfectible, albeit in a manner that will require much more than an appreciation of the imperative of ecological process.

At this juncture it is possible to get a glimpse of the dangerous tendency in Landscape Urbanism to mythologize nature, despite strong denials to the contrary. The evidence is the absence of urban realism, such that social conditions like ghettos and segregation — ironically, or perhaps tellingly, a product of Landscape Urbanism's CIAM progenitors — are omitted from the ecologically imbued discourse. Search "slum," "poverty," "ghetto," "white flight," "racism," "poor people," or even "segregation" in the Landscape Urbanism manifesto and you will come up empty-handed.[13]

The fallout of this alarming duality was well covered by William Cronon and his colleagues in *Uncommon Ground: Rethinking the Human Place in Nature* (1996). He argued that wilderness, the "ideological underpinning" of the environmentalist movement, is a highly problematic concept because it is viewed as something wholly separate from, among other things, urban social problems. True to form, the Landscape Urbanist interpretation of addressing human–nature duality is to confuse culture with *infrastructure*, offering as a solution the "fluid exchange between (natural) environmental and (engineered) infrastructural systems."[14] Clearly, this is not a search for synthetic thought in the tradition of Patrick Geddes, Benton MacKaye, or Lewis Mumford, who derived their principles of human–nature integration in a way that engaged humans as social and economic beings. Limiting themselves to the separation between nature and "infrastructural systems," Landscape Urbanists give themselves license to remain aloof from the everyday inhabited world — exactly what Cronon, like Jane Jacobs before him, warned against.

The continuation of the old dualism sets up an obvious conflict between environmental ethics and social justice. Malthusian predictions of environmental collapse, always lurking within Landscape Urbanist discourse, are readily interpreted as elitist and authoritarian because they turn a blind eye to the root problem: a class-based, racist social structure. Without this connection, Landscape Urbanists fall prey to "colonial nature talk" every bit as much as mainstream environmentalism. Conjuring up a weakly developed Marxist connection cannot be relied upon for anti-authoritarian cover. As many in Cronon's book argued, the only legitimate recourse is to position humans and their social and economic problems at the center of environmental concerns, to insist that the problems of the urban (or rural) poor must inform environmental goals.[15] This orientation seems to be entirely lacking in Landscape Urbanism.

Immune from social agenda, Landscape Urbanists now avoid the myriad social problems that form-based urban designers in the Jacobsian empirical tradition have been toiling with: housing segregation, food deserts, pollution, concentrated poverty, traffic congestion, bad schools, affordability, safety, accessibility. For designers, there must be great personal liberty in being released from these clichéd concerns. The detachment is made complete by blocking the participation — via the obscure conceptualizations and metaphors of post-structuralism — of average citizens in the task of creating an "emergent urbanism." By the same token, urbanists who do concern themselves with such engagement risk being ridiculed for reducing their designs to a formulaic accommodation of the overly programmed predictabilities of everyday life.

But this is where the channeling of Marxism again provides some measure of vindication. Since concern with form, or "spatial order," belies the truth that history and process cannot be controlled, the Landscape Urbanist approach to social concern — fluid, indeterminate — can leap over neoliberal sellouts who, because they have been unwilling or unable to "revolutionize the geographic subconscious," are only stoking new modes of capitalist aggression.[16] Fretting over "walkable urbanism" can be interpreted as nothing more than a shallow attempt to provide an antidote to suburban boredom or, worse, gloss over the internal contradictions of capitalism. Sticking to landscape — free of buildings — the Landscape Urbanist is less prone to getting implicated in Mayor Bloomberg-style spectacles of corporate consumption.

With Marxist backing, then, one can avoid the jejune claim that static urban form plays a role in determining whether cities are equitable or diverse, or that the location of sidewalks, schools and grocery stores matters, or that those tiresome elements of "traditional space making" have meaning. The "right to the city" of Lefebvre and Harvey is the right to change the *process* of urbanization, to challenge the "hegemonic liberal and neoliberal market logics," which have little to do with urban superficialities like access to urban resources.[17] As long as the designer steers clear of developer-backed mega-projects — sticking to "landscape" and letting someone else get mired in the capitalist backing required for built form — he or she is free to pursue a wide range of fluid compositions.

It is in the pursuit of these socially aloof, fluctuating design concepts that Landscape Urbanists can claim to be changing urbanism fundamentally. Their agenda far exceeds the mere task of designing better public spaces, cleaning up brownfields, and reprogramming industrial sites. With the intellectual cover of ecology and Marxism, infused with poststructuralist pomp, they are able to offer up a revolution in city-making, a new way of "shaping and shifting the urban settlement" by exploiting tensions, teasing out contradictions, and pinpointing scalar complexities. It is the stuff of art and poetry now validated by an environmental and revolutionary rhetoric.

To the more conventional, urban form-oriented urban designer, these positions render "place-making," and the social goals it entails, trivial and hopeless. Above the neoliberal fray, and under the pretense of a more ecologically sensitive approach to urbanity, the aestheticizing of the "fragmented and chaotically spread" city throws in the towel on centuries of collective urban wisdom to declare only that cities are landscape. Uncovering the urban voids of discarded industrial capitalism, Landscape Urbanists are offering nothing more than *reprogramming* — open-ended, strategic models, an "ad hoc emergence" of "performative social patterns" that will eventually "colonize" the voids.

The "indeterminacy and flux" of ecology and the "spatio-temporal production processes" of Marxism are both being called upon to undermine the central importance of figural space, pedestrianism, "projects" and, ultimately, social justice, social diversity and social equity too. Through the loose interpretations of Landscape Urbanism, the Marxist–ecological supporting structure helps sustain a mythic adherence to "instability," of "process and scaffoldings," of a "system of emptiness" and "a resilient structure of voids," of a "layered, non-hierarchical, flexible and strategic" landscape, of chance encounters and accidents in the production of "alternative urbanisms."[18] Pending revolution, the translation to justice, equality, and the day-to-day challenges of urban dwellers fades to black.

Landscape urbanism can be appreciated as a creative body of ideas to draw from for retrofitting brownfields, reprogramming "seemingly banal surfaces," and demonstrating how to read cities as "dynamic systems of flux." But since indeterminate ecological flows are the sole basis for pursuing spatial pattern and urban form, because social and political problems do not measure up to what is deemed to be the more imperative issue at hand, i.e., "to locate urban fabrics in their regional and biotic contexts,"[19] on the topic of advancing social objectives, Landscape Urbanists can never be relied upon.

Endnotes

1   M'Closkey, Karen. 2008. Without End: Mats, Holes, and the Promise of Landscape Urbanism. In Douglas Kelbaugh and Kit Krankel McCullough, Eds. *Writing Urbanism: A Design Reader*. New York: Routledge, pp. 120–26.

2   Harvey, David. 2000. *Spaces of Hope*. Berkeley: University of California Press.; see also Ley, David. 1987. Styles of the times: Liberal and neo-conservative landscapes in inner Vancouver, 1968–86. *Journal of Historical Geography* 13, 1: 40–56.

3   The full quote is: "Industry will decentralize. There is no city that would be rebuilt as it is, were it destroyed — which fact is in itself a confession of our real estimate of our cities." cited in Hilberseimer, Ludwig. 1949. *The New Regional Pattern*. Chicago: Paul Theobald. Quote is taken from Charles Waldheim's course syllabus, GSD 3341 Ford's Fields: readings in urbanism, ecology, and industrial economy, isites. harvard.edu/fs/docs/icb.topic844607.files/GSD%203341%20Fords%20Fields%20Spring%202011.pdf.

4   Waldheim, Charles. 2010. Notes toward a history of agrarian urbanism. *Places:* places.designobserver.com/feature/notes-toward-a-history-of-agrarian-urbanism/15518/

5   Cited in Mumford, Eric. 2000. *The CIAM Discourse on Urbanism*. Cambridge, MA: MIT Press, p. 38.

6   Sert, Jose Luis. 1944. *Can Our Cities Survive? An ABC of Urban Problems, Their Analysis, Their Solutions*. Cambridge: Harvard University Press, p. 150.

7   Mumford, op cit., p. 38.

8   Ley, David. 1987. Styles of the Times: Liberal and Neo-Conservative Landscapes in Inner Vancouver, 1968–86. *Journal of Historical Geography* 13, 1: 40–56.

9   Waldheim, Charles. 2010. On Landscape, Ecology, and Other Modifiers to Urbanism. *Topos: The International Review of Landscape Architecture and Urban Design*, 71.

10 Harvey, David. 2000. *Spaces of Hope*. Berkeley: University of California Press.

11 Spencer, Douglas. 2012. In the name of being: Critical regionalist Landscape Urbanism, a critique. *Critical Terrain*. terraincritical.wordpress.com/2011/02/01/in-the-name-of-being-critical-regionalist-landscape-urbanism-a-critique/ De Meulder, Bruno and Kelly Shannon. 2010. Traditions of Landscape Urbanism. *Topos*, 71: 70.

12 M'Closkey, op cit., 2008.

13 I refer to *The Landscape Urbanism Reader,* edited by Waldheim.

14 Corner, James. 2006. Terra Fluxus. In Charles Waldheim, Ed., *The Landscape Urbanism Reader*. New York: Princeton Architectural Press, pp. 21–33.

15 See, for example, Di Chiro, Giovanna. 1996. Nature as Community: The Convergence of Environment and Social Justice. In William Cronon, Ed., *Uncommon Ground: Rethinking the Human Place in Nature*. New York: Norton, pp. 298–320.

16 Harvey, David. 2010. Quote from David Harvey's Urban Manifesto: Down With Suburbia; Down With Bloomberg's New York by Greg Lindsay, Wed Jul 21, 2010, fastcompany.com/1673037/david-harveys-urban-manifesto-down-with-suburbia-down-with-bloombergs-new-york

17 Lefebvre, Henri. 1968. *Le droit a la ville*. Paris: Anthropos.

18 Waldheim, *The Landscape Urbanism Reader*.

19 Corner, op cit., p. 24.

6

A General Theory of Sustainable Urbanism

Andrés Duany

The Crises

THERE ARE GREAT CRISES UPON US, and three are of such magnitude that they may well be permanent. They are climate change, the exhaustion of inexpensive energy, and the evaporation of national wealth. Because these crises are all downtrends, there is a general feeling that they are related, and there is in fact an objective lynchpin: the lifestyle of the American middle class — the way we drive around for ordinary daily needs, dwell large on the land in commoditized real estate products, and how we secure our food heedless of the negative consequences. That lifestyle, and that we're now exporting it worldwide, is the cause of all three crises. That lifestyle can be summarized as "suburban sprawl."

Designers have become fully engaged in reform, and while the first generation of responses has been restricted to buildings (LEED), they are now addressing the urban scale (LEED-ND). We have agreed on the name for this approach — it is to be "Sustainable Urbanism" — but confusion remains, as there are several paradigms that are serious contenders to that title. Among these are the Old Urbanism, the now-mature New Urbanism, and the nascent Landscape Urbanism. There is that other, but given the seriousness of the situation, Irresponsible Urbanism may now be dismissed from the discourse.

The Contenders

The term Irresponsible Urbanism was derived from Rem Koolhaas' piece "Atlanta," which concludes, "The city is out of control, let us be irresponsible." From its origins in the Garden City, this paradigm has been gradually dumbed down through decades of inbreeding at the Urban Land Institute, to a vegetative state in the care of today's libertarian fringe. But it is not yet dead. One of the tasks of Sustainable Urbanism is to retain what Irresponsible Urbanism did well: being marketable, relatively inexpensive, and easy to administer. If the alternatives do not succeed, Irresponsible Urbanism may rise again. Remember that suburban sprawl is the *idiot savant* of urban planning, able to sucker the sympathy of polemicists such as Herbert Gans, Denise Scott Brown, and Charles Waldheim, as if its problem were the absence of a suitable aesthetic. But, in the end, Irresponsible Urbanism's aestheticized critical stance is not suitable for the seriousness of the situation, and cannot be considered a contender.

The Old Urbanism was informally defined by Alex Krieger when he asked, "But isn't the New Urbanism just the Old Urbanism?" The Old Urbanism is in resurgence as it becomes common knowledge that living diversely and densely, walking, and taking transit, is an environmentally responsible lifestyle. A Manhattanite has half the ecological footprint of the average American. The predicament of Old Urbanism is that it is technically at odds with current environmental standards. The Manhattan we know is an ideal we could never attain today for a multitude of reasons — the first being the hundreds of streams buried in pipes that its urban pattern requires. While it is an environmental success in its secondary consequences, it is thought to be an environmental disaster in its technical premises. The Old Urbanism values nature not at all — and those days are over.

Despite Alex Krieger's question, the New Urbanism differs from the Old Urbanism in many ways — one being that in the past, cities used to compete with other cities, but today, cities compete with their own suburbs. New Urbanism is technically pitted against Irresponsible Urbanism's polymorphic agility, which is enabled by culture, economics, codes, and standards. The New Urbanism seeks to level the playing field so that the market can freely operate and mitigate the enormous physical impact of Irresponsible Urbanism--but does not eliminate it. Its predicament is that it is capable of combining the best *as well as the worst* aspects of both the urban and the suburban.

Landscape Urbanism is also a hybrid. Having its origins in the techniques developed by Olmsted and Mc Harg, updated with the "green" touchstones of native plant species, naturalistic hydrological systems, and corridor typology. These innovations are now offered as structuring for buildings — not just as their appendages — thereby reaching for the mantle of an urbanism. But that claim is more than it can bear. With techniques limited to replicants of nature, Landscape Urbanism cannot avoid the ruralizing of even high-density schemes (the obverse of New Urbanism's urbanizing of low density). Its rabid bias against streets and any sort of spatial definition reduces the public realm to being primarily therapeutic; rustic walking, rooting about with edible planting, and communing with nature are surrogates for the social activity fostered by Old Urban and New Urban places. Even Landscape Urbanism's vaunted engagement with "infrastructure" amounts to buffering arterials, improving the design of stormwater apparatus, and decorating parking lots with porous paving. But an urban paradigm cannot be based on the implantation of natural vignettes in the residual places between buildings, particularly as it can be abused as green camouflage for the so-called "unprecedented typologies" of big box retailers, junkspace office parks and residential high-rise clusters. Such practices certainly cannot be considered sustainable, any more than can suburban sprawl.

The Challenge

How to assess the contenders for Sustainable Urbanism, when there is not yet consensus within the environmental discourse? One way to approach the challenge is to establish a theory that can provide the test while itself being qualified by the integrity and usefulness of its testing process. Like the best theories, it must possess that mystique of technique that underpins credibility in the modern political forum. And its metrics and protocols must be based on natural processes, so that the politically powerful environmentalists may be conscripted among the assessors rather than remain intransigent NIMBYs. Moreover, the theory must be simple enough to be administered by a bureaucracy that is accustomed to the robotic protocols of Euclidean zoning. A theory that is not operational and cannot be widely applied does not respond to the scale of the current crises.

The Theory

Would the Rural-to-Urban Transect (referred to as "the Transect") serve this rather abstract challenge, as it has so many utilitarian ones?[1]

The Transect is adapted from a scientific method of analyzing habitats. It is the concept of concatenated habitats based on geography ranging from wilderness to urban core. By integrating an environmental methodology for habitat assessment with a zoning methodology for urban design, the Transect breaks down the customary specialization, enabling

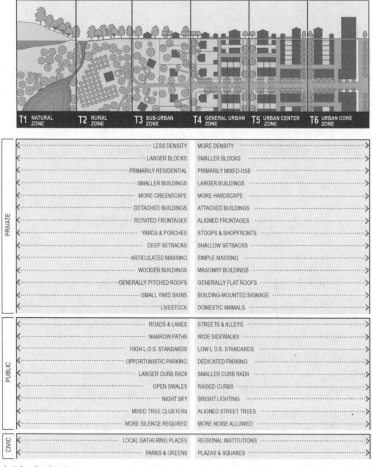

Credit: Duany Plater-Zyberk & co.

Fig. 6.1.

A SAMPLE ALLOCATION OF AN ELEMENT ALONG THE TRANSECT
FOOD PRODUCTION

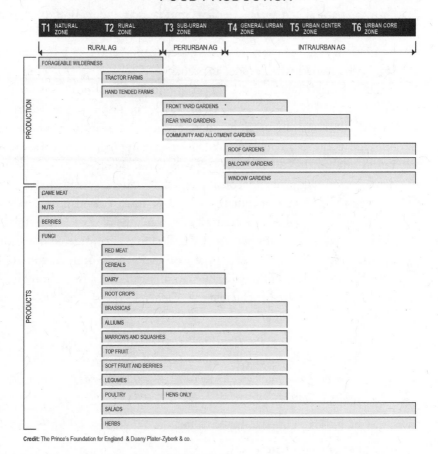

Credit: The Prince's Foundation for England & Duany Plater-Zyberk & co.

Fig. 6.2: *A sample application from the (freeware) SmartCode. There are some thirty such Transect-based modules.* See TRANSECT.ORG

environmentalists to consider the design of the cultural habitats and urbanists to protect the natural ones. It allows both interests to analyze and project the mix of human and natural elements that symbiotically create healthy environments. The Transect today is a freeware operating system available for zoning codes and other technical standards intended to replace the current system of zoning. It has proven to be a powerful taxonomic engine for the many disparate elements that would constitute a Sustainable Urbanism.

As a General Theory of Sustainable Urbanism must mediate value, the Transect proposes as a common currency the concept of *diversity* — which both the natural and social sciences employ as an index. Both biological and economic activity is based on transaction (of currency, of atomic composition, of heat, of beauty, of goods or services). A currency is designed to efficiently evaluate what is ceded in exchange for what is gained. A protocol for such transactions is physically, economically, or politically sustainable so long as it is balanced — or a fair trade. For instance, the American NIMBY regime arose with the consciousness that suburban sprawl was not a fair trade; that a housing subdivision or shopping center was a downward trade for the loss of a farm or woodland. Before suburban sprawl, development was generally considered a fair trade: a pristine pasture on riverfront might be lost, but the village or town gained in return was considered good value. For example, the wetlands of the Charles Towne Peninsula were lost, but the City of Charleston was considered much the upward trade. Today that exchange would not have been acceptable if what had replaced them was a suburban sprawl like nearby Hilton Head.

The Transect could elucidate a General Theory of Sustainable Urbanism with an equation:

> *At any point on the Rural-to-Urban Transect, the aggregate density of the social and natural diversity after urbanization must be equal to or greater than the natural diversity prior to urbanization.*[2]

$$N: \sum [Ds + Dn]post \approx > N: [DN]pre$$

N   = a constant
Ds = the socioeconomic diversity per unit of land, after urbanization
Dn = the natural diversity per unit of land, after urbanization
DN = the natural diversity per unit of land before urbanization land, after urbanization
Dn = the natural diversity per unit of land, after urbanization
DN = the natural diversity per unit of land before urbanization

The graphs of Figure 6.2 use this equation to compare the paradigms contending for Sustainable Urbanism as an illustration of the General Theory.

A GENERAL THEORY OF URBANISM

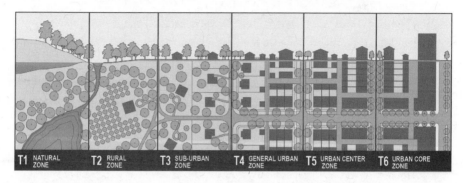

| T1 NATURAL ZONE | T2 RURAL ZONE | T3 SUB-URBAN ZONE | T4 GENERAL URBAN ZONE | T5 URBAN CENTER ZONE | T6 URBAN CORE ZONE |

Fig. 6.3a - TRADITIONAL URBANISM - PRIVILEGES SOCIO-ECONOMIC DIVERSITY

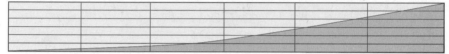

Fig. 6.3b - LANDSCAPE URBANISM - PRIVILEGES NATURAL DIVERSITY

Fig. 6.3c - NEW URBANISM - VALUES NATURAL & SOCIO-ECONOMIC DIVERSITY

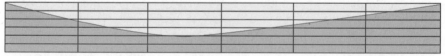

Fig. 6.3d - SUSTAINABLE URBANISM - EQUALIZES NATURAL & SOCIO-ECONOMIC DIVERSITY AT ALL T-ZONES

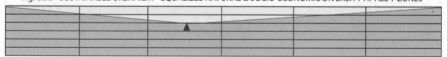

Credit: Duany Plater-Zyberk & co.

Fig. 6.3a: *With the Old Urbanism, the socioeconomic diversity of the T6 Urban Core correctly rates higher than T3 Sub-Urban. But there is a conceptual problem, as this single metric assigns a lesser value to T2 Rural — and T1 Natural has no value at all. The Old Urbanism created value by creating jobs, housing, shops, and entertainment. Diversity was achieved by their organic proximity within pedestrian sheds when transportation was scarce and expensive. The positive environmental consequences of the Old Urbanism are carbon-based: mitigation of tailpipe emissions, through mixed use, walkability, and transit viability. The negative is that land must be denatured by paved-network continuity into a commodity suitable for compact building. The Old Urbanism manifests an excellent environmental performance, but it cannot be inaugurated or extended without eliminating nature.*

Fig. 6.3b: In Landscape Urbanism T3 Sub-Urban rates higher than the T6 Urban Core-- which has the worst performance. This is the result of the absolute privileging of natural diversity, revealing the serious conceptual flaw of this paradigm. Landscape Urbanism has no metrics to assess the urban side of the Transect. With only half the tools, the Urban Core's social diversity does not register except as impervious pavement and denatured heat island. Places like London and Manhattan are rated as enormously negative ecological footprints. Such urban patterns are technically a problem and not within the repertoire of solutions.

Figure 6.3c: The New Urbanism assigns T3 Sub-Urban the lowest value, as it has the lowest index in both social and natural diversity, thereby, at least, improving upon the other two paradigms. With an array of tools ranging from the urban boundary for the preservation of nature at T1 and T2 — and transit orientation enabling density at T5 and T6, the New Urbanism is capable of recognizing diversity at the critical extremes of the Transect; however, it is unable to justify the persistence of the suburban single-family house, except as driven by market preference — a regrettable political necessity to implement its agendas elsewhere along the Transect. This flaw precludes the New Urbanism from becoming the paradigm for Sustainable Urbanism.

Fig. 6.3d: Sustainable Urbanism retains the "correct" high points of social and natural diversity of the New Urbanism, but it improves the performance of T3 Sub-Urban by integrating it technically to a green regime. T3 is redesigned by definition to compensate for its higher land occupation and transportation impact with requirements for energy generation, water reuse, recycling/composting, and food production. The ability to do this happens to coincide with its higher allocation of land per capita. A freestanding house handles these mitigating techniques better than urban building types of T5 and T6 (Figure 6.3 is an example of a food production protocol). The suburban thus becomes T3 Sub-Urban, with no opprobrium attached. A general theory of Sustainable Urbanism thus equalizes the environmental performance all along the Transect, retaining the choice that is integral to the politics of a market-based economy.

Summary

Both natural and social diversity are combined in various ratios along the Rural-to-Urban Transect. The high natural diversity of T1 Natural achieves the highest performance for Landscape Urbanism, while the high social diversity of T6 Urban Core achieves the highest performance for the Old Urbanism. But these two monovalent paradigms undermine their positive consequences by assigning an unwarranted high value to T3 Sub-Urban. The New Urbanism values the blend of both natural and social diversity at T1 and T6, while correctly devaluing the performance of T3, which has the lowest indices of both, but has no protocol to mitigate T3 Sub-Urban, which thus persists. Sustainable Urbanism equalizes the combined level of diversity of all T-zones so that all, including the Sub-Urban, are justified environmentally, and the market can exercise its preferences. The equation of the General Theory can determine if a transaction to the urban can fairly justify the loss of nature.

Endnotes

1   See www.transect.org and Duany, Andrés and David Brain. 2005. *Regulating as if Humans Matter. In Regulating Place: Standards and the Shaping of Urban America*, edited by Eran Ben-Joseph and Terry S. Szold. New York: Routledge. Pp. 293–332.

2   This type of equation contains both immeasurables (indices of diversity) and incommensurables (the natural and the social). Unlike in the hard sciences, approximate metrics may constitute equations in the social and environmental sciences, as they serve to elucidate a trend. A discussion of this appears in Farmelo, Graham. 2002. *It Must Be Beautiful: Great Equations of the Modern Science*. London: Granta.

7

Landscape Urbanism: The Zombies of Gund Hall Go Forth to Eat America's Brains

JAMES HOWARD KUNSTLER

LONG ABOUT THE LATE 1990S, anxiety beset the mandarins in the architecture schools when a reform movement calling itself the New Urbanism began to excite interest around America, and elsewhere. The New Urbanists proposed a revival of traditional city-making principles as a sovereign remedy for the practical absurdities, economic quandaries, ecological terrors, and spiritual disorders of twentieth-century land-use planning. What's more, the New Urbanists functioned in the real world of property development and had gotten scores of new projects underway, beginning with the demonstration project of a new town at Seaside, Florida.

This anxiety was most acute at the Harvard Graduate School of Design (GSD), the Vatican of modernism. After more than seven decades and countless iterations of dogma, and a vast record of built mistakes, it had little left to offer but a pretense of ideological correctness, in particular that it represented "the cutting edge" of design innovation reaching toward an evermore technologically dazzling future. The New Urbanism (NU) especially galled it, with its menacing porches and picket fences, those totems of bourgeois small-mindedness. Eventually, the GSD folk began to grok that the NU was about way more than these minor details, but rather a wholesale reordering of the human habitat into a coherent and comprehensible design theory that ran from the relations between buildings to the ordering of streets, neighborhoods and regions. Worse yet, the NU incorporated codes — the DNA of urban design — intended to be legible to both practitioners and their customers, ordinary people. The NUs were against mystification! How vulgar.

In elite architectural circles, mystification was the supreme weapon wielded by their warriors-of-the-cutting-edge. Harvard's Aegnor at the time was Rem Koolhaas, the Dutch architect who used mystification the way Stanford White had used a T-square. Koolhaas viewed the predicaments of overpopulation, resource depletion, financial instability, and consumerism as fundamentally hopeless, and had adopted the career strategy of going with the flow of the entropic zeitgeist, with all its delirious confusion. Hence the buildings he designed were intended to confound the people who used them or saw them, to produce a delicious sense of anxiety, the characteristic emotion of the era. Of course, many others in the *starchitect* firmament — Libeskind, Holl, Eisenman, Mayne, Hadid, et al — were working along the same lines, toward the effect of making cities everywhere more incomprehensible and alienating. When Koolhaas was first hired to occupy an eminent chair at the GSD, he devoted himself to a study of consumerism and produced a book about shopping. The joke was on everybody.

Meanwhile, The New Urbanists gradually occupied, shall we say, the *field of operations* where so much of the normal stuff of everyday life got built: the places where people lived and carried on commerce. In the booming economy of the millennium — which was, in fact, the last great gasp of the cheap oil era — their services were in demand from ambitious developers skeptical of suburban sprawl and all of its dismal schlock components. Mainly, they strove to build mixed-use, walkable places at a scale agreeable to human neurology, with attention to regional tradition. The New Urbanists were ambitious, too, about reforming the crusty accumulation of planning and zoning law that mandated a sprawl outcome practically everywhere in the USA and made it nearly impossible to assemble a human habitat worth living in. These reformers sent forth potent lecturers into unfriendly quarters, such as the Harvard GSD, which regarded the NU agenda with diffident contempt. But the threat to the mandarins' ideological power put the fear of God in them.

They had done almost nothing for ages to address the manifest horrors and hazards of American suburban sprawl. How the folks chose to live out there in the "flyover" states was not their thing. The mandarins' thing was keeping up with fashionable theory within the rigorous parameters of the modernist canon of styles. One of the reasons they objected so vehemently to the New Urbanism was that they only understood it in terms of style, and so the most trivial elements of the movement — the porches and picket fences — drove them crazy. This was to be expected as the dirty secret of modernism's American branch was that it had always been about style ever since it arrived from Germany with Walter Gropius in 1937 (who was hired straight off the refugee gangway by Harvard).

In the event, Gropius shed all his old Brave New World Bauhaus social engineering baggage at the immigration line and replaced it with a Horatio Alger kit bag of personal ambition, in which Cambridge intellectualism melded with American razzle-dazzle hucksterism to create a market for a new intellectual fashion imported from Europe. Before long, modernism successfully morphed from its original social program (housing for proles) to the official style of corporate America (glass-skinned office towers for the over-class). Architects could make a lot of money designing towers with big floor-to-area ratios, and corporations could get a lot of prestige for the buck from dressing their headquarters in the sleek new modernist raiment, which required no costly ornament. In the post war era, it also helped that Hitler and Stalin had completely discredited anything neo-classical. After the Allies defeated them, modernism became the official architectural style of the Free World, representing democracy and decency.

Pretty soon, urban design — that is, the officialdom of planning — caught up with the architects when the long-fermented ideas of Charles-Édouard Jeanneret (aka Le Corbusier), which had been laughed out of Paris since the 1920s, were adopted all over America. I refer here to the notorious piece of mischief the Ville Radieuse or Radiant City, the "buildings in a garden" format, the basis for the new public housing projects, quickly to become slums of vertically concentrated poverty. This bundle of ideas then went on to infect all other realms of city planning — especially as joined with the well-intentioned monomania of the traffic engineers, whose extract from "Corb" was to keep the cars comfortable above all other considerations. By the 1950s, these behaviors were becoming encoded in the post-war planning laws that would mandate suburban sprawl.

One result of this activity was the cumulative impoverishment of the urban streetscape. Between the sleek glass-box office buildings set back behind pointless landscaping displays or "plazas," both of which discouraged ground-floor retail, and the widened streets with their traffic lanes all turned one-way (and on-street parking removed), which allowed the cars to go faster, downtown pedestrian life withered until it was below the necessary critical mass for shopping, which duly moved to the new suburban retail ghettos mandated under single-use zoning — the highway strip, and then the mall. The pattern was set and continued to proliferate until the collapse of the housing bubble starting around 2007.

During this period, the mandarins in the elite architecture schools did nothing to oppose these practices. In fact, they sponsored them and taught them to their students who, in turn, went out into the officialdom and practiced all the humdrum duties of administering parking standards and doing statistical analysis — which was what remained of urban design with all the artistry removed. In academia, the art module was vested in the design of individual buildings and the cult of the individual genius-architects who conceived them. This program followed several parallel tracks.

One track was the aforementioned practice of maximum mystification. The more the genius-architect was able to confound the ordinary public with rhetoric, the more he/she would appear to be a wizard, a supernatural being, authorized by dint of superior powers of intellect to traffic in concepts beyond the ken of the common folk. Since narcissistic personalities were attracted to this racket, they naturally believed their own metaphysical bullshit, and easily derived support from both their fellow narcissists and the sycophants they attracted.

They engaged in generating ever-newer intellectual fashions to support career movement in the Big Business that higher education had become after the troublesome social commitments of the 1960s were demoted to the Kennedy School of Government and its imitators elsewhere. New intellectual fashions were required in order to wade through the swamps of accreditation for the PhD and enter the sinecured ranks of tenured professorship. A striving young scholar in the doctoral marshes had to generate an original idea, and often an entire thought-system used to arrive at it, in order to soldier through the dissertation ordeal and qualify for a faculty job.

This racket was in turn supported by the ideological politics of the day, namely the *struggles* of females, racial identity groups, and homosexuals against the age-old domination of hetero Caucasian males. It hopped on the express bus of the post-structuralism fad, which described all human endeavor in terms of "power relations" and all reality as "constructed" — meaning, if you wanted to change who was in charge of things, you could simply employ rhetoric to manipulate reality according to your needs. Under such a thought regime, reality was a fungible and chimerical commodity. Such obvious relativism created stresses that might not have been salubrious for the collective mental health of a culture, but it hugely benefited ambitious narcissist intellectuals who could claim that reality was whatever they said it was. And it did pave the way for management changes in the universities. Anyway, a great many ambitious hetero males were going off into the greener pastures of an over-financialized economy, so fewer were even competing for the plums of academe. The net result was that a lot of female PhDs manufactured in the Boomer Generation bubble landed in department chairs in the humanities, and the study of literature in particular entered a wilderness of *Theory* from which it has not since reemerged.

But the traffic in metaphysics affected all other quarters of the academic world, except for the hardest sciences, and it was especially suited to the architectural scene, a fairly low-paying vocation, like teaching, with all the additional hazards of small business, if you actually opened a practice. Anyone who succeeded in architecture in a major way became a kind of superstar, but very few did. Many of the wannabe superstars gravitated to the superstar training academies, of course, where the metaphysical bullshit thickets were in full flower. Theory larded with mystification was the ticket to a thriving career in the building arts.

Another track that ran through the architectural programs of recent years was the obsession with technology. Computer-aided-design (CAD) software had made it possible to tweak and torque construction materials in just about any manner — at least on the screen — and emerging architects were using this ability more and more to make bold statements by creating forms that had never been seen before: swooping curvilinear facades, constructed amoebic blobs clad in exotic metals, and UFO-like fantasy structures with no aesthetic precedents or practical justification. This ability to shape buildings in any conceivable way played neatly into the cult of the supernatural genius-wizard insofar as one could endlessly *innovate* novelties — and nothing was more central to the cult than the ability to produce *sui generis* novelties — to wow the public (and mystify them, too). It was the very essence of *the cutting edge*, the place so far out that nobody had any reference for what was produced there. It left the practice of architecture in a kind of circus of wizardry.

These stunts depended on a particular kind of economy, too: the late stage crackup-boom economy of the Peak Oil era, which, accompanied by Peak Credit creation, had left huge pools of deployable money around for real estate ventures, especially for non-profit institutions like museums, symphony halls and college libraries. These projects benefited from the staggering profits in innovative financialization (i.e., the racket in mortgage-backed securities and their derivatives) as newly minted billionaires and their cohorts vied with their checkbooks to have galleries and auditoria named after them. The Guggenheim Museum turned itself into a franchise and began replicating itself all around the planet like an especially fecund alien life form, and every second-tier city got a new museum of this or that. Monumental buildings such as museums and college libraries were exactly the types that lent themselves to grandstanding, so each new one became an opportunity for an attention-getting architectural stunt. To be such a genius-wizard of innovative cutting-edge forms, and to garner such superstar commissions, along with the superstar adulation, became the great aspiration of young architects, while the whole faculty and its programs were bent in the service of this aspiration. In the end, they managed to turn architecture into just another branch of the fashion industry.

Such ventures in metaphysics, high fashion, celebrity and novelty ultimately redounded in the realms of pure status-seeking. The Ivy League outfits obviously carried generations-long accretions of status. The name *Harvard* alone on a C.V. might denote a nice fat five million dollars additional expected lifetime earnings for an alum, on an actuarial basis. But it took some effort to maintain this status aura. Where status as attached to fashion is concerned, it is in the unfortunate nature of fashion that sooner or later it falls out of fashion. The audience or customer base tires of it and yawns and then the mob is on to the next fashion, leaving the old *mode du jour* looking pitiful and its followers ridiculous. Thus the pursuit of fashion, of novelty, becomes an exhausting process, a hamster-wheel of futility — even potentially humiliating, as when Mr. Koolhaas turned on the sycophants at Harvard with his prankish graduate program in...

shopping, as if to say: *here, you conclave of status-seeking, fad-following, celebrity-obsessed boot-lickers, is the one field of study worthy of your craven, tawdry, lost souls.* At the time, given just how demoralized they were up at Gund Hall, the GSD headquarters, they were probably thrilled to bend over and take it up the rear from the exalted, demigodlike, uber-genius-wizard Koolhaas.

At this point of moral and vocational exhaustion, around the turn of the new millennium, some other things were going on in the world which even designers preoccupied with the trivia of fashion could not fail to notice, if only as peripheral annoyances. One, as averred to above, was this bizarre phenomenon calling itself the New Urbanism. For those engaged in millennial high-architectural fashion, with its sleek, exquisitely tortured surfaces and reflective claddings, the NU's work was laughable. Porches and picket fences were about as bygone as poke bonnets and hobble skirts. It must be some kind of joke perpetrated by a claque of backward-gazing, neoconservative ape-people unacquainted with the concept of progress.

This was, of course, a terrible strategic miscalculation on Harvard's part, and a few of them did begin to suspect that NU was onto something. It was hard, at first, to tell just what because the whole paradigmatic worldview at Gund Hall was focused on individual gesture buildings devoid of context. NU was all about the context, the human settlement as an integral organism of parts, elements, components and programs (in which, by the way, grand architectural gestures played only a minor role). NU was about the one thing that all of America had ignored since the end of World War Two: how the things we build relate to each other and to the terrain on which they are located. It was also concerned with the deeper structure of principles in nature that could be employed in the design and assembly of human habitats that were worth living in and caring about.

This was really the crux of the matter. Any nine-year-old in America could sense neurologically the appalling failures of the post-war built environment with all its zones of alienation and anomie, its thoughtless, off-the-shelf, generic arrangements of boring-unto-death housing subdivisions, big box PUDs with groaning out-parcels of clown-like fried food dispensaries, and horizonless wastelands of free parking. These were the mere surface disturbances of a way of life so out of whack with the larger ecosystem that one could literally sense portents of apocalypse in it. Not to put too fine a point on it, American society had made a range of tragic choices in the late twentieth century which, if not altered, were sure to make civilized existence impossible.

The GSD eventually began to catch onto this, and even sent some envoys to the annual convocations of the New Urbanists, who by then had formed a professional organization called the Congress of the New Urbanism, or CNU. The GSD folk brought the news back to headquarters and something started to ferment there. First, they realized that they were late to the game on this whole larger question of how the human habitat might be treated as a design exercise. All they could do was ridicule the NU for being so hopelessly retrograde and un-sexy as to look back in history for practices to emulate. History, all modernists knew, was a dusty attic full of obsolete claptrap that was nothing but an impediment to innovative genius at the cutting edge. To be "edgy," indeed, was the great personal tribute of the moment. The NUs were anything but edgy. Their *führer*, Andrés Duany, wore pastel button-down shirts and plaid ties rather than the standard-issue all-black garb of the cutting edge, which flattered the edge-people to think of themselves as like unto the Viet Cong, indefatigable revolutionary warriors!

What nagged at them, though, was the suspicion that something about this context thing rang true. Wasn't there something called Global Warming or Climate Change happening in the background of all the ribbon-cuttings for the countless new Guggenheim Museums? Wasn't there a realm loosely referred to as "the environment?" (Many professors remembered it dimly from their own college days.) Was there not something cutting edge about it? Could one not assume a heroic, sexy position in defending this "environment"? And what was there in the residue of the *praxis* (a favorite jargon morsel at the GSD) that might point the way to some new, cutting-edge approach to all this. The answer was: Ian McHarg (1920–2001) and his currently out-of-fashion manifesto from 1969, *Design With Nature*.

McHarg was a landscape architect who had settled into a nice job on the faculty at the University of Pennsylvania. Landscape architecture, much as it sounds, is the practice (*praxis*) concerned with shaping a piece of property, generally to prepare a site for building or in the design of parks and gardens. LA, for short, had been architecture's muscle-bound stepbrother for most of the twentieth century, charged with the grunt work that called for front-end loaders and bulldozers to push dirt around. But as the late 1960s gave birth to the environmental movement, it took a new place in the order of things and found a voice in McHarg. *Design With Nature* was a call to action for respecting the planet at a time when many other such calls were issued and the public's awareness about keeping the Earth whole was keen. LA was particularly concerned with directing water flows — hydrology — since water management is usually the most problematic site-planning chore. It also happened that the biggest environmental preoccupations of that day were air and water pollution. McHarg's larger philosophical agenda revolved around the notion that human activity was something in opposition to nature, a toxic alien presence on the planet, the footprint which needed to be minimized. He came to refer to humanity as a "planetary disease."

From *Design With Nature* sprang hundreds of PUDs (Planned Unit Developments) of garden apartments nestled in bosky, *natural* settings and sheathed in *environmental*-looking cedar, and scores of university housing "complexes" bermed into the terrain (with plenty of free parking), and, to be fair, a set of water management methods that worked their way into the now-substantial body of law that regulates environmental permitting. In any case, forty years later, McHarg's work was the lost signpost that the GSD had been searching for in its quest to get off the hamster wheel of futility that was the *starchitecture* racket and into something fresher, newer, edgier, with more sex appeal. Finally it could shake off the growing embarrassment over its failure to address the larger context of the built environment — *territory* occupied by the hated New Urbanists.

The Harvard GSD found its avatar in Charles Waldheim, an associate dean at the University of Toronto, a sedulous contributor to the professional journals, and an especially deft theorist conversant with all the post-structuralist lingo that had infested the humanities and fine arts programs since the 1970s. He had conveniently coined the term "Landscape Urbanism" as a way to make the profession seem more up-to-date, edgy and sexy, and in him Harvard found the perfect field marshal to carve out some of its own *territory* on the battlefield of urban design where, so far, it had been subject only to humiliation. Waldheim was anointed dean of the GSD's Landscape Urbanism program in the summer of 2009.

He came out swinging immediately with an overt declaration that his new field was "a critique of the disciplinary and professional commitments of traditional urban design and an alternative to 'New Urbanism.'"[1] He accused the NU of failing "to come to terms with the rapid pace of urban change and the essentially horizontal character of contemporary auto-mobile-based urbanization across North America and much of Western Europe." This enfilade exposed foremost a bizarre feature of Landscape Urbanism's purported ethos: while supposedly predicated on sound eco-logical *discourse*, LU had no conception whatsoever that the suburban development program of the past ninety-odd years had reached its sell-by date, that the last thing you would want to do as an ecologically minded urban designer (i.e., of human habitats) was promote the idea that we could continue living a car-dependent lifestyle, or that we would even want to, given the grotesque diminishing returns involved. Waldheim assumed that the *horizontal* spewage of sprawl would continue indefi-nitely, and that there was no need to arrest it, merely a charge to refine and improve it. He showed next-to-zero awareness of the global energy resource quandary, or its relation to the disorders of capital formation and all the related dilemmas of epochal economic contraction. In essence, he was enlisted to serve Harvard's chief institutional aim: defense of the sta-tus quo, that is, the cherished old dogmas of modernism. The giveaway was in his statement that LU amounted to "a critical and historically informed rereading of the environmental and social aspirations of mod-ernist planning and its most successful models."

In point of fact, modernist planning had no successful models. It had only a long record of failure embodied in the 1972 demolition of one of its signature projects in the USA: the Corbu-inspired Pruitt-Igoe sub-sidized housing complex in St. Louis, MO, a mere eighteen years after the thirty-three towers-in-a-park opened for business. Modernist urban planning had amounted to repeated, cruel experiments on the poor with untested building typologies delivered in unprecedented mega-quanti-ties with the explosive results of massively concentrated poverty: crime, drugs, family disintegration, misery. What remained of modernist urban planning beyond that was little more than traffic management. Indeed, one of the reasons that Landscape Architecture had discredited itself in recent decades was that most of its remunerative work came from the decoration of parking lots with bark mulch beds and juniper shrubs.

In the spirit of the reigning ideology of the campus, with its incessant prattle about *power relations* between the sexes, the classes, and the ethnicity cohorts, Waldheim inveighed against "privileged" groups and "wealthy elites" — as though wealthy elites had never been seen around Harvard. (The NU project at Seaside, Florida, was a constant target of attack by GSD profs, who regarded it as an affront to decency for being an exceptionally successful beachfront real estate venture — as if some programming error had prevented it from becoming subsidized housing for the indigent or a retirement village for coal miners.)

Waldheim's chief ally was James Corner, chair of the LA program at a sister university, Penn, where Ian McHarg had roosted back in the day. Corner was an even more florid metaphysician than Waldheim — where Waldheim merely strove for obfuscation, Corner achieved nearly complete opacity. Corner was preoccupied with the "imaginative and metaphorical associations" lurking in the underlayment of landscape studies, which was another way of stating that it might represent whatever anyone said it was, a tactic straight out of the post-structuralist playbook where an ever-shifting reality could be manipulated by means of rhetorical *narrative*. Hence the title of Corner's seminal *text*, "Terra Fluxus," an opposition to the age-old notion of terra firma. Consistent with these shifting sands of reality, and the primary axioms of post-structuralism, was his assertion that terms such as "landscape" and "urbanism" were "contested," that there was some question as to what each meant, especially in relation to each other. (Indeed, one of the chief consequences of the suburban fiasco was the loss of any clear distinction between the rural and the urban, an unfortunate condition that had a great deal to do with the pernicious incoherence of American planning-and-zoning law.) Corner's *narrative* intention was simply to wrest the *territory* of urbanism away from the detested traditionalists who revolved around the New Urbanist forces and reoccupy it for the axis of modernism. In short, Landscape Urbanism, in its full-dress metaphysical uniform, was designed to allow the modernists to pretend that they were interested in things urban.

Over the past decade, the Landscape Urbanists came up with their own iconic projects. The two best-known showpieces were by Corner's commercial LA firm, Field Operations — a prankish name intimating crypto-military activities (on the cutting-edge battlefield). One of these was the High Line, a linear park built on an old elevated railroad spur that ran north from Manhattan's Meatpacking District to the old marshalling yards of Hell's Kitchen. The other was a gigantic brownfield remediation job commissioned by the City of New York to make something of the huge, capped, decommissioned garbage dump on Staten Island known as the Fresh Kills landfill.

The High Line was a great success, but aside from Corner's metaphysical jargon — "disciplinary categorizations," the "spatial frame," "spatio-temporal production processes," and so forth — what did it actually amount to? Essentially a one-off adaptive reuse of an urban ruin: the elevated trestle built so mightily as to sustain the enormous weight of railroad locomotives, a structure that had been too difficult for New York's Department of Public Works to demolish. The damn thing had stood in place for decades after the trains stopped running on it until thickets of mature ailanthus trees sprouted in the old track bed and it became the haunt of adventurous teen stoners. Now it happened to be the case that this part of Manhattan contained the least amount of park space of any neighborhood on the whole island, so the project was certainly welcome and extremely popular when completed. Also, at the exact moment the High Line opened in 2009, the Meatpacking District happened to be the epicenter of the downtown boho scene where the art world met the fashion world, with bars stuffed with supermodels and movie actors and a scenester hotel — The Standard — which became a casual theater of sexual display when its denizens began performing erotic stunts through the glass curtain wall windows for strollers below. Talk about the cutting edge! Was this not the reified essence of it! High-minded art + celebrity + live amateur porn!

Typologically, though, the High Line was an oddity of urban construction, a freak. It wasn't as if other American cities possessed this sort of ruin begging to be given the same treatment, or the kind of population densities found in Manhattan to justify it, or the nexus of art, fashion, showbiz, and money to provide excitement. There was a sort of historical precedent for using obsolete linear constructions in the transformation of European city walls to boulevards and ring roads as industrial cities expanded beyond their old boundaries, as for instance in Paris and

Vienna. But nobody had ever claimed that it represented a comprehensive body of urban design theory. The High Line was surely a fortuitous amenity for the neighborhood, but did it represent a great stride forward in urban design practice, something that would be widely replicated? Of course not. The final cost, by the way, was an astounding $30,000 per linear foot.

Corner's other big commission, the Fresh Kills landfill remediation project, was something else. There had never been any previous industrial revolutions in human history, only the current one that took off around the year 1800, and the question of what to do with the enormous accumulated detritus left in its wake posed a new set of problems. The brownfield site at Fresh Kills was a set of island mounds surrounded by marshes and tidal creeks, over two thousand acres in all, about twice the size of Central Park, on a remote corner of Staten island, bisected by a freeway. The program was to turn the old dump into a park, reestablish the natural ecology of the place as far as possible, and build some amenities in the way of boat launches, nature study pavilions, performance venues, and public gathering places. It was also supposed to include a memorial to the 9/11 disaster, since a lot of debris from the World Trade Center ended up there after the cleanup. The old landfill contained a whopping amount of entombed toxic garbage, with an elaborate network of pipes arrayed throughout the various mounds to siphon off the methane gas it exuded. But otherwise the stuff was not going anywhere. The master plan included, naturally, a vehicular roadway system and parking lots — since the cutting edge assumed that America's happy motoring program would continue indefinitely — and a network of bike and foot paths would also be supplied, as in any park.

In other words, it was ... just a park. It would be a very large park, for sure, in the most suburban borough of New York City. There was nothing metaphysical about it. The master plan did not propose any particular changes to the adjoining hodge-podge of subdivisions, shopping strips, malls — in fact, the new park would connect with a colossal network of already-existing parks at the center of Staten Island. As an exercise in landscape architecture, there was nothing particularly innovative to it, and there was nothing describably urban about it, apart from its proximity to where a lot of people lived. Even its brownfield remediation elements were pretty superficial, dealing only with the topmost layers of the old dump; soils and surface water flows — the nastier elements involving capping, plumbing and draining — were already done, and it remains to be seen how they would work, or what kind of effluents would ooze out of the thing over time.

If Corner's Fresh Kills project evinced anything, it was the very conventional impulse to ruralize city real estate wherever terrible technological impacts had occurred. In its most vulgar instances, this impulse showed itself in the universal yammer for "green space" or "open space" wherever an American downtown had suffered some gross mutilation. The public never asked for new and better buildings. They had no faith that contemporary architecture could deliver anything worth living in. Rather, "nature" was seen as the default remedy for mutilated urban fabric. And so ten thousand bark mulch and juniper shrub ensembles have been implanted in town centers from Bangor to El Segundo as *Nature Band-Aids* in an attempt to cover up the failures of urban planning.

The truth of the matter was that America suffered not from a lack of "open space" or green space, but from properly designed *closed* space — that is, from streets and public spaces defined by buildings that functioned in ways consistent with the human brain's cognitive and social needs. You'd go to places like Missoula, Montana, where the public clamored for "open space" in their misguided attempt to fix a business district that simply contained too many low, ugly buildings deployed on overly-wide streets with excessively fast traffic flows. Meanwhile, you could walk out of town in any direction for ten minutes and be in the biggest wilderness in the Lower 48 states. In short, the public was deluded. Having spent most of their lives in dreary suburban environments, they had no idea what a good town was — nor did their municipal leaders and appointed officials in the planning departments, so they'd just given up and asked for "nature" instead.

The Landscape Urbanism movement (if that's what it was) simply went along with this vulgar misunderstanding of how the urban human habitat might be designed and assembled, dressed in pretentious post-structuralist metaphysics. They were not interested in buildings at all, except for what might already be there, as in the case of the High Line. Whenever their plans even indicated the possibility of future new buildings, their renderings depicted apartment slabs-in-a-park straight out of a 1927 Bauhaus pattern book, but more arbitrary. Nor did they understand in any dimension the sweeping changes underway in twenty-first century economic life: the worldwide scramble for resources and most particularly the growing shortage of capital that would eventually prevent many municipalities from ever being able to finance or maintain gigantic projects such as Fresh Kills. They paid lip service to the possible contraction of cities, but they only understood it in terms of ever-expanding suburbs. They had no idea that people in the year 2050 would be living a whole lot differently than they had in 2005.

When all was said and done, the Landscape Urbanism project was a lame defense of the bankrupt old mandarin ideology that had corroded into little more than a never-ending exercise in status-seeking, especially at Harvard, where status now meant more than anything, including the quality of any ideas. The Landscape Urbanists perceived that there were moral, fashion and sex-appeal brownie points to be garnered in the craze for being "green," and, at least for the moment, there were commissions to be earned by LA firms in proposing various green-ups — whether they were new parks on old brownfields or cockamamie schemes to grow zucchinis on vertical surfaces (innovative urban farming), or the conversion of broken-down waterfronts into esplanades. None of it was materially different from the kinds of work Robert Moses had done back in the mid-twentieth century. None of it was consistent with what the future really required. It represented a new form of intellectualism in which pretending to be smart was just enough to get ahead in the world.

Endnotes

1   Lecture: "Planning, Ecology, and the Emergence of Landscape." 46th IFLA World Conference, Rio de Janeiro, October 22, 2009.

8

Landscape Urbanism:
Supplement or Substitute?

Paul Murrain

Becoming a Landscape Architect

IN PRIMARY SCHOOL, I LOVED TO DRAW TOWNS. Along with a friend, I was allowed to spend many hours in art class drawing from memory the plan of my hometown, on an enormous sheet of white paper hung on the wall at the back of the classroom. Walking to and from school we would check out the streets to see if we had drawn them correctly, how they connected to others, and where the shops, churches, schools, playgrounds and businesses were. To me this was architecture. No building was particularly special, even though some seemed more significant than others. The architecture existed to make something else, something more collective and whole. I couldn't articulate that at the time, of course, but over the years I realized its significance. Architecture and urbanism were one and the same.

When the time came for me to choose a vocation, I applied to several architecture schools in the UK and paid them a visit. What I saw in the studios, on the wall, and on the drawing boards left me utterly bewildered. I saw objects, most of them barely understandable to a seventeen-year-old who had grown up in a normal place. Anything remotely resembling urbanism was nowhere to be seen.

So I walked out hoping and believing there must be some other profession that did what I wanted to do. Town planning of course; the title speaks for itself, you learn to plan towns. To this day I still can't figure out what was going on. The only illustrations I saw — and there was barely any — were brightly coloured blobs, arrows and stars where towns once were, or ought to be. Town planning in the UK was not about planning towns.

What was left but landscape architecture: the architecture of the landscape? Towns and cities were not in that title but at least it was the right scale, I thought. Once in the academy, I learned this was not the case. Covertly I was being taught to despise cities, to improve them by fragmenting them, to realize that unless everything was enmeshed in or surrounded by "green," projects had little legitimacy. Humans had suffered from desolate urban environments. The greener the better, the lower the density the better, the more culs-de-sac that terminated on open space the better. And yet landscape architecture did teach me one essential thing: the true meaning of the word ecology — the branch of biology dealing with the relations of organisms to one another and to their physical surroundings. When extended to human ecology, it distinguishes the interaction of people with their environment. It was through my lectures in ecology that I came to understand the complexity of interactions between all things, at all scales. That sounded remarkably like towns and cities to me.

Unfortunately, the lessons of ecology never translated to human settlement. While complexity in the plant and animal world was considered paramount, complexity in the human habitat was dismissed. As long ago as 1958, the remarkable William H. Whyte, writing in *Fortune* magazine along with the likes of Jane Jacobs, encapsulated this tendency:

> Everyone it would seem, is for the re-building of our cities, and with a unity of approach that is remarkable.... But this is not the same thing as liking cities. Most of the re-building under way and in prospect is being designed by people who don't like cities. They do not merely dislike the noise and dirt and the congestion. They dislike the city's variety and concentration, its tension, its hustle and bustle. The new redevelopment projects will be physically in the city, but in spirit they deny it — and the values that since the beginning of civilisation have always been at the heart of great cities.[1]

And so it is with Landscape Urbanism. It does not partipate in urbanism. It becomes a substitute for it. As someone who has a degree (with distinction) in landscape architecture I condemn it for that reason enough. I was rescued a few years later by a masters degree in urban design.

In the *Landscape Urbanism Reader* Charles Waldheim opens by saying:

> Landscape urbanism describes a disciplinary realignment currently underway in which landscape replaces architecture as the basic building block of contemporary urbanism. For many, across a range of disciplines, landscape has become both the lens through which the contemporary city is represented and the medium through which it is constructed.[2]

Great urbanism has never tolerated such crude and simplistic distinctions. Neither landscape nor architecture should be thought of as the basic building block of urbanism, distinct from one another. Architecture has rarely been the single building block of urbanism. If today it attempts to be so, then I agree with Professor Waldheim's demotion of it. But you don't have to develop a new specialist called a Landscape Urbanist to challenge or critique it. Traditional urbanists have been successfully doing so for three decades and with more rigors regarding the necessary continuity.

The landscape has a profound influence if we begin to understand how settlements begin, where and why they grow: how it affects their siting, form and structure. Doubtless incurring the dismissal of Landscape Urbanists, the landscape has, in the process, often been radically modified to create some of the most functional and beautiful places on Earth; places that have therefore become sustainable by their adaptability and desirability.

In his 1997 *Landscape Urbanism Reader,* the seminal document of this movement, Waldheim acknowledges that many North American Cities grew as if sprung from the earth; but he does not give any meaningful examples to study. If he means that once upon a time, regional climate, geology and materials influenced urban form, who can argue?

And there are also US cities that were imposed on the landscape, doing little more than maximizing the breezes, while seeking to dominate the landscape for human purposes. Some evolved badly, some wonderfully.

The results Waldheim describes as commodification, cities for tourism. The more relevant question is why do millions flock to imposed, "artificial" places like San Francisco, Savannah and Charleston, amongst others? As Andrés Duany reminds us of the lamentable state of suburbia, "people visit these towns just because they are towns — to experience the difference."

One could agree with Waldheim's observation that North Americans have spent an enormous amount of their time in built environments characterized by decreased density, easy accommodation of the motorcar, and public realms plied with vegetation. An unmitigated disaster, but there are few within the design professions who have contributed more to masking that immense problem over the last eighty years than landscape architects.

Where did this reduction, from within the ecological traditions of landscape architecture, come from? Anti-urban philosphies and movements have been with us for centuries of course, but in relatively recent times we must turn to Ian McHarg.

Ian McHarg: Anti-Urban Through and Through

The late Ian McHarg has much to answer for in this regard, although at least he had a comprehensible system of evaluation that could be linked to outcomes. His theories had a rationale to back up a self-confessed dislike of cities. The urbanism was to be shoved into the space left over after everything else had been evaluated as being of higher value.

Having suffered the rejection of urban places in the form of a course with Ian McHarg's *Design with Nature* as compulsory material, I grant that it is a monumental work by a remarkable man. But it was published in 1969, not 1869, when Charles Dickens was taking us on hard journeys through urban London. Why was McHarg still so moved? Perhaps it was his childhood experience growing up in industrial Glasgow, where the adjective "grim" accompanied the noun "city."

McHarg castigates suburban sprawl, but he castigates the traditional city even more vehemently:

> Call them no place although they have many names. Race
> and hate, disease, poverty, rancour and despair, urine and
> spit live here in the shadows. United in poverty and ugliness,

their symbol is the abandoned carcasses of automobiles, broken glass, alleys of rubbish and garbage. Crime consorts with disease, group fights group, the only emancipation is the parked car.[3]

In this is the remarkable, ahistorical presumption that the rural idyll never exhibited poverty, race and hate, disease, rancour, and despair. It is either ignorance or prejudice to infer that this is the inevitable and universal condition of the city.

Rubbishing Philadelphia

McHarg cites research entitled "Mental Health in the Metropolis, The Midtown Manhattan Study," wherein "twenty percent of the population was found to be indistinguishable from the patients in mental hospitals"[4] Amazingly, 175 pages later in a chapter entitled "The City: Health and Pathology," he quietly mentions that this study *sadly excluded the entire subject of the physical environment.* And yet McHarg dedicates the chapter to declaring that Philadelphia — a *physical* environment — is riddled with every kind of pathological problem.

Maps of physical disease abound, followed by maps of social disease: crime, suicide and infant mortality (Figure 8.1). Then comes mental disease, followed by maps of atmospheric pollution, and on it goes. He points out that it is premature to predict correlations, but suggests density might have something to do with it. This assertion is lost in the assassination of Philadelphia, the city where McHarg lived, taught and practiced. The chapter displays a plethora of maps that rubbish the city, and by implication, every other city. It displays a rabid hatred for cities.

What then when an article on Philadelphia, written in 1994 by Marion Laffey Fox, begins: "Gracious as a curtsy, Philadelphia exudes beauty, culture and a bi-level attitude where frivolity and flamboyance are tempered by modesty"?[5] Fox goes on to acknowledge that there are "pockets of the usual urban decay, but on the whole it is wonderfully preserved on a human scale."

The superlatives continue: "breathtaking museum mile … studded with classical buildings mimicking the best of 19th century Paris.…. Philadelphia is its neighborhoods, a tightly sewn patchwork where people live together based on varied traditions, common goals synonymous with

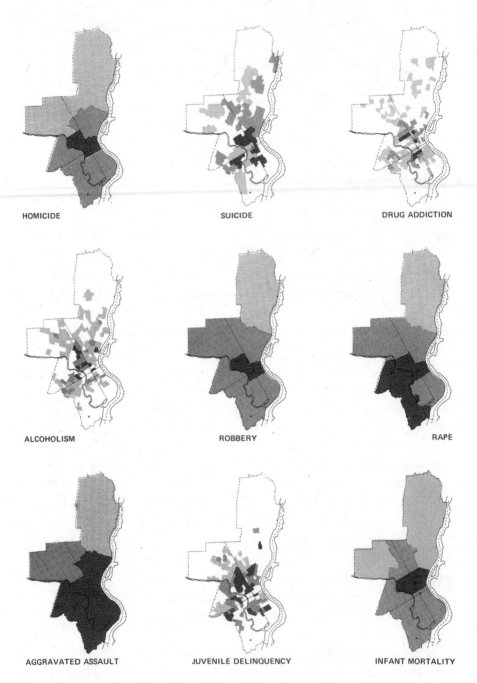

Fig. 8.1: *Philadelphia through the eyes of McHarg. Pathological with no redeeming features.*
SOURCE: MCHARG, I.L., 1969. 'DESIGN WITH NATURE'. THE NATURAL HISTORY PRESS, GARDEN CITY , NEW YORK

friendship, safety and a rich, welcoming atmosphere .... the University of Pennsylvania, swirls with students, landmark academic architecture, world class arts institutions and museums..... quiet Delancey, Panama and Cypress Streets invite strolling."

The article then quotes Mayor Edward G. Rendell: "When Philadelphia was founded by Quaker William Penn, as the 'City of Brotherly Love,' 313 years ago, his vision of diversity and tolerance planted the roots for what we are today ... a city of dozens of colourful neighbourhoods whose combined cultures make us the most fascinating and livable city in America" (Figure 8.2).

Approximately twenty-five years elapsed between that article and McHarg condemning his city to the ashes. Clearly, there has been great progress in that period, but Philadelphia has not been disassembled into tiny ecological villages to make it healthy and beautiful. It has not been stuffed full of green space fragmenting its structure to make it livable. It has been invested in, managed and cared for. That is all. It is a great gridded North American city of quality and substance.

Does McHarg's work have any redeeming features? Yes. It teaches holistic systems, ecological relationships in the full sense of the word. It proposes an ecological rationale for regional planning that is still woefully

Fig. 8.2: *Rittenhouse square, Philadelphia.* Source: Paul Murrain.

lacking. It rightly condemns mindless sprawl and the rights of any individual to abuse their land.

But analyze the work closely. The urbanism that he proposes is tiny and fragmented, given legitimacy only if labeled "villages." In truth, these are simply the residuae after all the other environmental criteria have been satisfied. They are fragments with no structure or purpose other than to be inoffensive to anything or anyone nearby. He proposes no function that would turn them into interactive places: no notion of what they must contain to be self-sustaining.

Design With Nature attacks suburban sprawl but it doesn't replace it with urbanism, nor with any strategy for coping with the urban issues we face today. There is an obvious explanation: McHarg neglected to include urbanism as part of his theories. Most of his disciples do the same.

McHarg may have been flawed, but he had far more rigor in his argument than Landscape Urbanism, which is a response to suburbanism that continues to build all the ingredients of "town" but no town.

With Landscape Urbanism the "landscape" is the surrogate structuring device for the fundamentals of urbanism. Behold the British and North American New Towns of years ago, and their exports across the world, to see the problem clearly.

As an example: Milton Keynes used to sell itself as the "City of Trees" and proclaim that it would be possible to drive through the city on unfettered highways and not see a building. Imagine if Amsterdam, Boston, Paris, Berlin and Charleston retrofitted to this model!

Real Landscape Urbanism.

What are we to make of the rejection, by McHarg and now the Landscape Urbanists, of urbanism? Why do they impose its total absence in their discourse, asserting that urbanism has had little to teach us in overcoming the planning failures of the last sixty years?

We can contrast the McHargian/Landscape Urbanism view with that of Thomas Sharp, who offered this insight in 1947, just as the first attempt to deconstruct urbanism was taking hold:

> The way to maintain the invaluable contrast between town
> and country is to keep these two utilities as pure as possible.
> We need to get back to the age-old conception of the town

as pure town and the country as pure country … along with
the preservation of the countryside; the preservation of the
town must be attempted. The two are interdependent: one
rises to beauty or falls to ruin with the other. It is true to
say that only through the rehabilitation of the town can the
countryside be saved, that the true way to save the countryside is to build true urban towns.

To do these things we shall have to overleap the degradation of a hundred years. We shall have to try and recapture
something of the Renaissance spirit of pride in our physical
environment and particularly in that part of the environment, the town, which is our special personal deliberate
creation from nothing.[6]

The brilliance of his observation is its simple directness: that for the
country to be the country, the town must be the town. This had nothing to do with greenery in town, nor with efficient energy use, drainage
or recycling. It had to do with the difference between substituting and
supplementing.

Is this view too romantic, or no longer relevant to the sustainable
imperative? Both critiques are levelled at Sharp's observation. And yet,
the number of people who inhabit, and willingly pay to do so, those
neighbourhoods, towns and cities, often in great natural settings, support the idea of urbanism in its traditional form. It is impossible to list
the number of great neighbourhoods, villages, towns and cities in use
today — in the circumstances of modernity — that refute the simplistic
dismissal of earlier urbanism.

Siena, Italy, offers an excellent example. Camillo Sitte, as Hegemann
and Peets remind us, investigated the causes of its peculiar aesthetic
charm: the old and somewhat forgotten methods of *setting buildings*.[7] For
example, Piazza del Campo is located in a natural amphitheater between
three hills. The streets follow the ridges and valleys and run radially into
the plaza. The city hall sits between the Campo and a market square at
a lower level. The citizens gather in the Campo for special civic events
as well as general exchange on a daily basis. The fountain celebrates the
aqueducts from the hills. The paving focuses on the drain that takes the
water away. Social and natural cycles are understood and celebrated.

The loggia of the city hall overlooks this urban setting and commands the scene, providing a unique transition. Move through the building or cross the loggia and you look down at the market place. Produce is displayed along with a truly stunning view to the productive landscape beyond, a landscape that laps up against the hard urban edge. The siting of the city hall commanding these two related, sustainable functions of town and productive landscape is unsurpassed Landscape Urbanism. Why is such an example excluded physically and intellectually from the *Landscape Urbanism Reader*?

Frederick Law Olmsted: No Landscape Urbanist

Olmsted features intermittently in Landscape Urbanism's discourse, often critically because of shifting landscape fashion, but also respectfully as a result of his linear park and greenway interventions for cities. And yet, Frederick Law Olmsted was not a Landscape Urbanist because he understood the difference between *supplementing* as opposed to *substituting* urbanism. He believed that urban life was unhealthy for body and soul; foul air, vice and congestion; the usual dystopia advanced by utopians.

But there is a key distinction between Olmsted and the Landscape Urbanists. Olmsted did not see parks and tree-lined streets as intrusions breaking up the city. He sought them as settings of contrast — *the park as haven*, as a supplement to civic interaction. Thus in 1870, in an article for the American Social Science Association entitled "Public Parks and the Enlargement of Towns",[8] he acknowledged the inevitability of cities: "The poorest who cannot find employment in the city, will come to the country, and these as soon as they have got a few dollars ahead, are crazy to get back to the town." The evidence was Paris absorbing half of the increase of population in France, and Berlin growing twice as fast as all Prussia. Olmsted did not view this as a moral epidemic and wrote instead of the intimate connection between the growth of towns and "the dying out of slavery and feudal customs, of priestcraft and government by divine right, the multiplication of books, newspapers, schools and other means of popular education ... transportation and various labor-saving inventions."

There were no abstractions about the city. Olmsted grasped what the city was and why it was to be solution and salvation rather than nemesis.

He wrote: "Compare advantages in respect simply to schools, libraries, music and the fine arts. People of the greatest wealth can hardly command as much of these in the country as the poorest work girl is offered here in Boston at the mere cost of a walk for a short distance over a good, firm, clean pathway, lighted at night and made interesting to her by shop fronts and the variety of people passing." Olmsted, that most revered landscape practitioner, was extolling the virtues of the nineteenth-century city. He was not advocating its deconstruction.

Olmsted also championed and designed elegant suburbs that took advantage of streetcars and railroads to provide a greener setting. But again, he saw this as a supplement to, not a substitute for, the city. Alluding to French colonial planning compared to the helter–skelter methods of settlement in the USA, he stated that whoever has observed such coordinated planning "will not believe that even the occupation of a farm laborer must necessarily exclude his family from a very large share of urban conveniences."

Olmsted did worry about towns growing too large, life expectancy being lower and, of course, the declining quality of the air. He was concerned about density resulting in "a tendency to regard others in a hard if not hardening way." He worried that the sheer weight of numbers on the streets would provide "no relief from it at all in our waking hours." He argued that air is disinfected by foliage and sunlight, and lamented the absence of trees on streets. He wanted sufficient space to allow trees to flourish.

But Olmsted also made an astute and, to some, surprising observation that: "Numerous small grounds so distributed through a large town that some one of them could be easily reached by a short walk from every house, would be more desirable than a single area of great extent, however rich in landscape attractions it might be." In a similar vein, he differentiated between "exertive" recreation and "receptive" recreation, the former being exercise and sports and the latter being music and the fine arts. He further subdivided receptive recreation into "gregarious" and "neighbourly." He regarded the promenade of the Champs-Elysés as the greatest experience of "gregarious receptive recreation" and valued the *alamedas* of Spain and Portugal as great promenading places. He spoke of the social value of landscape — of people coming together in New York's Central Park and Prospect Park. He wanted tree-lined avenues and boulevards to serve as convenient communicators between the districts of the town.

Neighbourly receptive recreation was "where the prattle of children mingles with the easy conversation of the more sedate." Where he proposed more of such spaces, he was arguing the need to supplement the urbanism rather than substitute it: "The park should as far as possible complement the town."

The Park as the Complement

While agreeing with Frederick Law Olmsted on the subject of parks complementing and supplementing towns, it is interesting to see how his views fare today. What is different from the days when Olmsted was bemoaning the environmental condition of nineteenth-century cities is that the air is now cleaner (though car emissions still plague us) and we have far better sanitation, cleaner energy, and very few noxious industries. Social equity and carbon reduction remain significant challenges — but that is not exclusive to cities. My main point is this: despite problems we must diligently address, there has never been a better time to inhabit a street-based city. In Olmsted's day, the large urban park was a refuge from crowded streets, poor air quality, and sanitation problems. Olmsted thus observed how, in the 1870s, thousands flocked to a half-finished Prospect Park in Brooklyn.

And yet, when I visit *large* parks in cities today, I am struck by how unpopulated they actually are — almost desolate from Monday to Friday; less than overflowing on the weekend. Hardly anyone is there in the hours of darkness. They are, in fact, massive thromboses to natural movement for a great deal of the day, week or season. As a resource in the city, they are significantly under-used. This is not true of the myriad of smaller parks and squares.

Two recent experiences illustrate my point, all occurring on good spring and summer days, in centrally located parks in major cities, and in locations surrounded by millions of people, including tourists, residents and workers — people of all ages, wealth and status.

First in London, where St James's Park merges with Green Park that in turn merges with the great Hyde Park. From west to east, fusing them all, they are similar in extent to Central Park in its north-south axis. The illustrations were taken at lunchtime on a summer's weekday in Green

Park. I chose that time deliberately to factor in the thousands of office workers immediately around the park and in Piccadilly Circus. It was the height of the tourist season. The Queen's residence of Buckingham Palace is approximately two hundred meters from where these photographs were taken. Thousands of people were milling around outside the palace. The shopping streets of Mayfair and Bond Street are close by, the density pathological by professional planners' standards.

The photos speak for themselves: there was hardly a soul (Figure 8.3). The layout, that of the English Landscape School, controlled and simulated nature. The mature trees were magnificent, the filtered light exquisite. The contribution to central London was one of serenity and emptiness.

I encountered a similar experience in New York City at Easter time the same year. The weather was fine, if a little cool. Times Square — all pavement, even where some of the heavy traffic has been removed and the space given over to cafe seating and cycle lanes — was heaving with

Fig. 8.3: *Green Park, London. A supplement to the vitality of the nearby streets.*
Source: Paul Murrain

Fig. 8.4: *South Central Park.* PHOTO PAUL MURRAIN

people, as were all the spaces in Midtown where Broadway crosses the orthogonal grid. It was classic Manhattan street life.

I walked a few blocks further north into the southern end of Central Park. Some people were there, mainly gathered around the children's playgrounds and the rock outcrops. The basketball courts were in use, the usual joggers were on the carriage drive, all examples of Olmsted's exertive recreation. But the park itself was empty by comparison (Figure 8.4). The number of people present was insignificant compared with Times Square, Herald Square and Union Square. People were *choosing* the urban milieu in far greater numbers than the large central park (Figure 8.5).

This is not a criticism of large urban parks, nor a plea to repurpose them. The fact that these large tracts are almost empty is *precisely why they matter,* just as Olmsted pointed out. They are a complement and supplement to the city, not a substitute for it. To be able to escape the city from time to time, and yet remain within it, is a worthy option. In this light, the Landscape Urbanist argument that "landscape" should replace streets, squares and the sophisticated networks of centuries is incoherent and unsupportable.

Fig. 8.5. *Times Square, New York City.*

Photo: Paul Murrain

Public Space: How Towns Are

For a movement that claims to have the answer to the current predicament of cities, it is alarming how little of Landscape Urbanism's effort is devoted to the crucial topic of public life. Much of what it promotes is an implicit or explicit condemnation of streets as the fundamental element of urbanism.

Kenneth Frampton, enlisted as a supporter, laments in Stanford Andersons "On Streets" that, despite the advent of "non-place urban realms," "the fact remains that an existential need for something that may be identified as a street seems to persist."[9] He seems surprised that, after thousands of years of streets being *the* essence of public interaction and exchange across cultures, they persist in the minds and aspirations of the populous. It is as if architects are being *required* to address the street despite a desperate desire to rid themselves of traditional urbanism.

Anderson himself eloquently summarizes the complete confusion endemic in those that seek alternatives to the street:

> This century's most pervasive models of the new city were ideal schemes of crystalline shelters in meadows with

occasional ways but no streets — openness and transparency in an innocent and undomesticated nature. This gave us plans devoid of streets and of any metaphor for guile, secrecy, danger, fear, and generally, the darker aspects of human nature and action. It was treated as a matter of some surprise that the removal of the street did not remove the darker aspects of human nature and action. Today, whatever our disappointments and fears in the use of streets, our strongest sense for most modern environments is of lost amenity and of fear so pervasive as to enforce total withdrawal from large parks and superblocks of single-use buildings in open space."[10]

On this point there seems to be some confusion within the seminal writings of the Landscape Urbanists. At times they condemn the spatial nature of traditional cities, and yet there is also the occasional nugget of praise for the grid and traditional streets and squares. Some authors have noted that the work of Allan Jacobs has "drawn attention from the design of the highway itself, championing instead the use of traditional urban forms such as street grids and boulevards." And yet *The Boulevard Book* is also condemned for its "equally nostalgic cast," arguing, in effect, that nothing more than sixty years old can be of value.[11]

Roger Scruton reminds us that space is made public by the nature of its boundary: a boundary both permeable and open to public uses. In this he makes a salient point that Landscape Urbanism can never deliver: "The wild countryside may be open to unlimited human movement, but it has no point of contact with the private world, no point at which to announce its public purpose. It is 'unbounded' not because it goes on forever, but because its perimeter has no mark. Lacking a boundary, it lacks the character of public-ness.... Nature is neither private nor public but merely beyond society".[12] In this assertion, Scruton reminds us of what our species must construct in order to achieve the interaction we must have: bounded, connected and legible space.

Many architects are supporting the tenets of Landscape Urbanism and ignoring the central importance of public life. This position frees them from having to adhere to a discipline greater than their own imaginations. It allows them not only to elaborate their individual objects, but also to move up in scale to design whole neighbourhoods in an artistic fashion. In this way, architecture and Landscape Urbanism are now colluding to deconstruct, and ultimately damage, the city.

Norman Crowe's book *Nature and the Idea of a Man-Made World* [13] is an antidote to the Landscape Urbanism doctrine. Crowe reminds us that the connections between the constructed world and the natural world are manifested in what we build — towns and cities, farms and gardens, architecture and works of civil engineering — those environments over which we have some direct control. Like the natural world out of which it is created, the built world operates in response to its own rules of change and permanence, by the interaction of contributing forces. Most important among those is our human nature, including our quest for meaning in the things we create. When we overlook the long-evolved ways of doing things, we do so at great risk.

Landscape Urbanism seems to deny both how cities *are* and what their management, our most complex task, requires. This is a form of simplistic utopianism, to pretend that we could or should abandon the spatial qualities that make cities what they are.

Endnotes

1   Whyte, W.H., Ed. 1958. *The Exploding Metropolis*. Garden City, New York: Doubleday and Co, p. 7.

2   Waldheim, C., Ed. 2006. *The Landscape Urbanism Reader*. New York: Princeton Architctural Press, p.11

3   McHarg, I.L. 1969. *Design With Nature*. Garden City, New York: The Natural History Press, p.20.

4   Ibid.

5   Fox, M.L. 1994. Philadelphia: Penn-Style Energy in a City Defined by its Dozens of Colourful Neighbourhoods. *Sky Magazine*. April, p. 51.

6   Sharp, T. 1940. *Town Planning*. London: Pelican Books, pp. 55-56.

7   Hegemann, W. and E. Peets. 1988. *The American Vitruvius: An Architects' Handbook of Civic Art*. New York: Princeton Architectural Press, ch 1.

8   Glazer, N and M. Lilla, Eds. 1987. *The Public Face of Architecture*. New York: The Free Press, pp. 222–63.

9   Anderson, S. 1978. *On Streets*. Cambridge, MA: MIT Press, p. 309.

10 Anderson, op cit., p. viii.

11 Waldheim, op cit., p.183.

12 Glazer, op cit.

13 Crowe, N. 1995. *Nature and the Idea of a Man-Made World*. Cambridge, MA: MIT Press.

Additional Works Cited

Olmsted, F.L. 1987. Public Parks and The Enlargement of Towns. In N. Glazer and M. Lilla, Eds., *The Public Face of Architecture*. New York: The Free Press. Pp. 222–63.

Scruton, R. 1987. Public Space and The Classical Vernacular. In N. Glazer and M. Lilla, Eds. 1987. *The Public Face of Architecture*. New York: The Free Press. Pp. 13–25.

9

Why Dogs Should Not Eat Dogs

DANIEL SOLOMON

T HE *LANDSCAPE URBANISM READER* has much in common with other sectarian tracts. It establishes an *ism*, and like many *isms*, it is a flowering of jolly good fellowship around a loose, marginally coherent, sometimes changing federation of ideas. One cannot reflect on this *ism* without considering the nature of *isms* in general.

The binding force, the very glue of all *isms*, is the otherness of others. It is obligatory for most religious leaders to mouth ecumenical sentiments from time to time, but one of the main things that believers in most things believe most deeply is that believers of other beliefs are fundamentally nuts or damned or both. So it is with Landscape Urbanism and New Urbanism, the former framed specifically to challenge and be offensive to the latter.

There is a certain absurdity in this debate, considering the larger (much larger) political crises it resides within — i.e., the dominance of climate-change-deniers, disbelievers in science or the value of research, and people who think physical planning of any sort is socialist tyranny. It is somewhat like the squabbles between the constructivists and the suprematists on the Bauhaus faculty, or the bitter feud between the Freudian and Jungian wings of the Berlin Psychoanalytical Institute — as if there wasn't something much more ominous to worry about in the last days of the Weimar Republic. With absolutely no one on the national scene making a cogent case for urbanism, environmentalism, or investment in the physical stuff of the nation, the NU–LU debate seems like a journey out into cold tundra of irrelevance.

But here we are, lodged between the covers of this book, horns locked in apparent conflict with people with whom we have much in common. To participate in this debate it is worth recognizing the utility in *isms*. To some degree New Urbanism has successfully exploited those benefits, an exploitation that seems to be the principal motivation for the formulation of the Landscape Urban-counter-ism. The Landscape Urbanist crowd observed that by packaging and wrapping an elastic ribbon stenciled with the New Urbanist label around the diverse works and thoughts of some talented people, it has been possible to fling those thoughts and works much further into the firmament than those same items would have traveled unpackaged. There is simple physics at work here.

Most *isms*, we must remember, have a pretty fixed lifespan. There is some dialectical process at work that destined the revolution of cubism a couple of generations later to become decor for the waiting rooms of dentist's offices. As ideas are disseminated, they are trivialized. Also, the followers of movements in the arts rarely have the ability or the charisma of the pioneers. New Urbanism has been headed for the equivalent of the dentist's office for a long time, and New Urbanists must credit their rival movement for jolting some new life into the carcass.

Landscape Urbanism also deserves credit for a brave and long overdue attempt to rescue landscape architecture from the abyss of irrelevance into which it flung itself decades ago. Through the efforts of Corner, Waldheim, et al, we and the world may someday be spared the little dribs and drabs of fake nature scattered everywhere, the oh-so-familiar landscape as artificial sweetener. Landscape Urbanism can claim a formidable array of large, important projects — New York's High Line, San Francisco's Crissy Field, Duisburg-Nord Park in Germany, Lurie Garden in Chicago among them. There is enough commonality in this list to lump them together as a movement and all of them are beyond the stretch of New Urbanism's elastic boundary and genius for appropriation.

Why not extract useful nuggets from Landscape Urbanism, from reasonable observations made in its name, and from some projects of stunning quality, consider where they may broaden "our" vision, and

While some of these grand episodes engage infinity and boundlessness, others do not. Boundlessness can be merely banal, and neither boundary nor its absence has a monopoly on the sublime. Think of a few cases:

- George Hargraves' reclamation of Crissy Field in the San Francisco Presidio is one such place, enjoyed by thousands every weekend. A small, former military airfield next to the Golden Gate Bridge was converted into a hundred-acre public park consisting of two large sections. The eastern half is a wetland reclamation, beachfront and lagoon — quite beautiful and a happy home for a great variety of squawking seabirds who don't seem to mind the proximity of their human roommates. The other half is a fifty-acre unbroken plane of lawn, subtly tilted toward the water, capturing the majesty of the Golden Gate with its glorious bridge framing the infinite Pacific beyond. When it was near completion with just the vast tilted lawn installed, I asked Hargraves' partner, Mary Margret Jones, what came next? She replied with a knowing twinkle, "NOTHING."

  Linda Pollak is quite right that this is a sublime urban place that the methods and preoccupations of New Urbanists, rooted in the enclosed ground of the figure/ground, would be unlikely to conceive.
- But what about another equally thrilling place that does depend upon the clarity of its boundary? Enter Central Park at East 90th Street and Fifth Avenue, walk a little and ascend the steps that lead to the path around the Central Park Reservoir. Head north and at the top of the Reservoir, turn and look south: a bounded space of stupendous scale, left and right the majestic street walls of Fifth Avenue and Central Park West, straight ahead the great striving skyscrapers of Midtown, and contained on three sides, the green carpet of the park, the world's most sublime juxtaposition of constructed urbanity and constructed nature. Every time you see it: *Gasp.*
- Or another that is not so easy to see. Try taking a small commuter flight out of Chicago, one that lets you walk across the O'Hare tarmac. Unlike other airports, the vast runways of O'Hare have a continuous visible perimeter of low buildings. That enclosed space with Airbuses and 757s taxiing around in it is a more stirring evocation of the scale and power of our technological society than any other I can think of — and it is the enclosure that makes it so.

- Conversely, the vast plaza built around the main buildings of the 2008 Beijing Olympics has no boundary or enclosure. It is just big, amorphous and stupid. There is nothing sublime about it, and it trivializes the great buildings it houses, including Herzog and DeMeuron's spectacular Bird's Nest.

One could go on and on with this list — great, majestic spaces with and without enclosure; big banal spaces with and without enclosure. The point is that neither dogma, NU or LU, is an adequate recipe for great urbanism. The problem lies with the very idea of recipes — looking to the pat and formulaic as opposed to seizing meaning from those occasional serendipitous interactions of circumstance and artistry that rarely follow anyone's rules.

Several of the LU essays make an undeniable point, that the New Urbanist cosmos does not engage large segments of what are inescapable parts of the contemporary landscape — vast infrastructure projects and facilities for the distribution of goods at the scale of the global economy; i.e., the IKEAs and Wal-Marts of the world. It is quite true that there is no such thing as New Urbanist International Airport.

One can only admire the ambition to seize control of these vast things and imbue them with civic virtue, but one wonders if any of these writers of manifestos has a real grasp of what they are taking on. Jacqueline Tatom resurrects the good name of landscape architect Lawrence Halprin as a kind of ur-hero who sought to expand the realm of landscape architecture in the 1960s by carving a role for himself in the planning of highway and transit infrastructure.

There are several concurrent confusions at work in the Landscape Urbanism's fascination with big infrastructure and their canonizing of Halprin. As it happens, I was an ear-wet junior fledgling in the Halprin office when most of that was going on. I was assigned to a basement purgatory to work on Halprin's open-ended cost-plus contract (what a deal!) to provide "consultation" to the mighty Parsons/Brinkerhof, Tudor/Bechtel joint venture that was actually designing BART (Bay Area Rapid Transit). My young companions in purgatory included Christopher Alexander, Art Gensler and Sandy Hirshen, later dean at the University of British Columbia. What we all learned together is how very easy it is for the role of urbanist / landscape architect to become that of cheerleader and window dresser for the brutal rapine of engineering pragmatism and momentum. BART and the California Division of Highways (which also employed Halprin) engaged in the worst urbanistic atrocities, made easier by Halprin's line of cosmetics and his blessing.

Really to engage transportation infrastructure, to shape it, control it, and integrate it with the urbanism of landscape and city, will require fundamental restructuring of the academic and professional relationships of civil engineering to landscape architecture, planning and urban design — a noble project, but not one for which Landscape Urbanism has yet provided an inkling of an agenda.

Nonetheless, the observation that New Urbanism is mute about essential components of the modern metropolis is hard to deny. The vast staging yards, warehouses and transit hubs of Newark, New Jersey, are fascinating, and constitute the life support of New York City. But it is a leap of unfathomable dimensions to see how the design logic of that infrastructure might affect how one builds within the fabric of the city. They are two different things, with the theory and practice of one having little to do with the theory and practice of the other. This is not an *our-subject-is-better-than-your-subject* argument. They occur in different places and serve different purposes.

Infrastructure and city fabric do become conjoined at certain points. One lesson that readers of figure/ground drawings know well is that there is a big difference between the *form* of urban space, as the citizens of the world's best cities and towns understand it, and the form of the landscape of processes that Landscape Urbanism celebrates. Hydrology is all the rage these days, and hydrology like traffic engineering is a form of fluid mechanics. No one would deny that the hegemony of the traffic engineer, ramming interstate highways through the heart of cities, was catastrophic a generation ago. New Urbanism's transect provides a useful guide as to when and where the great sweeping forms of drainage courses or other natural processes are destructive to the tighter, denser, more brittle forms of urban places. All of this does not seem beyond the realm of synthesis, accommodation, and mutual enrichment.

When it comes to finding common ground between NU and LU, James Corner is the most enigmatic of the Landscape Urbanist theorizers. He seems at times to have a balanced view of things, and his writing is laced with passages of intelligence and insight:

... antinomic, categorical separation between landscape and urbanism persists today not only because of a perceived difference in material, technical and imaginative/moralistic dimensions of these two media, but also because of hyper-professional classification, a construction complicated through competing power relations.

Or this:

... so-called "sustainable" proposals, wherein urbanism becomes dependent upon certain bioregional metabolisms, while assuming the place-form of some semi-ruralized environment, are surely naïve and counter-productive.

Bravo. Sounds a lot like New Urbanism to me. Or this:

This emphasis on urban processes is not meant to exclude spatial form but rather seeks to construct a dialectical understanding of how it relates to the processes that flow through, manifest, and sustain it.

The only bone to pick with this statement is the absence of a pause after "form". It is precisely the spirit of *rapprochement* and synthesis between LU and NU ideas that poor old Earth, sagging under the weight of seven billion souls, is rooting for.

To date the major work of Corner's career is New York's splendid High Line. The response of a number of New Urbanists to High Line show that NU is at least as riven with divergent, contradictory viewpoints, and occasional bad sense, as LU. Twenty years ago New Urbanism was launched as a powerful idea. It is an argument of such compelling logic that, like other powerful ideas, it has lingered and spread. And like other powerful ideas, it has mutated as it has metastasized and gotten weird in multiple ways. It now includes minutely prescriptive, compulsive codifying, pseudo-positivism à la LEED-ND, and the secret style police (Geheimstil Polizei — GESTAPO?) that have come to dominate what most people now think of as New Urbanism. Most troubling (to me at least) is the quest for formulaic universalism, exactly what New Urbanists thought was absurd in the trajectory of CIAM. This quest revealed itself in the widely voiced NU objection to High Line as a one-off, not a model that could be repeated in Peoria. GOOD GOD, how crazy! Whatever happened to contextual urbanism, the love of place, *genius loci*, wasn't that what we were all about?

Ironically, much of the special power of High Line is captured and conveyed in a figure/ground drawing that Corner, Pollak, et al view with such disdain. It is an infrastructural fissure in the city grid of just the right scale — not an erasure like an interstate highway ripping through the city, but a crack in the Big Apple just big enough to reveal the magical inner secrets of its blocks. While a figure/ground elegantly describes the spatial qualities of High Line, it says nothing of the brilliance of the interventions of Corner and his collaborators to capture those qualities and transform them into a beautiful, public place of great vitality. If High Line cannot occupy an honored place in a canon of New Urbanism, it is the canon, not High Line, that is deficient.

There is not a clear answer to the question of whether NU and LU are complementary (though mutually critical) or resolutely oppositional movements. The oppositional option is bad for all, and bad for the world. Conversely, grafting the good ideas of LU and the legitimate critique of NU into something operational (the name doesn't matter) may help provide relief to a beleaguered planet, teeming with too many humans frantically seeking sustenance, wealth and pleasure. How happy Mother Earth would be, if we just got it together and came to her rescue. That is what we can hope for and — with a tad more generosity, fewer polemical exclusions, and less dukes-up pugnacity on both sides — achieve.

Lest I end this on a naively sanguine and Pollyannaish note, I do think it is necessary to follow Landscape Urbanism to its occasional paddlings in the far shallow end of the pool. When Corner says that "landscape urbanism is first and last an imaginative project," he seems (sometimes) to mean "imaginative" as in imaginary, fictive, or nonsensical — a new formal "order" for the city based on unseen and arbitrary subterranean weirdnesses. The mining of miscellaneous invisible information generates shapes that the unaided brain within its prosaic boundaries of common sense could never conceive. Not a formal order based on use, social purpose, ecological process, geometry, or historical association. Just shapes! What fun!

Waldheim praises Corner and Corner praises Peter Eisenman and Laurie Olin for just these strategies.

This inspired concept is an archeological dusting off of an ancient *avant-gardist* trope, taken to its *reductio ad absurdum* in the 1950s and early '60s by the likes of "composer" Morton Subotnick and "dancer" Anna Halprin, who felt obliged by history itself to try to out-outrage their more famous contemporaries John Cage and Merce Cunningham. Operating from the premise that all sound is music and all movement is dance, they each devised "aleotoric" methods of composition — wheels of chance that generated "indeterminate" sequences of sound and movement, otherwise beyond the scope of human imagination. How cool we thought we were to have cultivated the ability to sit through hours of spastic gyration, accompanied by the shrieks, traffic noise, and banging garbage cans of the *musique concrete*. Of course, in this indeterminate, never-harmonious universe, the sound and movement could have nothing to do with each other, except to make the same interval of time seem endless. Hipness can open our sensibilities to the truly unbearable.

Those committed to an eternal avant-garde (and some New Urbanists as well) would do better to immerse themselves in the cryptic wisdom of that other figure from way back then, the composer John Cage. He claimed to live by the one rule that his fourth-grade teacher boldly emblazoned at the front of her classroom: NO SILLINESS.

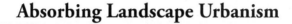

10

Absorbing Landscape Urbanism

BRUCE DONNELLY

THOUGH BOTH LANDSCAPE URBANISM AND NEW URBANISM have laudable goals, they are at odds. Largely designed to counter the "hegemony" of New Urbanism, Landscape Urbanism is in *principled opposition*[1] to its rival. It seeks to explode New Urbanism's repertoire of proven, standard, "normative" ideals by incorporating ecology more directly. In this chapter, I argue that New Urbanism should absorb the more successful aspects of Landscape Urbanism: its ecological-mindedness, its design motifs, and its use of competitions.

Ecology

The successful absorption of Landscape Urbanism's ecological stance requires first pairing it with other useful concepts. This is because, while New Urbanism seeks to create, or re-create, a norm for urbanism — an easily understood habitat that people know how to live in — Landscape Urbanism seeks to counter that norm as well as longstanding traditions by undoing standards and creating unfamiliar habitats.

Landscape Urbanism uses ecological performance as a way to critique current practice, but always with a layer of self-consciousness that sometimes seems unjustified. Chris Reed, for example, introduces four different stances towards ecology: *structured, analog, hybrid* and *curated ecologies*,[2] but these are not driven by the actual needs of plants and animals. Thus James Corner's project for the Delaware River waterfront proposed using dying plant material to indicate locations where remediation is needed — an example of Reed's *curated* ecology. West 8's Eastern Scheldt Storm Surge Barrier called for a theoretical sorting of birds according to color, much like the famed peppered moths that adapted to darker tree bark during the Industrial Revolution. Whether it ever worked (and deterioration has curtailed the experiment), the approach depended on the *idea* of birds standing on the *idea* of shells, not *actual* birds on *actual* shells. By this sleight of hand, a Landscape Urbanism project can escape the rigors of empirical evaluation.

In other projects without a constructed ecology, there is an echo of one. The High Line in New York, for instance, is designed to evoke the volunteer landscape that occupied the original train viaduct before it was made into a park. The abandoned viaduct had been colonized by plants that had to be removed for the safety of the structure. Now, they are evoked by carefully designed plantings between delicately shaped pavers, sometimes in combination with a reconstructed railroad track. In one part (25th to 27th streets), a pseudo-natural elevated landscape is treated with extreme deference. The walkway is built over the faux landscape as if over a wetland in a nature center. Visitors walk on a grating elevated above the viaduct's plantings on delicate stilts.

James Corner's project for the Fresh Kills landfill on Staten Island uses ecological remediation to create a functioning ecology in a carefully phased masterplan. But by using ecological remediation to drive its form, Corner turns the landscape into a critique of the normative urban park. As one writer put it, "Corner is among the handful of landscape designers who are taking the idea of an urban park into un-parklike territory".[3] This amounts to a critique of the conventional cultural meaning of a park, and one wonders why the word "park" is used at all. The core of the design is the process of change itself, not any final fixed feature. Thus mounds of garbage are to be covered over with soil, so that the pace at which the garbage settles, not a contractual timetable, triggers the next phase: planting. Eventually, abandoned equipment used to shape the mounds becomes part of the experience of the park. Even if the process does not work as envisioned, the design may still be considered a success because no single end state is imagined. Perturbations of the process would merely be ornaments to it, as flashing police lights are an ornament to Times Square.

In Michael Van Valkenburgh's project for the Lower Don Lands in Toronto, a wide, reconstructed riparian habitat splits a neighborhood into three parts. In renderings, the grassy wet habitat sunders the urbanism through a powerful symbolic gesture. In this case, the ecological functioning of the river seems a secondary matter to the assertion of nature's primacy over the built environment[4]. In his Brooklyn Bridge Park, Van Valkenburgh mixes several different strategies into the design. At the water's edge, these range from visibly artificial piers to embankments of riprap to constructed wetlands. His design meets various ecological goals, always with great complexity and showmanship.

In all of these projects and proposals, a frothy layer of critical stance creates an unnecessary division between ecology and cultural expectation. In a traditional park, for example, the design might revolve around a program for a waterside promenade, with a critical mass of overlapping activities along the way, such as play areas with seating and different cultural or recreational opportunities. In Landscape Urbanism, park design seems to revolve around the need for critical explication. The way it meets the water with riprap, for instance, seems more a commentary on glacial moraines than about providing a cultural resource within legitimate ecological constraints.[5]

How could these ideas be absorbed by New Urbanism? It would require swapping arcane ideas about ecological design in favor of something more measurable and grounded. Fortunately, some Landscape Urbanists, responding to critiques, are now providing what is needed.

In *Ecological Urbanism*, a book that overviews the current status of Landscape Urbanism, two essays propose useful metrics of ecological performance. Richard T. T. Forman critiques urbanism according to the degree to which it integrates habitat. He produces maps eerily similar to ones showing the movements of military campaigns.[6] It is a straightforward application of landscape ecology. The maps show patches of habitat within a regional matrix of urban and rural habitats. Similarly, Susannah Hagan suggests that ecological performance could be mitigated through built means such as plant berms and the shapes of buildings.[7] She privileges measurable ecological performance over esoteric ideas about ecological indeterminacy.

These metrics could augment the tools in New Urbanism that are already based on landscape ecology. The SmartCode, for example, is used

Fig. 10.1: *Brooklyn Bridge Park.*

to allocate development within a region according to ecological sensitivity, and smaller-scale elements (e.g., buildings and thoroughfare types) are allocated according to an urban-to-rural transect. Tom Low's *Light Imprint Handbook* [8] uses this sensibility — a locally derived urban-to-rural transect — to suggest appropriate design techniques for managing rainwater. Low's approach largely de-escalates the problem of managing stormwater by integrating it synergistically into a complete urban design. For instance, instead of the uniform application of curbs and inlets used intensively in conventional engineering, the *Light Imprint* method integrates rainwater management into everything from roadside swales and gravel driveways to reedy ponds. It is an integration of ecology and built form that respects and sustains both.

Motifs

Perhaps because New Urbanism is partly a reaction to the ill-conceived open spaces of the 1960s and '70s, civic spaces in New Urbanist designs rarely perturb the ground plane. New Urbanism shapes public space primarily through the vertical elements that surround it: buildings and trees. Landscape Urbanism, in contrast, makes use of certain motifs that are meant to perturb the ground plane. These motifs are:

- Plants on walls and roofs,
- Viaducts over and penetrating existing traditional urbanism,
- "Mat Urbanism," a term coined by Stan Allen for built space constructed in the ground plane,
- Artificial landforms, and
- Overlooks, particularly framed ones, which allow visitors high vantage points.

Green Walls and Roofs

While planted walls and roofs are not unique to Landscape Urbanism, they are frequently used within it. Planted walls in Landscape Urbanism take two main forms. They can be made by literally planting the walls, as in the work of Gilles Clément and Patrick Blank at the Quai Branly Museum in Paris (for Jean Nouvel). These are not simply walls on which vines have been allowed to grow but walls onto which plants and watering/nutrient systems are installed. The second kind uses trees planted on terraces to carry the foliage into the sky as in Il Bosco Verticale by Boeri Studio. The Netherlands Pavilion by MVRDV at Expo 2000 in Hanover is probably the most thought-provoking version of this vertical format. In either case, the same sorts of trees and shrubs that would be calming in any other setting become jarring in Landscape Urbanism.

Fig. 10.2: *The Quai Branly Museum*

Landscape Urbanism often uses green roofs that slope up from ground level to cover multistory buildings. Possibly the most photogenic proposal is Ken Yeang's idea for Zorlu Ecocity in Turkey, which combines sloping green walls with extensive green roofs over a podium and on top of towers. The School of Art, Design and Media at Nanyang Technological University in Singapore, by the CPG Corporation in Singapore, is a built example of a working green roof sweeping up from the ground. Such proposals are often combined with cultivation, as in SOA Architectes's La Tour Vivante in Rennes, France.

Green walls and roofs would have to be adapted for legibility and practicality before New Urbanism could absorb them. That adaptation is partly a matter of conquering technical issues of plant health and water intake, and partly a matter of legibility. In New Urbanism, attention-drawing designs are usually reserved for civic buildings, which are expected to assert their importance. Another approach would be to reserve green walls for blank or unattractive walls, such as garages facing apartments or on the sides of buildings facing neighbors. Green roofs, on the other hand, do not present much of a civic problem for New Urbanism. They are generally allowed anywhere that they can be healthy and use water frugally, and wherever they don't disrupt the privacy of neighboring buildings. But they should not complicate the reading of what is public and what is private. On civic buildings where public access is permitted, green roofs could slope up from ground level to give citizens treetop views. On private buildings, however, an overlay of public access over private structures would confuse the reading of public and private.

Viaducts

There is an example of a Landscape Urbanist viaduct that could be used as a model for New Urbanism: the High Line in New York, by James Corner Field Operations, Diller Scofidio + Renfro, and Piet Oudolf. It is probably the best known and most popular work of Landscape Urbanism. Yet we know from the earlier Promenade Plantée in Paris, also a reclaimed viaduct, that such a format can be compelling without transgressing the norms of familiar urbanism to the extent the High Line does.

The High Line is transgressive in the sense that, by penetrating through urban blocks, it violates the normal boundaries between public and private space. It is, in this way, different from the Promenade Plantée, which is located in the public realm, albeit bordered on one side occasionally by the private interiors of apartment blocks. The High Line penetrates two buildings, which gives park visitors the unusual experience of walking through buildings without entering them. In addition, its main pathway isn't just enlivened by various attractive plantings, as in the Promenade Plantée; its plantings often form unusual spatial configurations by feathering into the pavement or by incorporating gratings built as trestles over apparently untouched greenery.

Given the two precedents for reusing urban rail viaducts, one the flagship of the Landscape Urbanism and the other decidedly not, the Promenade Plantée may offer a more agreeable model for New Urbanism to digest. It offers compelling views and a compelling walk, but does so in a less transgressive manner — despite having a long bridge diagonally across an intersection. As with anything done within New Urbanism, there is an empirical requirement: it must be tested to make sure that enough people would use it. This is a safety issue. The High Line allows people in an already well-used area to enjoy light and air, but it would not work as well in a less-populated area. The Reading Viaduct in Philadelphia has been proposed partly as a way to draw people into a semi-industrial area; if it were to fail to draw visitors, it would be far less successful. A calming walkway across urban streets is a worthwhile model for New Urbanism, but only in some contexts.

Mat Urbanism

Stan Allen's concept of "Mat Urbanism" is about connecting various levels of buildings together by a rising ground plane. Alternatively, this can be done by building within a thickened ground plane so that spaces with loosely defined functions on different levels can be reached directly. The idea is not just to build underground but to expand the ground plane to more than one story in order to provide direct access to different levels. Allen mentions MVRDV's Villa VPRO, a headquarters for a broadcasting company, as a precedent.[9] It has stepped floors, ramps, roof terraces and gardens. These are intended to offer direct access to different parts of the building, and the different parts are meant to operate like a ground that can be appropriated for different uses, depending on the needs of the inhabitants. The combination of multi-level access and indeterminate function fits Allen's description of Mat Urbanism. The Cleveland Convention Center, by LMN Architects and Gustafson Guthrie Nichol, Ltd., may be considered "mat space." It is built underground, beneath a grassy "Mall" planned by Daniel Burnham. At the North end, the Mall is peeled up so that a lobby can be wedged under it. So not only is it a "thick mat" in the sense of having a thick cross-section with grass on top, it also has the open plan and loosely specified functions Stan Allen proposes.

The Lincoln Restaurant at Lincoln Center in New York by Diller Scofidio + Renfro in collaboration with FXFOWLE Architects is not a particularly influential version of Mat Urbanism because it has a single program and the space on top is not compelling on its own. On the other hand, the Olympic Sculpture Park in Seattle, by Weiss/Manfredi, is a good example because it uses a manipulated ground plane in order to bridge a roadway and a rail line, giving direct access to different functional areas above and below the new ground level.

Fig. 10.3: *The High Line, New York*
Copyright 2012 Bruce F. Donnelly

Mat Urbanism may be a useful approach for New Urbanism, at least for civic sites and buildings. Civic buildings are often approached from different sides, and the "Mat" concept can help resolve difficult topological problems of access for different classes of users, from service workers to legislators to citizens. In fact, the United States Capitol Visitor Center by RTKL (and supervised by the Architect of the Capitol) can be seen as an example of the Mat Urbanism concept. The visitor enters from a long distance in front of the west front of the Capitol into an underground foyer. To be consistent with New Urbanist principles, the formal artistic design of civic spaces and buildings would have to be respected, and important axial vistas could not be blocked. The Mall in Cleveland is an example where this blockage occurs, as the up-tilting convention center roof blocks the central vista.

Landforms

Landforms are a common motif in Landscape Urbanism. These are artificial hills or berms, which may be hollow inside or underneath. They may be part of a green roof or a "mat" or deployed on their own. Sometimes the landforms are deployed just to evoke natural forms. The Guadalupe River Park, by Hargreaves Associates, has landforms that are self-consciously inspired by braided river channels.[10] The mounds of garbage at Fresh Kills are landforms.

It is appropriate to distinguish them from hills that, even if artificial, appear naturalistic. Landforms are usually deployed in clearly unnatural locations. The Providence Pedestrian Bridge, by inFORM, draws a stylized landform halfway across the river, and tucks a café within it. It is clearly not "natural," since it bridges over water. The visitor on foot walks across its roof on a walkway and then steps down onto its terrace near the river, where it would be impossible not to notice that the whole structure is a bridge. Even when the landforms are not hollow, they are often visibly artificial.

The Santa Monica Civic Center Parks (formerly Palisades Garden Walk + Town Square), by Field Operations and other designers,[11] will be extravagantly artificial. With an extreme manipulation of the ground plane, James Corner has designed a square containing a spray of arc-like

Fig.10.4: *Overlooks as originally proposed for the Palisades Garden Walk + Town Square in Santa Monica,* © 2010 JAMES CORNER FIELD OPERATIONS.

hills of grass and foliage, with valleys of pavement in between. The typical elements of squares and plazas — pavement, foliage, fountains and artificial grading — are manipulated to create a series of artificial hills and valleys. Excavated wall terraces will augment the landforms.[12]

This artifice is the opposite of the naturalism of nineteenth-century parks — notably Central Park in New York. There, the intention was to look as natural as possible, even if a great deal of land had to be manipulated. Olmsted and Vaux used the natural-looking landforms as a pretense for grade separation between the road and pathway systems.

The pedestrian bridge in Providence and the Race Street Pier in Philadelphia, both by James Corner Field Operations, present a clear contrast between Landscape Urbanism and earlier conventions about naturalistic park design, which New Urbanists would be more likely to embrace. Landscape Urbanist parks have landforms that are stepped and look deliberately artificial. Even low grass plantings look contrived. The fact that both designs are on a pier makes the artificiality not only explicit, but *deliberately* ironic. Nobody will be fooled that the lush plantings were what nature intended.

Such irony is an uncomfortable fit for New Urbanism. Fortunately, however, planting over a void does not always have to be imbued with irony. The 1899 Wade Avenue Bridge over Rockefeller Park in Cleveland, by Charles F. Schweinfurth, carries planting beds over its arch so that shrubs grow directly above the roadway.[13] It appears rustic and natural (even though artificial in an Olmstedian way). Such unforced design seems the most beneficial way to use landforms in New Urbanism. Precedent shows how to integrate plantings into the design of a bridge, pier or other structure without drawing attention to their artificiality. The green sides of the Wade Avenue Bridge are only meant to soothe and comfort the pedestrian, not provide a cultural statement. With no ironic pretense, landforms could enrich the New Urbanist civic space repertoire.

Overlooks

Landscape Urbanism frequently uses high overlooks, sometimes with literal frames from which visitors can overlook the landscape below, as if through a proscenium arch.

One form of overlook is a terrace at the top of a hill or other high place. A typical type has been proposed for Hudson Park and Hudson

Boulevard on the west side of Manhattan, designed by Michael Van Valkenburgh Landscape Architects and others.[14] It provides an overlook as a kind of reward for people walking up to a bridge. The overlook attempts to draw people up the extreme grade change required to get there.

Another type of overlook has a literal frame like that of a proscenium arch. The High Line has two of these, at 10th Avenue and at 26th Street. Both have sloped seating reminiscent of a theater, suggesting that visitors look at the people below almost as voyeurs. A pair of framed overlooks in this genre is also found in James Corner Field Operations' original design for the Palisades Garden Walk + Town Square in Santa Monica, which has an ovoid, trellis-like structure with such a frame overlooking Ocean Avenue.

Overlooks are not new to landscape design. The arches over the stairs entering the platform of the seventh-century Dome of The Rock in Jerusalem might be considered an early example. Certainly Haussmann and Alphond's nineteenth-century Parc des Buttes Chaumont in Paris has numerous overlooks. *Framed* overlooks, however, are novel, and suggest another example of Landscape Urbanism's penchant for contrivance.

In either case, overlooks are not inconsistent with the principles of New Urbanism, especially if they can be used to get people to high and distant civic spaces that would otherwise go unused. Large grade changes usually discourage people from venturing up or down, and overlooks may help entice people to a higher level even when there is no intrinsic reason to do so. The voyeuristic aspect of framed overlooks, however, might be a more awkward fit for New Urbanists, who will likely want to wait and see whether the idea has any social value apart from landscape novelty.

Competitions

Charles Waldheim has suggested that competitions are a major way for Landscape Urbanism to spread,[15] suggesting that the normal procurement process has broken down. The idea is to use competitions to *drive* urban design. In Toronto, for example, the Lower Don Lands competition allowed the mayor's office and WATERFRONToronto to front-load the process with the winning design's vision, so that the rest of the planning and zoning apparatus would have to fall in line after the fact.

Waldheim notes that mayors Daley and Bloomberg (Chicago and New York, respectively) have used competitions and donors to drive a process that starts with grand visions. This is how the Friends of the High Line drove the development of the High Line. It is clearly beneficial to such a front-loaded process to have attention-grabbing designs and graphics that can be used to stimulate the imagination and maximize publicity. The more exciting a design is, the more likely it is to win, and ultimately to change the way of doing development on the target site. New Urbanism may be able to accept this approach, but the details of the competition — especially who juries it — will not be trivial matters. If the jury consists of two architects, a photographer, a structural engineer and Charles Waldheim, as the Lower Don Lands competition did, the selection may be driven predominantly by avant-garde status, something New Urbanism is unlikely to win.

The normal process in New Urbanism is to use a public charrette process to formulate a design and then, as justified through public participation, tailor codes to implement it. In Landscape Urbanism, where the idea is to impose a startling new vision (e.g., on a waterfront), a competition-driven approach involving insiders may ultimately work better for the eventual gathering of public and political support. It is worth noting that, when the public is consulted, New Urbanism fares well. The "People's Choice Award" of the *Reburbia* competition, sponsored by *Dwell Magazine* and Inhabitat.com, went to a New Urbanist proposal, the *Urban Sprawl Repair Kit*.[16] Marianne Cusato, another supporter of New Urbanist principles, won the People's Design Award in the Cooper-Hewitt National Design Awards of 2006.[17] New Urbanism, in other words, can appropriate a competition-driven approach, but only if it's possible to avoid being penalized for the lack of landscape bling.

Conclusion and Prospects

New Urbanism can consume certain aspects of Landscape Urbanist practice, especially its ecological-mindedness, some of its motifs, and certain ideas about the value of design competitions. Other aspects are less likely to be absorbed: its complex stances toward ecology, the problematic application of some of its favorite motifs, and the glossier, attention-grabbing approach to the implementation process.

Ecological sensitivity is now an imperative for urban development, and New Urbanism could pay more attention to the *visible* articulation of ecological concerns without succumbing to greenwashing. Most salient to New Urbanism is landscape ecology, for which Richard T. T. Forman's writings provide an accessible introduction.[18] Landscape ecology is concerned with the movement of animals, and offers insights into which places should be developed and which should be left undeveloped. The treatment of rainwater is another important ecological consideration, and New Urbanism is already developing a consensus about how to approach it. The caveat is that this treatment should not reduce the development capacity of land in all places, especially where higher intensity is necessary to avoid excessive outward expansion. Neither should it be used to justify outlandish design.

The characteristic motifs of Landscape Urbanism grab attention, and are therefore more suited to the civic spaces and civic buildings that play a strong role in New Urbanism. In general, it would probably not be in keeping with New Urbanist principles to apply these motifs to ordinary urban fabric.

Finally, the Landscape Urbanism's competition-driven approach may be most useful for sites that require wholesale redesign. Although this idea may not be appropriate for the repair of existing urbanism, it may be appropriate where an entirely new order is needed. This will generally happen in brownfields and other large in-town developments or redevelopments. Even then, of course, steps should be taken to ensure that the final design does not simply grab the imagination, but is also appropriate, practical and beautiful.

Endnote

1   Waldheim, C. 2010, February 17. Planning, Ecology, and the Emergence of Landscape. *Visions of the City Speaker Series*. Charlotte, NC: University of North Carolina at Charlotte, School of Architecture.

2   Reed, C. 2010. The Agency of Ecology. In M. Mostafavi, & G. Doherty, *Ecological Urbanism*. Baden: Lars Müller, pp. 24–29.

3   Sullivan, R. 2008, November 23. *Wall E Park*. Retrieved November 30, 2011, from New York Magazine: nymag.com/news/features/52452/

4   Michael Van Valkenburgh Associates, Inc., Project Projects, & CBH. 2011, January. *Lower Don Lands*. Retrieved November 30, 2011, from Michael Van Valkenburgh Associates, Inc.: mvvainc.com/project. php?id=60

5   Kent, F. 2011, December 15. Founder and President, Project for Public Spaces. (B. F. Donnelly, interviewer). N. Ouroussoff, 2010, April 1. *The Greening of the Waterfront*. Retrieved May 5, 2011, from *The New York Times*: nytimes.com/2010/04/02/arts/design/02bridge.html

6   Forman, R. T. 2010. Urban Ecology and the Arrangement of Nature in Urban Regions. In M. Mostafavi and G. Doherty, *Ecological Urbanism*. Baden: Lars Müller, pp. 312–23.

7   Hagan, S. (n.d.). Performalism: Environmental Metrics and Urban Design. In M. Mostafavi, & G. Doherty, *Ecological Urbanism*. Baden: Lars Müller, p. 2010.

8   Low, R. T. 2010. *Light Imprint Handbook: Integrating Sustainability and Community Design*. Charlotte, NC: Civic By Design.

9   Allen, S. 2001. Mat Urbanism: The Thick 2-D. In H. Sarkis, *Case: Le Corbusier's Venice Hospital and the Mat Building Revival*. New York: Prestel, pp. 119–26.

10 Czerniak, J. 2006. Looking Back at Landscape Urbanism: Speculations on Site. In Waldheim, C., Ed., *The Landscape Urbanism Reader*. New York: Princeton Architectural Press, pp. 105–23.

11 City of Santa Monica. 2010. *Meet the Team*. Retrieved November 30, 2011, from Santa Monica Civic Center Parks Palisades Garden Walk + Town Square: smciviccenterparks.com/home/2010/8/2/meet-the-team.html

12 Broverman, N. 2011, September 23. *Work Starting on Field Operations' Big Santa Monica Park*. Retrieved November 30, 2011, from Curbed LA: la.curbed.com/archives/2011/09/work_starting_on_field_operations_big_santa_monica_park.php

13 Photos available from the Historic American Building Surveys.

14 Hudson Yards Development Corporation, City of New York. 2011. *Hudson Park & Boulevard*. Retrieved November 29, 2011, from Hudson Yards Development Corporation: hydc.org/html/project/hudson-park.shtml

15 Waldheim, op cit.

16 Dwell, Inhabitat.com. 2009, August 9. *ReBurbia Winners Announced!* Retrieved November 28, 2011, from Reburbia: reburbia.com/

17 Office of the First Lady. 2007, July 18. Mrs. Bush's Remarks at the Cooper-Hewitt National Design Awards, Archived web page. Retrieved December 16, 2010, from The White House: President George W. Bush, via web.archive.org: web.archive.org/web/20070817085519/
http://www.whitehouse.gov/news/releases/2007/07/20070718-3.html

18 Forman, op cit., pp. 312–23.

Additional Works Cited

Google. 2010, November 30. *51.639222 N,3.711491 E*. Retrieved from Google Maps: maps.google.com/maps?q=51.639222,3.711491&hl=en&ll=51.63773,3.71192&spn=0.046078,0.111494&t=h&z=14&vpsrc=6

Toronto Waterfront Revitalization Corporation. 2007. *Lower Don Lands Innovative Design Competition Jury Report*. Toronto: Lower Don Lands Design Corporation.

Art Vitiating Life[1]

Michael W. Mehaffy

THE SAYING GOES that if you're a carpenter with a hammer, every problem looks like a nail. For modern practitioners of "architectural culture," the problems are the complex phenomena of urban life, and the specialized tools are the metaphoric expressions of sculptural art. The resulting "problem-solving by magical thinking" might be charming, if the consequences were not tied closely to an unfolding planetary disaster.

It is not art per se that is the problem. Art is as vital to cities as to any other sphere of life, and it can, as Jane Jacobs memorably argued,[2] profoundly enrich the structures of urban life. But the salient question is whether we are confusing the symbolism of art with the realities of life. If so, we may well be imposing art in a totalizing and life-damaging way. Worse, we may become mere industrial apologists, providing alluring packaging for untested, reckless, and ultimately destructive schemes of city making.

Some — and I am one of them — have concluded that just such widespread professional malpractice has indeed been going on for the better part of a century, and thereby serving as a convenient enabler (at best) of a pattern of wreckage across the face of the planet: eviscerated urban cores, soulless office campuses, drive-through Radiant Cities and suburbs. Most worrisome, this copious production of disastrous settlements is increasing at an ever-larger scale, and at the very moment that its most destructive results are reaching critical global levels: excessive emissions, depletion, devastation.

The history of this art-clouded regime reaches back at least to Peter Behrens, the father of corporate branding (i.e., the first to use architecture and its allied arts to create industrial product theming) and the effect of his marketing successes upon his extraordinarily talented young protégés. Three of them — Mies van der Rohe, Walter Gropius, and Le Corbusier — went on to work perhaps the most extraordinary transformation upon the built environment in history. For these and other early modernists, and for their hugely influential urban movement, the Congrès Internationaux d'Architecture Moderne (CIAM), architectural culture was a progressive and romantic project, and one inextricably linked to the astounding successes of the era's mechanist technology. The utopian exuberance of, say, Le Corbusier's 1924 *Towards a New Architecture*,[3] now seems touching: all the world's old reactionary horrors could now be swept away, and the art of industrial design would bring us to a rational new world, purified in the fire of industrialization. As Gropius put it, "Modern architecture is not a few branches of an old tree — it is new growth coming right from the roots." [4]

So this was, in every sense, the most radical of agendas, requiring not a mere change of styles but the elimination of virtually the entire gene pool of historical precedent, to be replaced in an entirely fresh new start. This revolution thus amounted to an enforced collective amnesia that forbade the reuse of virtually any previous lesson of good city-making. As with any revolution, there were many casualties: students were failed, faculty were fired, and curricula were burned.

Since then, the many failures of this regime have become evident, and the narrative has undergone a marked change. Now everybody, it seems, piles on to modernism and its old linear ways. Now the directive is to embrace not Platonic permanence but Heraclitan flux; not a single "grand narrative of history" but the chaos of many competing voices; not clear normative goals but merely the "irrigation of territories with potential" — in the words of one of the most articulate voices of this new sensibility (and most powerful critics of the old modernism), Rem Koolhaas.

But for all the talk of change, the underlying agenda is remarkably constant: the built environment remains above all a canvas for the staging of metaphoric art projects, as vehicles for new industrial development on an ever-larger scale. And on they come, the more extravagantly novel, the better — walking bugs on sticks, folded tacos, gigantic tube television sets, and, most recently, whole cities of undulating dissected planes. Patrons, corporations, governments and economic development agencies fund these marketable follies. Boards (and critics) review proposals and decide whether the neoplasms have the requisite power to stir men's (and the occasional women's) blood. Magazines relentlessly promote the images and students fall under the rapturous thrall of *neophilia* (as Doug Kelbaugh points out in his chapter). Sustainability advocates see no problem tacking on energy-efficient devices, along with magical images of greenness, to achieve the oxymoronic: *the sustainable new.*

To be sure, architecture can symbolize, dramatize and excite, and to some extent, has always done so. But architecture can also sever, stretch out, isolate and segregate. (Need I remind anyone of this?) It can destroy the tissue of vital human connections. It can facilitate — or prevent — patterns of connectivity between people, the ways they are able to interact, the ways they can or cannot solve problems, the resources they will use, re-use, or waste, and much else. As Jane Jacobs also pointed out, architectural city-making (especially of the superblock and wide freeway varieties) can accelerate the complex processes that cause a city core to transform into a depopulated slum.[5]

It's one thing to acknowledge and admit if we do not know how to reverse these failures — in itself a troubling admission of our collective incompetence at city repair — but to deny the existence of their effects, or rationalize them as beyond our power and go on merrily repeating the same mistakes, verges upon the old definition of insanity: repeating our actions with the expectation of a different result.

There is intriguing research from environmental psychologists suggesting that some of this "architectural myopia" may derive from a specialized training in the perception of objects over contexts.[6] The "carpenters with hammers" tendency is exacerbated by the specialized industry-serving role, going back to Behrens, of supplying art as product packaging. When it comes to branding and marketing, it's not context but *standing out* that gets rewarded and encouraged. Sell your commodity (your client, your firm, yourself) with neophilia: *New! Exciting!*

Into this environment stepped the New Urbanists, who, beginning in the 1980s, proposed to reform the CIAM errors within their own professions, which included not just architects but also planners, landscape architects, engineers, policy leaders, NGO activists, and even reform-minded developers. This cross-section of environmental agents did not just criticize but activated a series of urban counterproposals, of which some — but by no means all — have achieved their self-stated goals. In place of CIAM's superblock, segregated zones, unwalkable automobile arterials, and neoplastic buildings, New Urbanists advocated and built small blocks, mixed uses, pedestrian-friendly streets, and background buildings. In place of the segregating, severing and sterile patterns of CIAM, New Urbanists sought to connect people to each other, to their history, and to biologically enriched environments, often using recurrent or "revivalist" architectural languages as a reliable way to do so.

This recurrence of architectural language, especially, was met with a visceral reaction from the professional establishment. The New Urbanists were condemned for behaving as stylistic reactionaries, as transgressors of the post-industrial zeitgeist. Their attempted reuse of older pre-modernist types and forms as genetic material to try to make better modern cities was dismissed as inauthentic art, and thus, on its face value, very poor quality architecture.

This reaction is telling — particularly because reuse of forms and patterns was never before, in the long and successful history of settlement making, regarded as a bad thing in and of itself. On the contrary, it led to some of the greatest eras of renaissance, and the best-loved, most *sustained* places today. Far from requiring stolid copying, it opened endless possibilities of synthesis and genetic mutation. It was actually far more consistent with the most "modern" scientific ideas about adaptive evolution and morphogenesis of pattern, than with an almost century-old (and poorly examined) theory of mechanically determinist tectonics of form.[7]

But the New Urbanists deeply threatened the core modernist narrative of neophilia: the promise of a continually *new! improved!* art product, and its magical power to bring about a *new! improved!* industrial world.

Soon, a notable counterattack became organized, wielding an alternate brand of reformism. It would be called Ecological Urbanism, or Landscape Urbanism, and it would claim to preserve "architectural culture" against the art-philistines, while greatly expanding the metaphoric and aspirational treatment of ecology.

Some years ago, Harvard architecture professor Alex Krieger made one of the most memorable critiques of the New Urbanism: in many cases it was, he said, "sprawl in drag." [8] What he meant was that the underlying patterns of sprawl were still dominating, and no mere repositioning of buildings on streetscapes would be enough to change that. While the Charter of the New Urbanism was much more thoroughgoing than Krieger suggested, the criticism resonated for a number of projects.

Since then, many New Urbanists have tried to do more to combat sprawl — a gift of CIAM — and its profligate waste of resources. And indeed, they've had notable successes in formerly declining inner cities, HOPE VI mixed-income housing projects, and new LEED-ND (Neighborhood Development) certified projects. While the extent of the success is a subject of fair debate, there's evidence that these efforts are at least slowing the decline of factors like walkability, social capital, and public transportation. There is considerable urgency in this project, given the rapid Western-style (and CIAM-style) development in China, India and Brazil, with the potential to multiply the disastrous effects of resource depletion, carbon emissions, and other grim externalities.

But the New Urbanism surely has its flaws, and thus a series of competitors has arisen, each with its own critique — and each usually with some variation of the "X" Urbanism: Everyday Urbanism, Real Urbanism, Landscape Urbanism, Now Urbanism, and so on. Each reveals its own kind of backhanded compliment, in the suggestion that New Urbanism is "the team to beat." Indeed Charles Waldheim, one of the originators of Landscape Urbanism (LU), made clear its competitive aims: "Landscape Urbanism was specifically meant to provide an intellectual and practical alternative to the hegemony of the New Urbanism." [9]

Landscape Urbanism, according to Waldheim, rejects the New Urbanist idea that urban design can reform the auto-dominated patterns of the twentieth century and their negative social and ecological consequences. It seeks to provide an alternative to the "prevailing discourse" that sees, as he put it, "a kind of nineteenth-century image of the city, that said if we could put the toothpaste back in the tube of automobility, we could all get out of our cars, and live the right way, the kind of moral and just way, we could somehow reproduce some social justice and some environmental health that we feel as though we've lost." [10] According to

James Corner, another proponent, we must abandon the antiquated idea of urban public spaces as "vessels" or enclosures meant specifically to accommodate human activities. We should instead embrace "the staging of surfaces," which he describes as "continuities" of landscapes and buildings, across which river-like forms of infrastructure will flow, setting the stage (quite literally) for creative acts of collective imagination. This "terra fluxus," as he terms it, is a kind of gigantic sprawling horizontal mat on which artists will "stage" their ever-changing works. Those less concerned with the delights of imagination, and more with the needs of ordinary life, had better get out of the way: "And so it seems landscape urbanism is first and last an imaginative project, a speculative thickening of the world of possibilities."[11]

How do these new imaginative "field operations" (also the name of Corner's firm) manifest themselves? The LU schemes are often characterized by lush greenery forming abstract shapes. The designers are very clear that these shapes are not the product of human activity, physical or economic, nor of any other urban precedent. They are based on metaphorical generative forces. Here is Waldheim describing a scheme by Corner:

> What I want to draw your eyes to are these lozenge shaped, weird football shaped public open and park spaces. Corner's proposition here would be that the shape of the public realm, the shape of the parks and the plazas and the open spaces, would not be derived by urban precedent from models of the 19th century, would not be derived by walking radii of transit oriented development or other principles. It would be derived from a mapping of the plumes of the toxicity subsurface onsite.[12]

In fact there is no reason to suppose that a person *could* navigate such a surface to access transit or other daily needs. Landscape Urbanists accept river-like expressways and auto-dominated patterns — which is to say, sprawl: cumulative empty green space between disconnected buildings. Thus Alan Berger, in an essay in *The Landscape Urbanism Reader,* writes: "The phrase 'urban sprawl' and the rhetoric of pro- and anti-urban sprawl advocates all but obsolesce under the realization that there is no growth without waste. 'Waste landscape' is an indicator of healthy urban growth."[13]

There is more than a faint echo here of Le Corbusier, in his profoundly influential 1935 polemic (and CIAM blueprint) *The Radiant City:* "The cities will be part of the country; I shall live 30 miles from my office in one direction, under a pine tree; my secretary will live 30 miles away from it too, in the other direction, under another pine tree. We shall both have our own car. We shall use up tires, wear out road surfaces and gears, consume oil and gasoline. All of which will necessitate a great deal of work ... enough for all."[14]

The Landscape Urbanists, like laissez-faire ideologues, seem to grant sprawl a secure status as the result of inexorable forces, beyond the control of the designer to do anything other than artistic accommodation to a fait accompli. In each case there is no sense that sprawl arose as a result of defined historical choices — choices that can be understood and thereby, to some extent, changed by a new generation of designers, using an expanded conception of design. This omission permits a most extraordinary artistic blank check: as Rem Koolhaas put it, "since we are not responsible, we must become irresponsible." That is, we are free to focus in any way we choose on our imaginative art: "Since it is out of control, the urban is about to become a major vector of the imagination. Redefined, urbanism will not only, or mostly, be a profession, but a way of thinking, an ideology: to accept what exists."[15] Thus "what exists" — the city — becomes only the inert source material, and the place for "staging" our art.

This leads us back to the role of "art" in Landscape Urbanism. After Jacobs, let us suppose, for a moment, that the role of art is not merely to accommodate the artist's will-to-making, but also to elucidate the natural order of human life and to clarify, enhance and ennoble what Jacobs referred to as the "organized complexity" that ordinary people create around them every day. This is a very different, let us say "evolutionary" model of the design arts. It respects and accommodates the aggregation of small acts over years and even centuries. From such small acts, the larger urban patterns emerge and evolve, forming reusable clusters. So, gradually, the patterns of traditional urbanism self-organize: not authorial contrivances, but evolutionary consequences of the transcendent needs of human beings, facilitated and elucidated by the design arts.

For New Urbanists, these patterns may certainly (and should, for human benefit) be reused, under adaptive evolutionary protocols. This is because in natural systems (of which we are only a subset), it is evolutionary folly to discard useful problem-solving designs only because they have been used in the past, and are therefore supposed not "innovative" or "creative" enough. This only decreases the gene pool, and makes fitness less likely, not more so. Porpoises, to take just one obvious example, did not reject the dorsal fin pattern merely because sharks already used it three hundred million years earlier. (Now that's reactionary!) To do so would be poorly adaptive and anti-evolutionary, and likely to draw a swift negative selection by evolutionary process. Instead we need the best and most reliable genetic material we can get, from whatever source. A rare few heroic geniuses — even if they produced more than occasionally extraordinary and delightful follies — would not be enough.

But the program of novelty product theming packaging goes on largely unquestioned in the schools, in the critic circles, and with the star practitioners, whose work continues to proliferate in ever more rococo varieties around the world. (Students are almost all certain they too will win that lottery.)

The form language falls roughly into two classes: one, a permutation of the early industrial production geometries (line, plane, cube, cylinder, etc.) with varied new aesthetic draperies (chia walls, op-art patterns, etc); and two, neoplasms, generated often by computer and consisting of old mechano-industrial forms now sliced, diced, mutated, or presented as generated outputs of computer b-splines and other exotic generative functions. In each case the concept of the city remains fundamentally a neo-modernist art composition, reflecting singular instances of visual culture imposed on the landscape. So Peter Eisenman's City of Culture is "generated" by his code from the form of the old city — but not by the human and natural agents of complexity, as the old city was. Instead, the generator is but a single artist and his imagination, served by a vast army of technical implementers.

Landscape Urbanists, seen in this light, are yet another case in point. In a discussion at the Congress for the New Urbanism in 2011, Charles Waldheim gave a remarkably frank account of the primacy of "architectural culture" in Landscape Urbanism. While he said he accepted the New Urbanist ideas of planning around neighborhoods, the pedestrian, and the importance of an interconnected street network, he rejected the notion of buildings along a thoroughfare defining a "street wall" and enclosed space. Instead, he argued, Landscape Urbanists endorse something more akin to "open-plan urbanism," which accepts horizontality, surface mutations, and new kinds of spatial systems. By comparison, he suggested, the New Urbanists' ideas of spatial enclosure, no less than their architectural predilections, were reactionary and outmoded.[16]

The Landscape Urbanists' use of "open-plan" urban space harkens back to nothing so much as Le Corbusier's 1924 proto-sprawl "Towers in the Park," in which the landscape is an amorphous, visually arresting tableaux. The trouble with that model, as Bill Hillier and other analysts have demonstrated, is that it doesn't reflect the way people actually use, and coinhabit, public space.[17] It doesn't reflect the natural groupings of space arising from clusters of human activity within gradations of a public realm — a natural grouping for which the term "room" is probably as good as any other.

Nonetheless, the attack is telling. Once again, a simple fact of accommodation to human nature — a normal prerequisite for any good design — is seen, through the overspecialized lens of fine art, as insufficiently novel and ipso facto "reactionary." It demonstrates, the critics say, a woeful lack of creativity, a failure of "imagination." Could it be that, especially in an age of biological complexity, such a failure to understand the creative possibilities of evolutionary recurrence and genetic synthesis may be the ultimate failure of imagination?

It was Jacobs who first described — half a century ago now, remarkably — the usefulness of the new scientific models of complexity for understanding and acting effectively upon the "kind of problem a city is." It was a problem of emergent order, coming not from high-art design, nor from the province of other specialists, but from the interactions of people within the city. The variables of interaction were not just a few that could be easily controlled, nor huge populations that could be managed statistically, but interacting agents whose actions were, through this complexity-organizing process, "interrelated into an organic whole."[18]

This order could therefore not be commanded from the top down. At the same time, some top-down interventions were important and necessary, to catalyze important changes as, for example, for governments to use some urban structures as "chess pieces" in a kind of urban game. (Jacobs was hardly a libertarian ideologue, as some recent revisionists have proposed.) But most of the physical order would emerge from the inherent processes of self-organization that are seen in all living systems, and no less so in cities. The role of planners and designers, she insisted, was to empower and support these activities — not to sweep them away and impose instead a neoplastic order. She foresaw Charles Waldheim's "open-plan urbanism" in the CIAM model of diffuse superblock park-lands, whose colossal waste of space she described witheringly as "project land-oozes."[19] Once again, this was a misappropriation of visual order, and a confusion of art and life: "To seek for the look of things as a pri-mary purpose or the main drama," as she warned in her introduction, "is to seek no end of trouble."[20]

Now we have other forces acting on the emergent order of the city, to be sure: global capital, new regulatory constraints, increasingly frag-mented social agendas. But these are differences of degree from what came before, not kind — and they suggest similar expanded kinds of design strategies in response, working upon the same "kind of problem a city is." They recognize and even empower the bottom-up agents, by employing strategies that encourage the spontaneous formation of orga-nized complexity within the city. This expanded notion of design is one that incorporates and builds upon our collective intelligence, accumulat-ing as a treasury of reusable packets of traditional precedent. It is the contrary of intelligence to throw this treasury away in exchange for clever novelties, whether or not they qualify as anyone's great art.

Jacobs went on to chide Garden City planner Clarence Stein for affording his residents the construction of their own little school, and patting himself on the back for "involving the users." This, she says, was only token empowerment; Stein had already "staged" the parameters that he, the planner, found permissible.

It is hard not to conclude that the Landscape Urbanists have the same impoverished and tokenistic program, but on a much expanded scale. Though they highlight the occasional opportunities for users to mutate the scene, in the end, only specialized artists like themselves have the rare imaginative genius to plan the necessary great artworks across the landscape of the city. In the words of Jacobs, this art comes structured neatly into endless permutations of the same old CIAM agenda: "the superblock, the project neighborhood, the unchangeable plan, and grass, grass, grass."[21]

Endnotes

1   Portions of this essay appeared in *Planetizen* magazine, under the title "The Landscape Urbanism: Sprawl in a Pretty Green Dress?" planetizen.com/node/46262

2   Jacobs, Jane. 1961. *The Death and Life of Great American Cities*. New York: Random House. pp. 372–91.

3   This, as well as Le Corbusier's 1935 *Ville Radieuse* (translated in 1967 as *Radiant City*), should be required reading for all architecture students, as well as Sigfried Gideon and Walter Gropius. Yet incredibly, at this writing we are informed that both *Ville Radieuse* and *Radiant City* are out of print.

4   Gropius, Walter. 1962. *Scope of Total Architecture*. New York: Collier Books. p. 83.

5   Jacobs, op cit., pp. 270–90.

6   See for example the citations discussed in Mehaffy, M. and N. Salingaros, Architectural Myopia: Designing for Industry, Not People. In Shareable.net. shareable.net/blog/architectural-myopia-designing-for-industry-not-people

7   Sigfried Giedion's 1935 *Mechanization Takes Command* is probably the best explication of this philosophically questionable theory (especially by today's standards). Yet it is still an extremely influential theory among architects, professors and students, and still a mostly unquestioned foundation for later postmodernist and poststructuralist design theories.

8   See e.g., Krieger, Alex, metropolismag.com/pov/20101108/krieger-to-duany

9   Waldheim, Charles. 2010, Feb. 17. Lecture to UNC College of Arts and Architecture. Available at vimeo.com/12992244

10 Ibid.

11 Corner, James. 2006. Terra Fluxus. In Waldheim, Charles, Ed., *The Landscape Urbanism Reader*. New York: Princeton Architectural Press.

12 Waldheim, Charles, op cit.

13 Drosscape. In Waldheim, Charles, Ed., *The Landscape Urbanism Reader*. New York: Princeton Architectural Press. p. 203.

14 Le Corbusier. 1935. *The Radiant City*.

15 Koolhaas, Rem. Whatever Happened to Urbanism? In Koolhaas and Bruce Mau. 1995. *S, M, L, XL*. New York: Monacelli. p. 969. Koolhaas is a favorite of the Landscape Urbanists, often drawing approving references — as for example in James Corner's essay Terra Fluxus, also quoted herein.

16 These remarks are taken from the author's notes, and personal discussions with Charles Waldheim at a following dinner. Any errors are the author's.

17 See for example, Hillier, B. and O. Sahbaz, 2008. An Evidence Based Approach to Crime and Urban Design: Or, Can We Have Vitality, Sustainability and Security All At Once? From spacesyntax.com website. Retrieved March 24, 2012 at spacesyntax.com/oldsite/Files/MediaFiles/Hillier%20Sahbaz_An%20evidence%20based%20approach_010408.pdf

18 Jacobs, op cit., p. 433.

19 Jacobs, op cit., p. 110.

20 Jacobs, op cit., p. 14.

21 Jacobs, op, cit., p. 22.

12

Marginality and the Prospects for Urbanism in the Post-Ecological City

MICHAEL RIOS

L ANDSCAPE URBANISM HAS RISEN OVER THE PAST FIFTEEN YEARS as
part of an ecological turn in urban design and as a strategy to repurpose leftover void spaces and infrastructure in the city.[1] Some of its
distinguishing characteristics include landscape as a medium of urban
analysis and projection and the shift from built form toward temporal
processes. Under the rubric of Landscape Urbanism, proponents draw
from a number of fields including environmental planning, landscape
architecture, landscape ecology, cartography, and GIS.

Landscape Urbanism has emerged at a time when the political economy of cities has changed dramatically, as reflected in new relationships
between the state, the market, and civil society. One manifestation is the
rise of growth coalitions comprised of political leaders, real estate developers, and philanthropists. The adoption of sustainability into the cultural
economy of cities coupled with the need to address environmental and
infrastructural needs has positioned Landscape Urbanism as an increasingly
preferred approach over New Urbanism. The focus on large-scale, highly
visible, and capital-intensive projects in major cities contrasts sharply with
the growing social and economic disparities of the urban population. In the
rush to find eco-cultural products that can be leveraged to increase global
competitiveness, austerity measures deprive the poor of social benefits,
and neighborhoods deemed as underperforming are abandoned.

In this chapter, I reflect on the prospects for urbanism in a world defined by growing social inequality in the post-ecological city. Drawing from Jacques Rancière's work, I highlight how different images of the city and forms of urbanism serve a political purpose by determining what is made visible in the urban landscape and what can be said about it. For discourses such as Landscape Urbanism this amounts to privileging an ecological over a social representation of cities. This ecological turn has been motivated by political economic concerns: the rise of the cultural economy, adoption of a sustainability agenda among growth coalitions, and regeneration schemes for large stretches of the post-industrial landscape. The emergence of this "post-ecological" city is characterized by the abandonment of legitimate environmental thinking in favor of a mindset that rationalizes ecology through cultural hegemony, consumption, economic efficiency, and de-politicization.[2] The critical question in the post-ecological city is not how it can be planned or designed to address environmental issues, but rather how the illusion of the ecological city has been maintained while perpetuating a system that benefits powerful interests and inherently exclusive priorities.

Landscape Urbanism is complicit in this regard. This is not to suggest that New Urbanism have been successful in advancing social equality in practice. Both movements avoid what the current urban crisis brings to light — the perpetuation of social inequality and the avoidance of the most marginalized citizens *and* places. Redressing this will require policies and design practices that integrate a new social-ecological understanding of urbanism "from above" with urbanism "from below" to engage the spaces of marginality. At a minimum, this would include reconciling different images of the city; incorporating social processes into resiliency; and repairing neglected parts of the urban ecosystem. The future projection of urban life will ultimately rest on addressing these social-ecological issues.

Invisibility in the Image of the City

In *The Politics of Aesthetics,* French philosopher Jacques Rancière argues that politics is the struggle of the unrecognized for equal recognition in the established order.[3] In relation to politics, Rancière identifies different regimes that compete for the "distribution of the sensible" — a system of self-evident facts of sense perception made visible to the public. The *ethical regime* entails images and forms of art in relation to the ethos of community whose purpose is to educate the citizenry and their role in the communal body. The *representational regime* liberates art from social norms and establishes itself as a separate domain with its own operative language and criteria.

What can be drawn from the work of Rancière is that aesthetics is more than the appearance of space. Aesthetics is at the core of politics, not as the art of politics, but in terms of what can be seen and what can be said about it. From this perspective, urbanism can be viewed as "ways of doing and making" that intervene in the general distribution of ways of doing and making. Urbanism also serves a purpose in maintaining modes of being and forms of visibility. As a field that produces future visions of the city, both creative and symbolic, urbanism is a boundary-making practice that identifies what is common to a public, the form of its visibility, and that of its organization. The point is that urbanism, like art, can either repress modes of being as invisible or reveal new sensory possibilities that instigate novel forms of political subjectivity. Debates over the future trajectory of urbanism can be viewed from this lens. Urbanism employs different and competing images of the city that parallel regimes of artistic practice.

Landscape Urbanism uses representational techniques across a range of territorial and temporal scales to envision new spatial imaginations that challenge the figural city. The outcome has been a shift from architecture to landscape as a medium of analysis and projection. With the ascribing of agency to the ecological over the social world, Landscape Urbanism makes no claims on behalf of the "public good." By contrast, New Urbanism is clear about the ethical basis of its project in articulating a civic purpose of urban design. Over the past thirty years New Urbanism has expanded its constituent audience to include policy-makers and elected officials, among others. A key to the New Urbanism's success has been its ability to frame issues of common concern across different scales ranging from federal policy to building form. This includes a shared identity that aims to address the ills of suburban landscapes and automobile-dominated environments through traditional forms of urbanism. Of course, whether New Urbanism has made progress in addressing social inequities, ethical proclamations withstanding, is a matter of considerable debate.[4]

The persistence of representational (Landscape Urbanism) and ethical (New Urbanism) preoccupations in urbanism has had the effect of perpetuating invisibility of the most marginalized in our cities at a time when urban sustainability has risen in the public's consciousness. There is a need to shed light on marginality, not as an expression of urban anxiety, but as a way to expose the "political" in urbanism. The political is about making choices about what is seen and unseen in the city, a reflection of power in urbanist discourse and practice. It is from this position that I will sketch out the prospects for urbanism and how a focus on marginality can draw attention to, recognize, and offer new possibilities to address social inequality. The city moving toward sustainability will remain an illusion as long as the issue of race in the city is avoided and disparities persist between the wealthy and the poor.

Green Illusions in the Post-Ecological City

The incorporation of "sustainability" into the agenda of cities, including the redress of derelict land and infrastructure, now dominates landscape and ecological approaches to urban planning and development. Beginning in the early 1990s, a significant number of government-supported brownfield remediation projects were implemented to catalyze development and increase waterfront accessibility. In addition, a number of competitions such as the High Line, Downsview Park, and Fresh Kills Park helped to reimagine large urban sites with a view to developing strategies for post-industrial landscapes.

It is important to consider the political economy undergirding these ecologically inspired redevelopment efforts, especially trends that have emerged since the 1970s. One includes the rise of growth coalitions. Under regimes that blend elements of civil society, the state, and the market, human welfare and regulatory oversight was transferred outside of historical state responsibility.[5] The move toward entrepreneurial forms of urban governance is widely interpreted as a manifestation of the state's devolution under neoliberalism — a form of economic liberalism in response to crises in financial markets and changes to labor production as the result of a globalized economy. State re-scaling has been identified as a diffusion strategy to shift citizen expectations of social welfare to regional and local scales of governance.[6] These processes affect how public goods are distributed, resulting in highly differentiated geographies of urban development.[7]

A second outcome of a globalized knowledge economy and increased competitiveness among cities is the rise of cultural industries.[8] This symbolic economy rests on social and physical attributes of the city as a raw material from which to produce and market culture for consumption purposes. Chief among these are art institutions and creative labor, but also included are other competitive advantages such as place identity and natural assets. While initially centered on a select number of global cities as hubs of the informational society, the cultural economy has expanded to cities that range in size and geographic location as regional economies have changed.[9]

Landscape Urbanism seems to align well with these political economic trends — growth coalitions and the marketing of cultural economies — because it offers infrastructural strategies that are politically appealing, flexible to changing market conditions, and in keeping with the tastes of cultural elites. An emphasis on international design competitions has also curtailed citizen involvement in the name of public expediency, a standard byproduct of neoliberalism.

More recently, cities have incorporated sustainability objectives for different reasons and with mixed results.[10] Many of these practices include greenhouse gas reduction goals, emission inventories, and green public sector operations.[11] Urban environmental risk is also an increasing concern, especially after Hurricane Katrina, generating a new push for post-disaster planning and disaster recovery.[12] The evidence of the human and financial cost of such disasters is mounting: 79,000 fatalities and 200 million people were affected annually by disasters during the 1990s.[13] Moreover, data from the Organization for Economic Co-operation and Development, a member organization of thirty countries including the United States, indicate that financial costs arising from disasters have risen from \$2 billion to \$70 billion a year between the 1960s and 1990s. Given these dire statistics it is not surprising that sustainability has been incorporated into the agenda of growth coalitions despite scant evidence that local initiatives can address climate change without significant changes to federal and statewide policies.[14]

The initial impetus for these practices began with "sustainable development" some twenty-five years ago and was a wake-up call about finite resources and the need to plan cities for ecological and economic stability.[15] Sustainable development has been defined as "development that improves the long-term health of human and ecological systems."[16] In practice, however, much of the attention is on the environmental accounting of carbon sequestration, carbon reduction, and lessening dependence on non-renewable energy sources in the form of carrying capacities and ecological footprints.[17] Given the difficulty of measuring social outcomes, it is not surprising that the relationship between ecological impacts and economic output has been prioritized over concerns about social equity.

With the focus squarely on economic growth over social concerns, environmental modernization has advanced the argument that the economy prospers as it moves toward the adoption of environmentalism. Central to ecological modernization is equating environmental management with industrial development.[18] Key characteristics of environmental modernization include the use of technology to achieve carbon neutrality; the internalization of environmental externalities through economic means; new forms of governance to set sustainability goals and systematize monitoring; and lifestyle approaches that try to weave environmentalism into consumption practices.

The adoption of these practices can be viewed positively when considering the projected effects of climate change on cities. Yet these priorities also describe what I call the post-ecological city — the economic rationalization of environmental issues as a response to market crises, the greening of the cultural economy, and a strategy to secure citizen consent to de-politicize local environmental concerns. For those engaged in the planning and design side of urbanism, important questions emerge: How does urbanism reproduce the post-ecological city? In the absence of discussions about the differential effects on urban inhabitants of environmental concerns, are urban designers helping to sustain the illusion of true sustainability? What, if anything, can be done to foster an understanding of these entanglements to move toward a more socially informed idea of urban sustainability?

Ghostly Matters: How Sustainable is Inequality?

Absent in current debates over the right course for urbanism is the growing social inequality of cities. This growth can be attributed in part to increases in transnational and transregional migration due to globalization.[19] For the US, demographic growth and the subsequent rise in inequality falls squarely on Latino populations. While migration to the US does not account for overall population growth, between 1990 and 2010, the Latino population more than doubled in size, an increase of 28.1 million people, now totaling 16 percent of the total US population.[20] Current demographic projections show the Latino presence will account for 46 percent of the total population growth in the next two decades (as compared to 24 percent for non-Latino whites). This has instigated a number of discussions about "Latino urbanism" and place-making in these communities.[21] There is no consensus about the particular form of urbanism appropriate to Latino communities, but it is clear that many of the places Latinos call home materialize the intersections of global, national and local forces in the built environment, as well as conflicts over how history is depicted, the present is understood, and the future is envisioned. There is little doubt that migration will continue due to climate change and natural disasters. The National Academy of Sciences estimates that upwards of seven million climate refugees from Mexico will emigrate to the US before this century's end.[22] The reality of an increasingly global and multi-ethnic society suggests a need to better understand new social formations, the changing cultural landscape, and the effect on cities.

How can urban sustainability, and Landscape Urbanism in particular, respond to these changing social dynamics? With regard to current debates about the "right to the city," there is a need to consider whose rights and what city the planners and designers have in mind, and whether ecological forms of urbanism perpetuate marginality. To what degree do ecological approaches to design give us the "freedom to make and remake our cities and ourselves"?[23] Some planning scholars have theorized the possibilities for this agency through insurgent forms of citizenship that claim new rights of urban inhabitation.[24] Others note how new social formations, especially immigrants and refugees, destabilize notions of core and periphery, which instigates a coming to terms with the reshaping of cities by marginalized populations.[25] What can be drawn from this work is that participation in a political community is a defining characteristic of citizenship and that new subjectivities serve a pivotal role in shaping the spaces of the city. However, these expressions of the "right to the city" stand in stark contrast to the current state of urban sustainability.

Citizenship and the right to the city have become a battleground for an unexpected confluence of sustainability and anti-immigration rhetoric. One manifestation is the "greening of hate," or the "greenwashing of nativism," as social critic Andrew Ross has suggested.[26] In *Bird on Fire: Lessons from the World's Least Sustainable City,* Ross writes about the possibilities for sustainability in Phoenix and argues that sustainability can only be achieved through social and political changes that redress the claims of the least powerful and most marginalized, not through technological fixes. Among other problems, he documents the growing nativist activism that uses the rhetoric of climate change and population control to fuel anti-immigration sentiment.

Some use the term "eco-apartheid" to describe how affluent non-Latino white communities benefit disproportionately from green economic development, while communities of color fall further behind. It is highly problematic that economic gains under "urban sustainability" bypass the very communities most in need of development, workforce creation, toxic cleanup, and environmental stewardship. Other places are witnessing the greening of the ghetto where nature is part of a planning agenda that uses *terrain vague* as test beds for urban sustainability projects — e.g., the reclaiming of vacant parcels for urban agriculture or hydroponic farms — as part of a larger discourse of regeneration that aims to reimagine marginalized urban places, and not always in ways that benefit local inhabitants. Implicit in these landscape-oriented place-making discourses is a devaluation and disregard for urban places whose histories mean little more than the blocking of profit and cultural consumption. What is at stake is the use of "nature" to render the marginalized invisible. Inequality in the city is perpetuated because of a failure to operationalize sustainability in social terms.

Arrested Development:
From Smart Growth to Smart Decline

Strategies being promoted for abandoned and depopulating neighborhoods include planned shrinkage and smart decline.[27] These concepts have been applied to an analysis of Rust Belt cities and, more recently, to parts of the Sun Belt, which have experienced population loss since the foreclosure crisis. Using housing as a proxy for neighborhood decline, some scholars have laid out a convincing argument to discourage new housing production in the form of de-densification policies, relaxed zoning codes, and tax incentives to assist in resident relocation.[28] Related strategies include the consolidation and shrinkage of government service areas and the conversion of residential lands into areas for recreation, urban forestry, agricultural production, or the grazing of livestock. The timing could not be better to consider these proposals given current austerity measures as well as the downturn in regional housing markets. In addition, it would appear to be a logical strategy for many inner-city neighborhoods that have experienced decline for decades.

However, there are elements of planned shrinkage and smart decline that need to be unpacked and problematized. One is an over-emphasis on physical solutions when the actors responsible for, and those effected by, these interventions are under-specified. The creation of urban voids as an inversion of smart growth does not address the failed legacy of urban renewal that resulted from racist policies, the annihilation of working-class and poor neighborhoods, and lack of attention to socio-economic and cultural dynamics. The revaluation of vacant land for agricultural production under the guise of "weak urbanization" is one manifestation of the post-ecological city that conflates agrarian living with urban renewal and conceals the environmental costs of decentralized landscapes through localized consumption discourses of "slow food" and "locavorism."[29] A related issue concerns the organizational capacity of redevelopment agencies, development specialists, and planning and design professionals, who often know little about local neighborhoods, the livelihood of residents, or the informal economies that sustain them. Spatial planning techniques seem trivial when an evaluation of the impacts to the most vulnerable populations is what is really needed.

These critiques aside, planned shrinkage is a provocative thesis about reimagining opportunities in marginalized neighborhoods as an alternative to the growth model. In some cases it will be an effective strategy, but will need to be sensitive to historical inequities and account for the territorial rights of citizens. This would require new forms of community governance, organizational infrastructures, and participation by residents that are most affected. Alternative uses for vacant and cleared land should be an outgrowth of these deliberative structures, but need to address environmental health concerns and be coupled with physical interventions and economic strategies that improve livelihood and enlarge the community commons. For example, the deconstruction, not demolition, of buildings should be tied to workforce development so that salvaged materials and other surpluses gained from related employment are recycled back into community economies. These are just a few examples that begin to suggest a social and ecological understanding absent in the contemporary practice of either Landscape or New Urbanism.

A Social Ecology of Urbanism

What future do conflicting narratives of place and sustainability offer to marginalized populations? As I have argued, struggles over place are manifested in the "greening of hate," territorial and social isolation in the planning and design of urban space, the reimagining of inner-city neighborhoods for consumption purposes, and the planned shrinkage of underinvested, marginalized neighborhoods. Sustainability will remain an illusion if ecologically based approaches continue to avoid the social and material consequences of inequality.

The challenge, however, goes beyond technical solutions or debates about the horizontal and vertical city. At issue is the crisis of urban imagination in addressing the persistence of social inequality and the marginalization of both people *and* places. A new social ecological understanding of urbanism is needed, one that understands the relationships between people and their environments, beginning with the premise that ecological problems are deeply social in nature and cannot be separated from larger political and social dynamics. The failure to recognize this is evident in urbanist discourse that gives little consideration for existing sociopolitical structures and the differential effects these have on citizens and the communities they inhabit.

Adopting a social-ecological perspective would be a first step forward. In simple terms, social ecology centers on the relation between people and place: the human experience that includes the individual and the interactions and relationships between people and their environments. Here, the environment is comprised of both social and ecological worlds and is inclusive of different social groups, institutions, the built environment, and physical landscapes. From a critical but operative perspective, social ecology draws attention to different scales of inequality, but also provides a framework for possible strategies to address inequalities. It helps to ensure that institutional and political ecologies are accounted for in urban analysis and design. It would instigate a greater concern for the inclusion of social objectives into urbanism, incorporating what are currently treated as social externalities in the distribution of environmental resources and in the design of public landscapes. A social ecology of urbanism would draw attention to the causes and effects of social and environmental problems, as well as the solutions to those problems, with particular attention to environmental degradation and social disparities.

A social-ecological approach to urbanism can be effective in not only shaping the built environment and landscapes, but also staging new spaces of production and exchange, as well as institutional and policy decision-making. This is a strategy for changing *both* social and ecological settings across multiple scales of intervention. By incorporating form *and* process, it would also consider the spatiotemporal aspects of place-making and acknowledge that places are historically contingent, assemblages of different ideas and practices that have material consequences. These assemblages involve negotiations between groups whose histories are intertwined and are situated in territorialized space.[30] Conceptualizing place in this way acknowledges the complex entanglements in which planning and urban design are situated, but also helps to open new spaces for practice. Place-making is an important means by which groups negotiate different social imaginaries of location and, in the process, create new spaces in the city. As a setting for rights claims, place also draws attention to the political and raises important questions — which rights, for whom, and how are entitlements manifested in material terms?

Several areas offer possibilities for Landscape Urbanism to engage the spaces of marginality if urban sustainability is to be achieved. The first concerns reconciling different images of the city. Multiple and competing knowledge claims exist about the "good city" and depend on who employs them, for what purpose, and with what results. A reading of the city that brings together an urbanism "from above" with urbanism "from below" is needed if inequality is to be taken seriously. The former, as embodied by architects, landscape architects, and planners, creates the representations and future projections of the city that, although not always intentional, conceal the sensibilities of multiple publics and render invisible the everyday practices and livelihoods of people. Henri Lefebvre called this "the illusion of transparency" which conceals the fact that the spaces of the city are socially produced to serve powerful interests.[31] Urbanism "from below" is the experience of marginalized citizens — their struggles, hopes and fears — as they seek to order their coexistence in urban places. These are the individuals and groups that do not figure into images of the city projected by urbanists and whose presence disrupts normative visions of urban life. Imagining the city within the liminal zone of these different urbanisms can integrate current approaches, acknowledge the coexistence of social and ecological worlds, and address inequality in an explicit manner. Strategies that engage the local citizenry are worth considering, especially in the wake of urban austerity, housing foreclosures, and high levels of unemployment.

A second area concerns resiliency as a key concept in ecological approaches to urbanism. Resiliency is often described as the ability of an ecosystem to absorb energy through adaptation and internal modification in response to external changes or threats, without undergoing a radical change into a qualitatively different system. Resiliency is an important component in landscape ecology that aims to improve the functioning of ecosystems within urban development. This is a distinguishing feature in the theory and practice of Landscape Urbanism, but there is a need to better integrate social aspects of resiliency that mirror this goal. A fundamental challenge is to develop robust ecological strategies while also creating greater self-reliance on local resources, institutions, and human capacity. Adaptability, flexibility, survivability, and self-organization are some shared characteristics. Important to social resiliency is an engaged and educated citizenry that can achieve a self-balancing relationship between environmental, economic and social forces.[32]

Resiliency is relevant to cities and communities that are vulnerable to natural and human disasters and offers an alternative to the status quo, i.e., overly deterministic and formulaic approaches to planning and urban design. Socio-ecological resiliency in urban design would need to respond to changing conditions and users over time, and adapt form to process. Examples include designing and constructing modular houses to expand or contract in the future without adding significant costs to homeowners; financing a public fund through tax increments to support environmental restoration projects and/or future disaster relief; or developing workforce housing in close proximity to existing employment centers or multi-modal transportation infrastructure. These examples draw many parallels with the central tenets of Landscape Urbanism, i.e., adaptability over time, staging of sites, and infrastructural programming, but are piecemeal, lack scale, and are not integrated with the high-profile design commissions centered on formal, civic landscapes. Moreover, there is an unmet need to transform abandoned sites in neighborhoods whereby socioeconomic strategies are directly incorporated into the remediation and regeneration of public landscapes.

A third, related area relevant to Landscape Urbanism involves repairing neglected parts of a city's urban ecology in low-income neighborhoods. This is materially relevant for those communities that suffer from a disproportionate amount of macro environmental health problems that manifest locally in the form of contaminated lands, proximity to polluting industries and waste treatment facilities, and exposure to frequent flooding. Also, despite having high amounts of vacant land, these places often have the least parks and healthy, affordable food is scarce. This has public health implications in terms of the lack of accessible and safe locations for physical activity as well as the prevalence of food deserts in low-income neighborhoods. These and other environmental injustices can be rectified through thoughtful planning and design, but will require a nuanced reading of these landscapes in terms of energy and material flows, their potentiality, and the livelihoods connected to these places in a real, material sense. It will also need to take stock of what J.K. Gibson-Graham identifies as "community economies" comprised of existing and latent community assets and alternative forms of labor and enterprise.[33] The task is to develop "a post-humanist ethics of community economy" that "acknowledges the blurred boundaries of humans, the natural environment and others that make life possible and shape the character of life."[34]

In sum, a social-ecological understanding of the city calls for a different theory and practice of urbanism; one that questions the logic of the post-ecological city and the mirage that keeps the professional disciplines from making visible the unhomely aspects of urban life that continue to haunt the city. If sustainability is a main goal of urbanism, we can no longer avoid the inequalities that persist at different scales of place-making. A social ecology of urbanism instigates an awareness about human and non-human relations, and the social and political consequences of decisions within policy, planning, and institutional decision-making. Thus, a supplementary image of the city would instigate the design of new social, ecological, and physical relationships to address inequality head-on. The liminal zone of boundaries — between different urban livelihoods and between the social and the ecological — provides a space, a grounding, from which to consider the prospects for urbanism in the post-ecological city. The aim of urbanism should not be to placate dominant discourses of aesthetics or form, but rather to reflexively engage with unfamiliar terrain where different visions of the city, the social and ecological, and the local and the global all collide. This new aesthetics of urbanism registers *place* as a site of world-making to make visible an inclusive image of the city and the multiple worlds we inhabit.

Endotes

1   Shane, Graham. 2003–2004. The Emergence of "Landscape Urbanism." *Harvard Design Magazine*, Fall/Winter 19: 1–8.

2   Blühdorn, Ingolfur. 2000. *Post-Ecologist Politics. Social Theory and the Abdication of the Ecologist Paradigm*. London and New York: Routledge.

3   Rancière, Jacques. 2004. *The Politics of Aesthetics: The Distribution of the Sensible*. London and New York: Continuum International Publishing Group.

4   Pyatok, Michael. 2000. Martha Stewart vs. Studs Terkel?: New Urbanism and Inner City Neighborhoods that Work. *Places* 13,1: 40–43; Clark, Paul W. 2005. The Ideal of Community and its Counterfeit Construction. *Journal of Architectural Education* 58, 3: 43–52; Harvey, David. 2005. The New Urbanism and the Communitarian Trap. *Harvard Design Magazine*, Winter/Spring 1: 1–3.

5   Mayer, Margit. 1994. Post-Fordist City Politics. In Ash Amin, Ed., *Post-Fordism: A Reader*. Oxford and Cambridge, MA: Blackwell; Painter, Joe. 2000. State and Governance. In Eric Sheppard and T. Barnes, Eds., *A Companion to Economic Geography*. Oxford: Blackwell. Pp. 359–76.

6   Harvey, David. 1989. *The Condition of Postmodernity*. London: Basil Blackwell; Hall, Tim, and Phil Hubbard. 1996. The Entrepreneurial City: New Urban Politics, New Urban Geographies? *Progress in Human Geography* 20, 2: 153–74; Purcell, Mark. 2002. The State, Regulation, and Global Restructuring: Reasserting the Political in Political Economy. *Review of International Political Economy* 9, 2: 298–332.

7   Smith, Neil. 1984. *Uneven Development: Nature, Capital, and the Production of Space*. Oxford: Basil Blackwell; Smith, Neil. 1992. Geography, Difference, and the Politics of Scale. In Joe Doherty, Graham Elspeth and Mo Malek, Eds., *Postmodernism and the Social Sciences*. New York: St. Martin's Press. Pp. 57–79.

8   Zukin, Sharon. 2000. *The Cultures of Cities*. Oxford and Cambridge: Blackwell; Scott, Allen J. 2000. *The Culture Economy of Cities*. London: Sage Publications.

9   Amin, Ash, and Steve Graham. 1997. The Ordinary City. *Transactions of the Institute of British Geographers* 22, 4: 411–29; Short, John Rennie. 1999. Imagineers, Boosterism, and the Representation of Cities. In A. E. G. Jonas and D. Wilson, Eds., *The Urban Growth Machine*. Albany: SUNY Press.

10 While, Aidan, Andrew E G Jonas, and David Gibbs. 2004. The Environment and the Entrepreneurial City: Searching for the Urban "Sustainability Fix" in Leeds and Manchester. *International Journal of Urban and Regional Research* 28, 3: 549–69; Jonas, Andrew E G, and Aidan While. 2007. Greening the Entrepreneurial City? Looking for Spaces of Sustainability Politics in the Competitive City. In Rob Krueger and David Gibbs, Eds., *The Sustainable Development Paradox: Urban Political Economy in the United States and Europe*. New York and London: The Guilford Press. Pp. 123–59.

11 Wheeler, Stephen M. 2008. State and Municipal Climate Change Plans: The First Generation. *Journal of the American Planning Association* 74, 4: 481–96.

12 Birch, Eugenie L., and Susan M. Wachter. 2006. *Rebuilding Urban Places after Disaster: Lessons from Hurricane Katrina*. Philadelphia: University of Pennsylvania Press.

13 Organization for Economic Co-operation and Development. 2003. *Emerging Systems Risks in the 21ˢᵗ Century: An Agenda for Action.* Paris: OECD Publications.

14 Betsill, Michele M. 2001. Mitigating Climate Change in US Cities: Opportunities and Obstacles. *Local Environment* 6, 4: 393–406.

15 United Nations World Commission on Environment and Development. 1987. *Brundtland Report.* Oxford: Oxford University Press.

16 Wheeler, Stephen M. 2003. Planning Sustainable and Livable Cities. In Richard T. LeGates and Frederic Stout, Eds., *The City Reader: Third Edition.* London and New York: Routledge. Pp. 486–96.

17 Rees, William. 1992. Ecological Footprints and Appropriated Carrying Capacity: What Urban Economics Leaves Out. *Environment & Urbanization* 4, 2: 121–30; Wackernagel, Mathis, and Rees William. 1996. *Our Ecological Footprint: Reducing Human Impact on the Earth.* Gabriola Island, BC: New Society Publishers.

18 Hajer, Maarten. 1995. *The Politics of Environmental Discourse: Ecological Modernization and the Policy Process.* Oxford: Oxford University Press; Gibbs, David. 2002. *Local Economic Development and the Environment.* London: Taylor & Francis.

19 Guarnizo, Luis, and Michael Peter Smith. 1998. The Location of Transnationalism. *Comparative Urban and Community Research* 6: 3–34; Peter Smith, Michael. 2001. *Transnational Urbanism: Locating Globalization.* Malden, MA: Blackwell.

20 US Census.

21 Davis, Mike. 2000. *Magical Urbanism: Latinos Reinvent the US Big City.* London: Verso; Mendez, Michael. 2005. Latino New Urbanism: Building on Cultural Preferences. *Opolis* 1, 1: 16; Rios, Michael and Leonardo Vazquez, Eds. 2012. *Dialogos: Placemaking in Latino Communities.* London and New York: Routledge.

22 Feng, Shuaizhang, Alan B. Krueger, and Michael Oppenheimer. 2010. Linkages among Climate Change, Crop Yields and Mexico–US Cross-Border Migration. *Proceedings of the National Academy of Sciences* 107, 32: 14257–62.

23 Harvey, David. 2008. The Right to the City. *New Left Review* 53: 23–40.

24 Douglass, Mike, and John Friedmann, Eds. 1998. *Cities for Citizens: Planning and the Rise of Civil Society in a Global Age.* Chichester, UK and New York: Wiley; Sandercock, Leonie. 1998. *Towards Cosmopolis: Planning for Multicultural Cities.* West Sussex, England: Wiley; Holston, James, and Arjun Appadurai. 1999. *Cities and Citizenship.* In James Holston, Ed., Cities and Citizenship. Durham, NC: Duke University Press. Pp. 1–18; Friedmann, John. 2002. *The Prospect of Cities.* Minneapolis, MN and London: University of Minneapolis Press.

25 Vidler, Anthony. 1992. *The Architectural Uncanny: Essays in the Modern Unhomely.* Cambridge and London: The MIT Press.

26 Ross, Andrew. 2011. *Bird on Fire: Lessons from the World's Least Sustainable City.* New York: Oxford University Press.

27 Popper, Deborah Epstein, and Frank J. Popper. 1987. The Great Plains: From Dust to Dust. *Planning* 53, 12: 12–18; Rybczynski, Witold, and Peter D. Linneman. 1999. How to Save Our Shrinking Cities. *Public Interest* 135: 30–44; Hollander, Justin B. 2011. *Sunburnt Cities: The Great Recession, Depopulation, and Urban Planning in the American Sunbelt.* London and New York: Routledge.

28 Hollander, *Sunburnt Cities.*

29 Waldheim, Charles. 2010. Notes Toward a History of Agrarian Urbanism. *The Design Observer:* places. designobserver.com/feature/notes-toward-a-history-of-agrarian-urbanism/15518/

30 DeLanda, Manuel. 2006. *A New Philosophy of Society: Assemblage Theory and Social Complexity.* London and New York: Continuum; Massey, Doreen. 2005. *For Space.* London: Sage.

31 Lefebvre, Henri. 1991. *The Production of Space.* Cambridge, MA: Blackwell.

32 Vale, Lawrence J., and Thomas J. Campanella, Eds. 2005. *The Resilient City: How Modern Cities Recover from Disaster.* New York: Oxford University Press.

33 Gibson-Graham, J.K. 2006. *A Postcapitalist Politics.* Minneapolis and London: University of Minnesota Press.

34 Roelvink, Gerda, and J. K. Gibson-Graham. 2009. A Postcapitalist Politics of Dwelling: Ecological Humanities and Community Economies in Conversation. *Australian Humanities Review* 46: 145–58.

13

Adaptive Urbanism

KRISTINA HILL AND LARISSA LARSEN

Introduction

CITIES ARE AN EMERGENT PHENOMENON. From a long human history of impermanent communities, cities appeared only five to seven thousand years ago.[1] The fact that the majority of the Earth's population now lives in dense, permanent settlements speaks to the advantages that these settlement types afford. Our human capacity to occupy, comprehend and manage cities as a cultural and biophysical phenomenon continues to grow over time. However, the depopulation of city centers in the middle of the twentieth century, the explosion of urban fringe growth (especially along rivers and coasts),[2] and current megacity growth rates provide ample evidence that cities are vulnerable to booms and busts. If our goal is to manage cities as just and sustainable human living environments, it's not clear that humans are meeting that goal on a global scale.

In recent literature, many urban design scholars have suggested different "urbanisms" in an effort to guide how we shape cities and neighborhoods. In the first section of this chapter, we begin by recalling the origin of the term urbanism and then use Barnett's[3] categorization system to illustrate how the many terms may be sorted into some logical order. We end the first section by highlighting some of the key characteristics of New Urbanism and Landscape Urbanism that help reveal their

priorities, strengths and weaknesses. In the second section, we argue that
the tensions between New Urbanism and Landscape Urbanism return
us to an older debate about the relationship between technology and
nature, specifically to the effects of industrialization and an industrialized economy on landscapes. Finally, in the third section of our essay, we
suggest that global climate change, one of our most pressing challenges,
requires moving beyond these past debates and ideological divides toward
a conception of adaptive urbanism. Adaptive urbanism recognizes the
interdependence of people and ecosystem services, and points to the need
for design interventions to consciously address urban social inequalities.

Organizing the Urbanisms

The term urbanism made its way into English from the French *urbanisme*, which came into use in 1801 to refer to a branch of study "dealing
with urban life." But it was not recorded in English until 1884, and by
1929 it was still referred to as a "newly-coined word" by the London
Times.[4] Before the nineteenth century, and the proliferation of the terms
urbanism and urbanist in the twentieth century, the only real predecessor to the term was "urbane" — an adjective used to describe refined
human behavior, not human settlements.[5] "Urbanize" originally referred
to improving people's manners, not expanding city districts.[6] In the
last twenty-five years, without conducting an exhaustive search, several
prominent schools of thought have arisen in the design and planning
professions that call themselves a form of "urbanism" — New Urbanism,[7]
Landscape Urbanism,[8] postmodern urbanism,[9] everyday urbanism,[10]
green urbanism,[11] and many more.

In a recent categorizing essay, Jonathan Barnett divided more than
sixty recently coined "urbanisms" into six categories:

- System urbanisms: frames cities as the product of systems, and a matter of systems design
- Green urbanisms: frames cities as linked to natural processes through
food and other materials
- Traditional urbanisms: emphasizes opportunities to learn from places
that evolved successfully
- Community urbanisms: emphasizes the need for wider participation
and power-sharing in cities

- Sociopolitical urbanisms: identifies political and social critiques of city life and city design
- Headline urbanisms: labels situations, rather than more fully organized points of view.

After reviewing a multitude of these competing notions, Barnett gives up and describes this proliferation as a process of self-negation, in which each aspect of the wide variety of urban conditions is given its own urbanism.[12] He also identifies some as "territorial claims," in which the central issue is whether the hegemony of architecture over landscape architecture will continue, or whether planning will reassert its claim to urban ideologies. But in his half-serious, half-humorous review of the various forms of advocacy involved in these various urbanisms, as in all "-isms," Barnett misses the opportunity to reflect on their origins, as well as the timing of this ism-explosion. While the proliferation of "isms" almost trivializes their intents, it also demonstrates our collective need for larger ideas that remind us of our priorities and advance our practices. In this essay, we feel compelled to briefly describe the key concepts and characteristics of New Urbanism and Landscape Urbanism as we see them. In these brief summaries, we hope to contrast each movement's design priorities and highlight some important strengths and weaknesses.

Dissatisfied with the perceived loss of community within many postwar suburbs, New Urbanism's primary focus is how we can "build" better communities through design and improve residents' quality of life. New Urbanists believe that mixing uses, offering a diversity of housing types, and including prominent public spaces builds better communities. By creating compact developments, neighborhoods are expected to facilitate greater social vibrancy and encourage walking over driving. New Urbanism has called for a more "human" scale. This has returned designers' attention to the pedestrian environment, to street connectivity, and to grid-based urban street patterns that simplify wayfinding. It has also meant that New Urbanist developments incorporate community public spaces, cultural institutions, and destinations that serve residents' needs. New Urbanism has become a social movement over the last twenty years. The reason for this success may be largely the result of its utopian aspirations and its clear identification of design elements.

But in applauding New Urbanism's aspirations and noting its popular support, we must also revisit two of its weaknesses. The first is its reliance on physical design to address social problems. While physical design can encourage walking and serendipitous social interactions through proximity, it cannot address the problems of housing segregation by income and race. Fainstein[13] notes that the New Urbanist towns and neighborhoods are, "only slightly less exclusive suburbs than the ones [New Urbanists] dislike." The history of urban renewal reminds us of how simplistic physical responses cannot overcome larger social problems of racism and poverty. Every designer and decision-maker must be wary of the logical fallacies and social consequences of advocacy based on environmental determinism. If the meaning of diversity in New Urbanist communities is to extend beyond the physical aesthetic to include social diversity then design efforts must be coordinated with public programs. In part, proponents for New Urbanism in the design and development community should feel some sense of relief that they alone aren't expected to solve some of society's most divisive problems. But by acknowledging that design can't solve larger structural injustices, New Urbanists must temper their expansive claims. Duany once stated his belief in, "the ability of architecture to transform society." This statement exaggerates the power of physical design, neglects the darker, potentially exclusionary side of community, and undercuts New Urbanism's positive contributions.

A second critique of New Urbanism is the movement's limited impact on reducing sprawl. New Urbanism's desires to reduce the need for private vehicle use and to construct well-defined (non-sprawling) edges have obvious environmental benefits. But while they may be potentially walkable, these neighborhoods have been less successful in reducing vehicle miles and preserving natural areas and agricultural lands. We acknowledge that ecosystems are not the primary focus of New Urbanists' concerns. Some New Urbanists would argue that a greater sensitivity to environmental issues has developed within the movement as low-impact development strategies have been incorporated into their design practices. So while the movement has successfully increased density within, most of the heralded examples are still located in exurban and suburban areas.

The primary focus of Landscape Urbanism is to reveal geomorphologies and other natural systems that underlay our human settlements. Waldheim states that Landscape Urbanisms offers designers two key insights. The first insight is that twenty-first-century cities are not like nineteenth-century cities. Therefore, we need to accommodate emerging urban functions and not simply emulate earlier models of urbanism. The second insight is that urban designers can protect the environment if they prioritize natural functions. Therefore — in contrast to New Urbanism, which saw the neighborhood, the block, and the street as the key urban design elements — Landscape Urbanism broadens the scale to a natural system (generally the watershed, but also to multi-scale systems of plant succession and animal dispersal), highlights ecosystem services, and sees infrastructure as an opportunity for revealing how natural and man-made systems intermingle. When asked how this newer movement differs from McHarg's regional environmental planning tradition, some Landscape Urbanists have stated that McHarg's notion of preserving the most desirable natural areas first and then integrating development in the remaining areas sets up an unnecessary opposition between human activity and natural systems. The popularity of this newer movement reflects increasing environmental concerns, the belief that by exposing the extent of natural systems within urban environments society will recognize their importance and fragility, and the perceived need for self-organizing, less capital-intensive solutions for large brownfield remediation efforts and park development proposals.

We agree with the need to recognize the intrinsic values of natural systems as part of the urban environment and highlight these systems, and we agree that people are active agents shaping environmental systems. However, we are concerned with two weaknesses within Landscape Urbanism. The first weakness is the movement's use of language and the obfuscation that imposes. From a lyrical perspective, the words of Landscape Urbanism sound intriguing. However, identifying the key characteristics based on the writing of leading proponents can be frustrating. Landscape Urbanists assert that flexibility, open-endedness, and indeterminancy are the hallmarks of their design practices. They believe that these hallmarks reflect the dynamism of ecological systems and that flexibility is essential in a time when social and technological changes happen rapidly. But when pressed to explain in greater precision what this explicitly means for design, Landscape Urbanists generally engage in a tautological style of debate that is impenetrable. The characteristics of flexibility, open-endedness, and indeterminancy can be used to avoid specific answers. Intermingled within these conversations are references to natural processes and environmental sciences. Again, language imprecision makes it hard to discern how this information contributes to their designs but we feel that Landscape Urbanists are largely inspired by information from the natural sciences. The intricacy and complexity of natural systems is amazing and should inspire us. However, instead of using this information only for inspiration and speculation, we believe that is important to use it to 1) create more resilient and adaptive systems and 2) advance our understanding of how we can measure the quality of these complex human-environmental systems.

Our second concern involves the issue of density and some Landscape Urbanists' acceptance of lower-density settlement patterns. We believe this concern involves the implications of boundary setting. We agree with Landscape Urbanism in their position that biophysical conditions must be considered when setting boundaries. Locating a site within a watershed instead of a municipal jurisdiction provides a more useful way to understand how water moves through a site as part of a larger system and how small site-specific actions can have cumulative impacts on water quality and quantity. But boundaries for environmental evaluation need to vary. When biologists create a quadrant of an acre or even a larger expense of several hundred acres to measure the presence of a particular species, the extent of biodiversity, or surface water quality, low-density settlements produce better environmental results than higher-density settlement areas. However, to advance environmental sustainability it is necessary to remember that the true boundaries of our collective impacts need to be measured at the global scale. Currently, cities occupy approximately three percent of the Earth's land mass but they accommodate more than half of the Earth's population. While the area of a city can't be self-sustaining, we must preserve natural areas and agricultural lands beyond our urban areas to supply our needs and absorb our wastes. As the demands of population and consumption continue to increase, urban patterns must increase in their density if we are serious in efforts to advance global environmental sustainability. Therefore, increasing urban density is imperative. Landscape Urbanists correctly note that city/suburban divides are meaningless from both natural system and economic perspectives. While this is true about these boundaries, that information doesn't mean that low-density patterns are permissible if we seek long-term, global survival.

Now we will step back to place New Urbanism and Landscape Urbanism within a larger debate that helps us to understand these two movements.

Echoes of a Classic Debate

We argue that there is in fact a common genesis to New Urbanism and Landscape Urbanism and that they — quite unsurprisingly — arise from one of the most persistent intellectual and popular tensions in Anglo-American society: our ambivalence about industrialization. When Leo Marx wrote his 1964 essay on the representation of machines in American literature, *The Machine in the Garden*,[14] he was writing about the fiction literature of the nineteenth century. But he wrote the book and amplified the motif at a moment in time when that ambivalence had broken out into culture wars over social authority, conflicts which reflected that same tension between un-checked industrialized systems driven by historical necessity versus a simpler, kinder conception of nature as an unbroken envelope around human lives.

This ambivalence about industrialization speaks to a long-standing debate about the unresolved relationship between people and non-human nature. The Marxist geographer Neil Smith[15] believes that this debate can be distilled to a question of whether nature is internal or external to the human. William Cronon[16], an environmental historian, recasts it by illustrating how nature is a "profoundly human construction" and thus internal to the individual. However, the cultural notions of nature as either the sublime or the frontier continue to place it external to the individual. Cronon notes that if we view nature as the sublime we "forgive ourselves the homes we actually inhabit … [and we continue the] dangerous dualism that sets human beings outside of nature". If we view nature as the wilderness frontier, we view modernity with hostility for destroying that frontier and thus ending, "the nation's [America's] most sacred myth of origin".

But beyond this uncertain place for nature is the question of sentiment. The modernism–postmodernism rift described by Charles Jencks[17] persists in these debates about machines and systems versus natality[18] and membership in a community of living things. At the root of it all is the turn to secular philosophy and governance that accompanied the Enlightenment, which fundamentally altered cultural and political hierarchies. Since the

Enlightenment made religious authority less important, where could new sources of authority come from? Will authority come from the narrative of industry and pursuit of efficiency, from a notion of systems, from nature, or from the community of human beings? If authority is ascribed to a source that mirrors human consciousness, whether secular or religious, then sentiment has a justifiable presence; if authority is vested in a machine-like logic of systems, then sentiment has no place except as a reminder of human illusions.

As we reflected on the ideas of New Urbanism and Landscape Urbanism when we agreed to write for this book, it occurred to us that these polemical schools of thought can logically be seen as splintered philosophical shards produced by the oedipal clashes between modernism and postmodernism. Where postmodernism embraced sentiment, New Urbanism also embraces sentiment and the attachment of meaning to symbols. Where modernism sought an unsentimental rejection of confining moral codes and aristocratic social orders, Landscape Urbanism rejects sentimentality in favor of representing the world and the city as amoral (not immoral), non-hierarchical, mechanical assemblages,[19] criticizing the small-mindedness of urbanists who denigrate the American love of automobiles, and rejecting what some see as the nostalgia inherent in New Urbanists' sentimental goals.

The reason these schools of thought have become polarizing for some in the design and planning professions is two-fold. First, both make aggressive territorial claims.[20] New Urbanism claimed city-making for architects, and sometimes bemoaned planners' lack of vision;[21] leading proponents of Landscape Urbanism claimed city-making for landscape architects, ideally based on the application of ecological knowledge.[22] By rejecting the traditional hegemony of building architecture as the discipline that claims to give form to city landmarks and districts, they prompted many practitioners in both architecture and landscape architecture to choose "sides" as a matter of positioning. Second, as a result of the Enlightenment's success in Europe and its former colonies, urban design professionals of all stripes must in fact make arguments to establish their authority in a secular world. In doing so, they have constructed a kaleidoscopic patchwork of sources for that authority. New Urbanism has tended to make moral arguments that build on the perceived evils of sprawl, adding functional arguments supported by less than complete evidence (for the pedestrian-friendliness of their formal strategies, for example). Landscape Urbanism has claimed its authority from landscape ecology, but its proponents are generally more fascinated with science as a source of unresolvable indeterminacies, rather than the progressive construction of theory via hypothesis-testing that would be familiar to most actual scientists.

It's not clear how New Urbanism can make claims that extend beyond moral ones without establishing a body of evidence for the relationships between traditional urban forms and human behavior, regional urban growth patterns, and psychological perception that form the basis of their advocacy. Some peer-reviewed research has certainly been published on these relationships,[23] but rarely by the best-known proponents of the New Urbanist school of thought and practice. And some of it shows tenuous or negative results, which should be acknowledged and addressed.[24]

To develop the ideas of Landscape Urbanism, its proponents would have to incorporate some of the insights and perhaps even the experimental methods of landscape ecology and other ecological fields.[25] Almost none of the science related to urban processes and systems is cited in the most widely read theoretical works on Landscape Urbanism.[26] Without that, the movement could easily continue promoting a kind of "systems nihilism," rejecting moral arguments in favor of a fascination with indeterminacy. It is also quite telling that both forms of urbanism have arisen in our current post-industrial era, when the elephant of industrialization has left the room and now pulls most of its strings in the Anglo-American political economy via the financial industry. Perhaps the philosophical and aesthetic aspects of our former production systems can be embraced on an industrial scale only once they have actually moved to Asia and are many steps removed from our immediate experience. Or perhaps hundreds of varieties of urbanism can only arise now because there is no longer any economic logic to urban expansion anymore, other than a recurring finance bubble and a long-term trend towards smaller households.[27]

Global Challenges Require Adaptative and Equitable Approaches to Urbanism

Our own work on cities is done from an epistemological perspective that might be called "normative functionalism," for the sake of building some constructive ambiguity into this debate. We seek active debates about the values of different functions, and we try to increase the successful performance of these functions through programmatic and formal strategies. We look to science for some of our methods, and in general rely on observation as a critical form of knowledge. But we also actively incorporate scholarship on human emotions and ethical positions in translating our observations into recommendations for cities. Cities must be as livable and as sustainable as possible. It is in that spirit that we'd like to consider some of the general ideas of Landscape Urbanism and New Urbanism in relation to what we see as the most significant challenges facing cities.

The new elephant in the room is rapid climate change, and we fully expect to see its effects over the next several decades and more. Our explicitly ethical position is that any "urbanisms" that don't address the pressing need for adaptation to these rapid, overwhelming trends are going to be obsolete very soon. From this position, we advocate specifically for forms and philosophies of urban adaptation that support the most vulnerable humans in our societies, who will be less able to adapt using their own resources. Public space and public funds should be used to increase our broader adaptability, since private funds will surely be used to the advantage of the groups that control them. Our basic philosophy is that today's imperative is for all designers to participate in adaptive urbanism, ideally in support of the most vulnerable human beings, who cannot easily adapt on their own.

Setting Priorities for Urbanisms

As we review the range of possibilities for urban function, we have returned again and again to the magnitude of the changes that climate trends predict over the next several decades. We believe that the disruptions that are predicted to come within the next hundred years are so significant that adaptation should be the primary focus of urban design and planning.[28]

In addition, we have noted that the economics of market-based urbanization have not been widely supportive of New Urbanism.[29] For their part, Landscape Urbanists have yet to promote alternative models of urban development that are ready for implementation. New economic conditions have already begun to emerge that will draw our attention away from Fordism vs. post-Fordism,[30] and these conditions are likely to increasingly constrain our visions for alternative futures that involve New Urban structures.[31]

Significant new burdens on public budgets will be produced by frequent extreme weather events, the gradual processes of reducing freshwater resources, and much higher rates of sea level rise — just to name a few obvious pressures that will result from climate change. Public budgets for infrastructure have already been drastically altered by disinvestment and reduced tax rates, and private asset values have declined precipitously with recent adjustments in the housing market. Current infrastructure projects will tie up the debt capacity of cities for decades, and may not allow them to respond to new demands for additional performance (e.g., holding more rainwater, protecting against more frequent storms, weathering under hotter conditions, protecting a growing residential land area). Coastal changes alone may produce another major readjustment in home values and related markets, as the reality of sea level rise and land erosion becomes apparent to potential buyers, lenders and insurers. In short, we believe that urban development pressures are going to change over the next twenty-five years in ways that will fundamentally alter our conversations about urban design and planning — forcing us to focus more on adaptation and the evidence-based (not purely theoretical) linkages between form and function.

One of our primary concerns is for the most vulnerable members of societies. While this includes many people living in developing nations, we are also deeply concerned about the many American families who are living close to their economic "edge." These at-risk families, who may be just one crisis away from poverty, have been recently estimated to include half of the US population.[32] As climate disruptions occur, producing extreme weather events that challenge public budgets to maintain basic infrastructure and social services, the people most at risk will have a thinner safety net and fewer resources to rebuild than in the past.[33] Climate change will force local, state and federal governments to replace the old "one disaster at a time" response strategy with broader, adaptive approaches.[34] Relatively wealthy families will use their resources to rebuild and eventually relocate as an adaptive response. But if many Americans are one crisis away from poverty, we may see a pattern for those families that looks more like the dislocations produced by Hurricane Katrina in New Orleans — in which people with fewer resources were forced to start over in new cities, to which they were evacuated both by choice and by chance, and could not afford to rebuild their former homes. Flooding will have more severe impacts on people without significant savings than on the wealthy. Urban planners and designers have already begun to develop innovations in stormwater detention as a way of mitigating additional flooding, but these have not yet been widely implemented.[35]

We will also see greater impacts on some neighborhoods, and on all people with cardiopulmonary illnesses, from an increased frequency of summertime heat waves and a related decrease in air quality.[36] Individuals and families are likely to adapt by buying more electrical appliances to cool their homes, producing more electricity demand and waste heat, which will add to the problem. Urban planning and design must address this problem quickly, developing tools that can help predict the performance of alternative programs, plans and designs.[37] Innovations such as green walls and stormwater evaporation trenches can add to the benefits of urban forests generally, but without reasonably accurate predictive models at site, district and metropolitan scales, investments may be made in many cities and districts that do not provide significant performance and health benefits.

We believe this is the time for urbanists to engage in a conversation that sets priorities. Cities in the developed world, and the much larger cities of the developing world, are going to face shape-changing problems driven by extreme weather, lost water resources, flooding and overburdened public budgets. Fundamental ecosystem services that all humans rely on today will be stressed as well; some are likely to be significantly reduced, placing additional burdens on human systems. Regional conflicts are likely to be exacerbated, and many people will be dislocated.[38]

If we look at the data and the trends they imply, the irrefutable priority should be on developing adaptive strategies for urban regions. These strategies will have to consider sentiment as well as systems. We will have to acknowledge human psychology and emotions in our future strategies, as well as the fact that most cities do not have the fiscal capacity to build infrastructure that will prevent major dislocations, even if our technological capacity were adequate — which is a debatable point in itself.

If designers and planners do choose to refocus on what we have called normative functionalism — i.e., structuring debate around the functions we want to provide in cities, using arguments that consider both evidence and ethical positions — we think that professionals and academics will need to position themselves along new lines. The oppositions of modernism and post-modernism might be replaced by a more basic recognition that the machine of industrialization has now fundamentally altered the garden of the environment. Humans are not in control of the changes we have set in motion and now must adapt on a global scale, altering familiar economic and political relationships and even, on the most basic level, altering our sense of what it means to be human in our time — when we can't assume that levees will control floods, cities will have enough water, or that we can cool our homes or breathe city air freely.

The aesthetic experience of people living in cities under these conditions might be a major factor supporting their ability to adapt and incorporate these new realities. Our definition of normative functionalism includes the aesthetic function of design and planning. We will need to activate our cultural strengths of resourcefulness, courage, and compassion to function as urban people, and as communal societies generally.[39] If we hope to develop refinements in our initial ideas over the next several decades of rapid change, designers and planners must begin to address this need today. Can the design of public space help urban communities be more resourceful, or courageous, or compassionate? Excellent design has prompted us to adapt and allowed us to experience shared emotions before — we think of the successful housing experiments of the nineteenth century, when rapid changes in the density of urban populations required adaptations that would support quality of life; infrastructure innovations in the same period that supported human health; and, more recently, memorial designs that have found success as sites of collective memory and places to experience shared emotions.

Components of the contemporary array of "urbanisms" — including the higher-density models of New Urbanism, and the process fascinations of Landscape Urbanism — will undoubtedly persist as necessary strategies in the coming period of rapid urban adaptation we have described in this chapter. The persistent ambiguous attitudes towards technology and industrialization that have been part of the Anglo-American intellectual world for hundreds of years will probably persist as well. But one thing is certain — we will definitely move beyond any dichotomous false oppositions between New Urbanism and Landscape Urbanism, since neither advocacy position is sufficient to address these challenges on its own. We hope something called "adaptive urbanism" or "equitable urbanism" may emerge to replace them. The sooner this happens, the better off we will be fifty years from now.

Endnotes

1　It is interesting to note that many of these early cities were significantly affected by an earlier era of climate change, expressed as changes in sea level: Kennett, Douglas, and James Kennett. 2001. Early state formation in Southern Mesopotamia: Sea levels, shorelines and climate change. *The Journal of Island and Coastal Archaeology* 1, 1: 67–99.

2　Beach, D. 2002. *Coastal Sprawl*. Washington, D.C.: Pew Oceans Commission.

3　Barnett, J. 2011. A Short Guide to 60 of the Newest Urbanisms. *Planning* (April): 19–21. See also Banai, R. and M. A. Rapino. 2009. Urban Theory Since A Theory of Good City Form (1981) — a Progress Review. *Journal of Urbanism: International Research on Placemaking and Urban Sustainability* 2, 3: 259–76; and Bass Warner Jr, S. 1996. Urban Discourse, a Reply to Robert A. Beauregard. *Journal of Urban Affairs* 18, 3: 233–36.

4　"urbanism, n". OED Online. December 2011. Oxford University Press. 16 February 2012 oed.com/viewdictionaryentry/Entry/276005.

5　"urbane, adj.". OED Online. December 2011. Oxford University Press. 16 February 2012 oed.com/view/Entry/220387?redirectedFrom=urbane.

6　"urbanize, v.". OED Online. December 2011. Oxford University Press. 16 February 2012 oed.com/view/Entry/220393?redirectedFrom=urbanize.

7　Katz, Peter. 1994. *The New Urbanism: Toward an Architecture of Community*. New York: McGraw-Hill.

8　Shane, Graham. 2004. The Emergence of Landscape Urbanism: Reflections on "Stalking Detroit," *Harvard Design Magazine* 19: 1–8.

9　Ellin, N. 1996. *Postmodern Urbanism*. Cambridge, MA: Blackwell.

10　Chase, J., M. Crawford, J. Kaliski, Eds. 2008. *Everyday Urbanism*. New York: Monacelli Press.

11　Beatley, T. 2000. *Green Urbanism: Learning from European Cities*. Washington, D.C.: Island Press.

12　Barnett, op cit.

13　Fainstein, S. 2000. New Directions in Planning Theory. *Urban Affairs Review* 35 (March): 451–78.

14　Marx, Leo. 1964. *The Machine in the Garden: Technology and the Pastoral Ideal in America*. New York: Oxford University Press. It is also interesting to note the link to technology and urban/rural conceptions related to the Cold War era effort to decentralize urban populations to mitigate losses in the case of nuclear war, described in detail by Farish, M. 2003. Disaster and Decentralization: American Cities and the Cold War. *Cultural Geographies* 10, 2: 125–48.

15　Smith, N. 1990. *Uneven Development: Nature, Capital and the Production of Space*. Cambridge, MA: Basil Blackwell.

16　Cronon, W. 1995. *Uncommon Ground: Toward Reinventing Nature*. New York: W.W. Norton and Company. Quotes on pgs. 23, 81 and 77.

17　Jencks, C. 1989. *What is Post-Modernism?* London: Academy Editions; see also, Harvey, D. 1990. *The Condition of Postmodernity: An Enquiry into the Origins of Cultural Change*. Oxford and Malden, MA: Blackwell; A. Duany and E. Plater-Zyberk present the core of an argument for the rejection of the values of modernism in *Suburban Nation: The Rise of Sprawl and the Decline of the American Dream*, New York: North Point Press, 2001, p. 11. Hirt develops the argument that New Urbanism is in many ways a postmodern idea, except for its lack of pluralism; Hirt, S. A. 2009. Premodern, Modern, Postmodern? Placing New Urbanism into a Historical Perspective. *Journal of Planning History* 8, 3: 248–73. Meyer noted the tensions between modernism and postmodernism vis-à-vis landscape architecture, with interesting consequences for a reading of landscape urbanism, in Meyer, E. K. 1994. Landscape Architecture as Modern Other and Post-Modern Ground. In H. Edquist and V. Bird, Eds., *The Culture of Landscape Architecture*. Melbourne: Edge Publishing. Pp. 12–34. Pearlman provided an interesting history of modernist urbanism and an early postmodern urbanism in: Pearlman, J. 2000. Joseph Hudnut and the Unlikely Beginnings of Postmodern Urbanism at the Harvard Bauhaus. *Planning Perspectives* 15: 201–239.

18 "Natality" in the sense of Hannah Arendt, who used the term to reflect on the ethics of living a "vita activa" in her book, *The Human Condition*, published by the University of Chicago Press, Chicago, 1958.

19 The term "machanical assemblage" has appeared in translations of Gilles Deleuze and Félix Guattari's book collaboration, *Mille Plateaux*. Paris: Les Editions de Minuit (1980), translated by Brian Massumi as *A Thousand Plateaus*. London and New York: Continuum (2004). A version of this concept was used in a book edited by Mohsen Mostafavi and Ciro Najle, *Landscape Urbanism: A Manual for the Machinic Landscape*, published in 2003 by the Architectural Association in London.

20 Barnett, J. 2011. A Short Guide to 60 of the Newest Urbanisms. *Planning* (April): 19–21. A. Krieger. 2005. In Praise of Un-Heroic Planning: A Response to Emily Talen's Challenge to Planning, *Harvard Design Magazine*, 22, Spring/Summer: 95–96.

21 Krieger, A. 2005. In Praise of Un-Heroic Planning: A Response to Emily Talen's Challenge to Planning, *Harvard Design Magazine*, 22, Spring/Summer: 95–96.

22 Waldheim, C. 2006. *The Landscape Urbanism Reader*. New York, Princeton Architectural Press. Steiner, F. 2011. Landscape Ecological Urbanism: Origins and Trajectories. *Landscape and Urban Planning* 100, 4: 333–37.

23 See for example: Lund, H. 2003. Testing the claims of new urbanism. *Journal of the American Planning Association* 69, 4: 414–29. Jacob, J. S. and R. Lopez. 2009. Is Denser Greener? An Evaluation of Higher Density Development as an Urban Stormwater-Quality Best Management Practice. *Journal of the American Water Resources Association* 45, 3: 687–701. Berg, H. E. and T. K. BenDor. 2010. A Case Study of Form-Based Solutions for Watershed Protection. *Environmental Management* 46, 3: 436–51. GARDE, A. 2006. Designing and Developing New Urbanist Projects in the United States: Insights and Implications. *Journal of Urban Design* 11, 1: 33–54.

24 See for example: Larsen, K. 2005. New Urbanism's Role in Inner-city Neighborhood Revitalization. *Housing Studies* 20, 5: 795–813. Bond, S. and M. Thompson-Fawcett. 2007. Public Participation and New Urbanism: A Conflicting Agenda? *Planning Theory & Practice* 8, 4: 449–72. Clarke, P. 2005. The ideal of community and its counterfeit construction. *Journal of Architectural Education* 58, 3: 43–52. Cozens, P. and D. Hillie. 2008. The Shape of Things to Come: New Urbanism, the Grid and the Cul-De-Sac. *International Planning Studies* 13, 1: 51–73. Evans-Cowley, J. S. and M. Z. Gough. 2009. Evaluating New Urbanist Plans in Post-Katrina Mississippi. *Journal of Urban Design* 14, 4: 439–61. Forsyth, A. and K. Crewe. 2009. New Visions for Suburbia: Reassessing Aesthetics and Place-making in Modernism, Imageability and New Urbanism. Journal of Urban Design 14, 4: 415–38. Winstanley, A., D. Thorns, et al. 2003. Nostalgia, Community and New Housing Developments. Urban Policy and Research 21: 175–89.

25 See for example: Kaye, J., P. Groffman, et al. 2006. A Distinct Urban Biogeochemistry? *Trends in Ecology & Evolution* 21, 4: 192–99. Colding, J. 2007. "Ecological Land-Use Complementation" for Building Resilience in Urban Ecosystems. *Landscape and Urban Planning* 81, 1–2: 46–55. Hall, M. H. P. 2011. A preliminary assessment of socio-ecological metabolism for three neighborhoods within a rust belt urban ecosystem. *Ecological Modelling* 223, 1: 20–31. Pickett, S. T. A., M. L. Cadenasso, et al. 2011. Urban ecological systems: Scientific foundations and a decade of progress. *Journal of Environmental Management* 92, 3: 331–62. Strohbach, M. W., E. Arnold, et al. 2012. The carbon footprint of urban green space — A life cycle approach. *Landscape and Urban Planning* 104, 2: 220–29. These are the types of basic and applied scientific observations and predictions that we would expect to underpin the theories of landscape urbanism, among others, if its proponents were genuinely interested in developing strategies for design interventions based on urban ecology.

26 Waldheim, C. 2006. *The Landscape Urbanism Reader*. New York: Princeton Architectural Press. Mohsen Mostafavi and Ciro Najle, Eds. 2003. *Landscape Urbanism: A Manual for the Machinic Landscape*. London: Architectural Association.

27 Buzar, S., P. E. Ogden, et al. 2005. Households matter: the quiet demography of urban transformation. *Progress in Human Geography* 29, 4: 413–36. Buzar, S., P. Ogden, et al. 2007. Splintering Urban

Populations. *Urban Studies* 44, 4: 651–77; Myers, D. and S. Ryu. 2008. Aging Baby Boomers and the Generational Housing Bubble: Foresight and Mitigation of an Epic Transition. *Journal of the American Planning Association* 74, 1: 17–33.

28 For a thorough, if conservative, review of the trends and likely impacts, see the most recent report of the International Panel on Climate Change (IPCC AR4 SYR (2007), Core Writing Team; Pachauri, R.K; and Reisinger, A., Eds., *Climate Change 2007: Synthesis Report, Contribution of Working Groups I, II and III to the Fourth Assessment Report of the Intergovernmental Panel on Climate Change, (IPCC).* and for a more recent example with relevance to urban populations, see Maantay, Juliana, and Stefan Becker. 2012. The health impacts of global climate change: A geographic perspective. *Applied Geography* 33, 1: 1–3.

29 Mayo, J. M. and C. Ellis. 2009. Capitalist dynamics and New Urbanist principles: junctures and disjunctures in project development. *Journal of Urbanism: International Research on Placemaking and Urban Sustainability* 2, 3: 237–57. Grant, J. 2009. Theory and Practice in Planning the Suburbs: Challenges to Implementing New Urbanism, Smart Growth, and Sustainability Principles. *Planning Theory and Practice* 10, 1: 11–33.

30 Stiglitz, Joseph E. 2007. Bleakonomics, *New York Times Book Review*, 00287806, 9/30/2007.

31 *The Economist*. 2011. Life in the slow lane. 00130613, 4/30/2011, Vol. 398, 8731: 29–31.

32 Allegretto, S. 2011. The state of working America's wealth. Briefing Paper. Washington, D.C.: Economic Policy Institute.

33 Fussell, Elizabeth. 2006. Leaving New Orleans: Social Stratification, Networks, and Hurricane Evacuation. Accessed February 10, 2012, understandingkatrina.ssrc.org/Fussell/

34 Trombetta, M. J. 2008. Environmental security and climate change: analysing the discourse. *Cambridge Review of International Affairs* 21, 4: 585–602.

35 For example, the series of workshops known as the Dutch Dialogues has identified a wide range of options for storing additional stormwater in the city of New Orleans (see dutchdialogues. com). An effort is underway to implement pilot projects via a new Water Management Strategy, which is being developed for the city of New Orleans by a group of local and international participants in the Dutch Dialogues workshops.

36 Mustafic, H., P. Jabre, et al. 2012. Main air pollutants and myocardial infarction. *Journal of the American Medical Association* 307, 7: 713–21; Wellenius, G., M. Burger, et al. 2012. Ambient air pollution and the risk of acute ischemic stroke. *Archive of Internal Medicine* 172, 3: 229–34; Weuve, J., R. Puett, et al. Ibid. Exposure to particulate air pollution and cognitive decline in older women. 219–27. Lai, L.-W. and W.-L. Cheng. 2009. Air quality influenced by urban heat island coupled with synoptic weather patterns. *Science of the Total Environment.* 407, 8: 2724–33; Merbitz, H., M. Buttstädt, et al. 2012. GIS-based identification of spatial variables enhancing heat and poor air quality in urban areas. *Applied Geography* 33, C: 94–106.

37 See for example new predictive models being developed at the University of Gothenburg, Sweden, which are being considered as evaluative tools by Swedish municipal authorities: Svensson, M., S. Thorsson, et al. 2003. A GIS model for creating bioclimatic maps. *International Journal of Biometeorology* 47: 102–112; Thorsson, S., F. Lindberg, et al. 2010. Potential changes in outdoor thermal comfort conditions in Gothenburg, Sweden due to climate change: the influence of urban geometry. *International Journal of Climatology* 31, 2: 324–35.

38 Martin, S. 2010. Climate Change, Migration and Governance. *Global Governance* 16, 3: 397–414.

39 Hill, K. 2011. Crisis, Poignancy and the Sublime. *Topos* 76, September: 47–50. See also a recent discussion and challenge to the so-called declensionist narrative, that cities have only negative impacts on the natural world: Melosi, M. V. 2009. Humans, Cities, and Nature: How Do Cities Fit in the Material World? *Journal of Urban History* 36, 1: 3–21.

14

Talk of Urbanism

JASON BRODY

THE DESIGN MOVEMENTS THAT ARE THE SUBJECT OF THIS BOOK have been advanced through talk in a variety of venues public and private, professional and informal. I define talk as any communication via language between speaker and an audience. In the early urban design conferences and in contemporary debates, across urbanisms ranging from the New to the Everyday to Landscape and Ecological, through touchstone concepts like design and sustainability, we make sense of our world through talk with others. The social nature of talk *moves us* — in the sense of spurring us to action as well as evoking empathy. Talk in this sense is largely moral, addressing what ought to be done.

Talk of urbanism is complex, contingent and embedded in practice. Discursive communities shape our talk by setting norms, framing ways of seeing, sustaining or closing debate, and ordering communicative relations between members and the larger world in which they operate. Talk of urbanism can be rational and sophisticated or ambiguous, contradictory, dishonest or inarticulate.

In this essay I address the talk of urbanism with the hope of rehabilitating the reputation of theorizing in discursive communities — not because we need more dogma, but because I believe that discursive communities and their often-tiresome refrains play minor but necessary roles in preparing design to guide urbanization through the very difficult years that lie ahead. To show this, I first discuss the role of language in constituting discursive communities. I then contrast talk employed by New Urbanism and Landscape Urbanism to cultivate their particular constituencies. In both cases, rhetorical dimensions of talk link audiences in common purpose by framing contrasts, articulating threats, and shaping normative visions. I conclude by discussing discursive communities' interactions with each other and with their environment. The discursive communities that develop through rhetoric enable specialized talk that advances urbanism far beyond what is possible when we toil in isolation.

Language and Discursive Communities

Talk is a richly creative medium. Though both tradition and social institutions discipline our use of language, they pose no great barriers to linguistic invention. The attachment of shared meaning to language is a Sisyphean endeavor in which language is continually formed and reformed through talk as new speakers use language in novel contexts.

So it is with most of the ideas we talk about in urban design. Indeed, the emergence in the fifties of a discourse of urban design is indicative of the power of talk to crystallize meaning — to call attention, in Bateson's words, to a "difference that makes a difference."[1] The early talk of urban design suggests four overlapping implications regarding the construction of leading ideas. First, talk of urban design was historically contingent, responding to the rapid proliferation of post-war suburbs through a renewed interest in the historic city core. Second, urban design had multiple determinants: it stemmed from architecture and planning, CIAM and Team 10, the historic city and metropolitan sprawl, and, to varying degrees, aesthetic, social, environmental and political dilemmas. Third, talk of urban design was embedded in practice, concerned with the arrangement of the functional uses of buildings and the roles that designers played in the shaping of the city. Finally, talk of urban design was normative. It made value claims about the city as a material and cultural object as well as arguments about who urban designers are, how they ought to pursue their work, and what connections should be made across the design disciplines. Speculative and provisional, this talk embedded within urban design a complex assemblage of information and ideas. The language of urban design and the discourse that that language signified were mutually defining.

The theoretical movements that are rife in urban design follow a similar pattern. Current urbanisms — New, Landscape, Everyday, Fluid, Fast-Forward, Ecological — are part of a long tradition of talk that frames urban design by appending a descriptive adjective to urbanism or the city. This kind of talk in itself is not a substitute for deep contextual thinking about particular dilemmas in the workaday practice of urban design, but it can accomplish real communicative work by shaping meaning of language and focusing the attention of an audience on a particular frame of interpretation. Importantly, talk of urbanism in this sense presumes — indeed, constitutes — a discursive community interested in the dilemmas, values, roles, and positions embodied in its discourse.[2] Underlying talk of urbanism are implicit claims of authority by designers over the shaping of cities[3] — claims that, needless to say, do not go unchallenged by politicians, the public, other occupations, or rival design discourses.

The language used to signify discursive communities matters. Naming is a claim that a difference is significant. Urban design discourses, though, are complex, contingent, embedded in practice, and normative. They are dynamic as well. Resilient discursive communities need appellations that, like New Urbanism or Landscape Urbanism, are tantalizingly ambiguous — suggestive enough to call attention to the substance of their discourse but sufficiently vague to be able to envelop multiple agendas, address multiple audiences, and sustain continued development of a discourse over time.

The "Talk" of New Urbanism

New Urbanist appeals to tradition such as "Traditional Neighborhood Development" are rhetorical strategies as well as sources of design principles. To some extent talk of tradition provides evidential backing; it also enlarges the audience for New Urbanism by communicating through concepts that are widely shared. Duany and Plater-Zyberk's appropriation of the neighborhood unit concept is a good example of this. Note how they stitch together a set of historic and contemporaneous examples in their talk of neighborhood:

> The nomenclature may vary, but there is general agreement regarding the physical composition of the neighborhood. The "neighborhood unit" of the 1929 New York Regional

Plan, the "quartier" identified by Leon Krier, the "traditional
neighborhood development" (TND) and "transit-oriented
development" (TOD) share similar attributes. They all
propose a model of urbanism that is limited in area and structured around a defined center. While the population density
may vary, depending on its context, each model offers a balanced mix of dwellings, workplaces, shops, civic buildings
and parks.[4]

— (Duany and Plater-Zyberk 1994).

Duany and Plater-Zyberk's synthesis demands a level of abstraction.
Though it calls attention to common elements of the examples cited it
glosses over both substantive differences among them and the contexts
from which they were drawn.

The conceptual stretching required for this maneuver is evidenced
by comparison of the best-known of Perry's original diagrams for the
neighborhood unit with two versions created by Duany and Plater-
Zyberk. Duany and Plater-Zyberk's first version of a neighborhood unit
(Figure 14.1) was a conscious imitation of Perry's diagram (Figure 14.2),

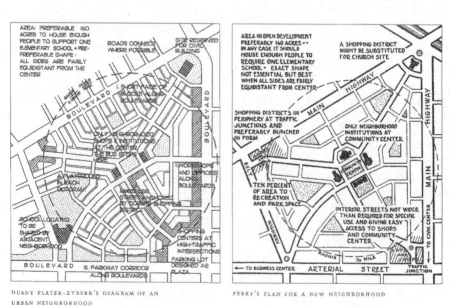

DUANY PLATER-ZYBERK'S DIAGRAM OF AN   PERRY'S PLAN FOR A NEW NEIGHBORHOOD
URBAN NEIGHBORHOOD

Fig. 14.1 and 14.2.

borrowing not just substantive ideas but also form. This stylistic imitation of Perry provides a clear context for interpreting innovations introduced by Duany and Plater-Zyberk (principally a better-connected street grid). Duany and Plater-Zyberk's latter version of the neighborhood unit (Figure 14.3) is a significant substantive and formal departure, however — substantive in dissecting the elementary school from the central core of the neighborhood and formal in departing from the pentagonal form of Perry's diagram.

If the latter version is more reflective of the principles underlying Duany and Plater-Zyberk's practice of neighborhood planning, it is the initial version that accomplishes the rhetorical work of embedding their ideas in talk acknowledged by a larger audience. The loss of fidelity inherent in amalgamating a set of nuanced and loosely related ideas into a general discourse (or in weakening articulation of their own principles to more closely mimic Perry's) is compensated by the strength of the community that the discourse nurtures.

The New Urbanists were particularly adept at using the villainy of modernist urbanism to rally the troops. As Yaro noted in a different

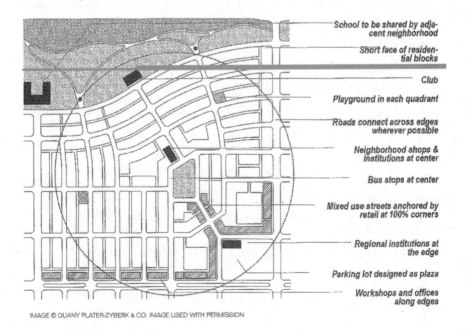

School to be shared by adjacent neighborhood

Short face of residential blocks

Club

Playground in each quadrant

Roads connect across edges wherever possible

Neighborhood shops & institutions at center

Bus stops at center

Mixed use streets anchored by retail at 100% corners

Regional institutions at the edge

Parking lot designed as plaza

Workshops and offices along edges

IMAGE © DUANY PLATER-ZYBERK & CO. IMAGE USED WITH PERMISSION

Fig. 14.3.

context, communities seem to respond to the perception of a common threat.[5] Thus New Urbanists often cast modern architecture as the villain in a story of how American urbanism lost its way. In *The New Urbanism: Towards an Architecture of Community*, for instance, Scully argued that "community is what America has most conspicuously lost, and community is precisely what the canonical Modern architecture and planning ... were totally unable to provide. This was so for many reasons; foremost among them was the fact that the Modern architects of the heroic period ... all despised the traditional city."[6] Kunstler went further: modern architects — "with the hubris of religious zealots," he says — "set out on a great purifying mission that damaged the whole physical setting for civilization in our time."[7] Daniel Solomon blamed Le Corbusier for misleading an entire generation.[8] Talk of villainy is moral talk. It can infuse a nascent community with a sense of righteous urgency.

Equally as telling is Duany and Plater-Zyberk's diagram[9] (Figure 14.4) that attempts to draw a distinction between conventional development and a preferred alternative. The effectiveness of this kind of diagram lies less in its sophistication than in the contrasts it draws. The diagram manipulates in a manner not unlike commercials for weight loss programs or baldness cures. Difference is brought into focus through the juxtaposition of suburban sprawl (the "before" picture)

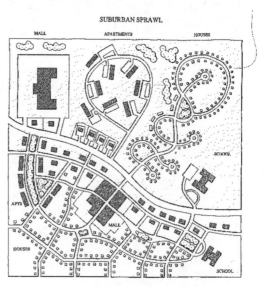

Fig. 14.4.

and traditional neighborhood (the "after"). The diagram makes stark distinctions between each and assigns them strong, even unreasonable, value judgments. Suburban sprawl in the diagram is essentially framed as a pathology that threatens our well-being. The diagram suggests not merely that one might be able to get around more easily in a traditional neighborhood (i.e., the rhetorical "after" picture) but also that our lives would be better, healthier and more rewarding for it. The binary juxtaposition pushes us to encounter each model as a whole, to ascribe blanket value judgments to each, and to choose between one or the other. The diagram operates as a sorting machine, obliterating subtlety and pushing us to either value traditional form over suburban sprawl or to reject the New Urbanists' claim altogether.

Whether we subscribe to these kinds of discourses or repudiate them, we tend to presume a level of rationality and detached professionalism in the talk of urbanism. Yet talk of urbanism is often inchoate, and it can exhibit the biases of advocates actively engaged in the construction, debate and winnowing of shared ideas and values. Rhetorical dimensions to our talk are geared towards the constitution of normative discursive communities that make critical value judgments and are actively invested in shaping the direction of urbanism's development.

The "Talk" of Landscape Urbanism

Like New Urbanism before it, Landscape Urbanism grew out of local conversations among a community of friends and colleagues — in this case within the Landscape Architecture and Regional Planning program at the University of Pennsylvania. Many of the thought leaders in Landscape Urbanism, including Alan Berger, James Corner, Anuradha Mathur, Moshen Mostafavi, Chris Reed and Charles Waldheim, either taught at or attended Penn (or both) in the early nineties. Beginning at Penn, they drew on landscape traditions to develop what has become an ambitious, dense approach to urbanism whose possibilities have yet to be fully realized.

Landscape Urbanism developed around two critiques. The first concerned modernism's impotency in directing urban change. Works like *Stalking Detroit*[10] and *Drosscape*[11] called attention to the waste and abandonment left in capitalism's wake, particularly in an era of industrial decline. They questioned the efficacy of the modernist project (driven by the rational plan and preoccupied with the spatial arrangement of buildings) to shape urbanism given the dominance of political, economic and technological forces. This criticism pointed towards a "fast-forward urbanism" that might "recognize the catalytic agency of form"[12] through opportunistic design strategies critically engaging neoliberal development.

Landscape Urbanism came into focus through a critique of the contemporary state of landscape architecture. In a series of articles in the nineties James Corner attacked the "cultural atrophy" of landscape architecture practiced as a design discipline.[13] Landscape Urbanists questioned the preservationist ethic implicit in the environmentally oriented practices that developed after McHarg's *Design with Nature*.[14] Corner argued instead for treating landscape as an "active instrument in the shaping of culture," drawing on central tenets of landscape architecture — including landscape, ecology, systems thinking and change over time — to inform a design practice capable of directing urbanism in a way that modernism could not.[15] Typical of discursive communities, Landscape Urbanism addressed specific practices developing out of multiple, historically contingent events.

One of the ways that the talk of Landscape Urbanism has advanced beyond these initial criticisms has been by mining the etymology of its language for deeper and more varied meaning. Corner, for instance, contrasted the representational connotations of *landskip* and *landschap* with the productive and cultural dimensions of the *landschaft*.[16] Girot and Mathur deepened landscape's meaning through explication of the cultural variants of *paysage* and the *maidan*.[17] In the same volume David Leatherbarrow drew on the etymology of *terrain, territory, textile* and *techne* in an effort to tease out implications of topological intervention[18]; Kwinter has engaged in similarly challenging etymological arguments.[19] Such hermeneutic work is inherently creative. Rather than pinning discourse back to definitions fixed by history it stalks the dusty imprints left in distant conversations for sources of inspiration and renewal. In this regard it is analogous to the inventive wordplay evidenced in the coining of terms like *landscraping*.[20]

Like most talk in urban design, Landscape Urbanism also developed through valorization of precedents. Projects like West 8's Schouwburg-plein and Peter Latz's Landscahftspark at Duisburg-Nord become

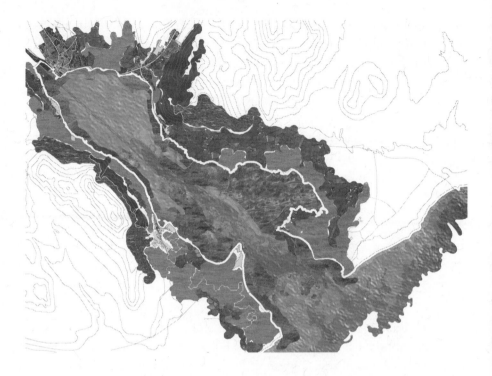

Fig. 14.5: *Tidal Ecologies.* JESSICA CANFIELD, ASSISTANT PROFESSOR, KANSAS STATE UNIVERSITY

exemplars that stake the territory of Landscape Urbanism by representing the promise of, for example, programmed surfaces, strategic indeterminacy, and ecological and cultural succession. Talk of precedent synthesizes a meshwork of ideas not into a singular agenda as much as an emergent sensibility. Competitions have been fruitful in this regard by providing forums for the development of and debate over a body of creative work offering a range of approaches to a common program.[21] Particularly significant has been Parc de la Villette. Both the Koolhaas/OMA entry and Tschumi's winning proposal presaged Landscape Urbanism with schemes eschewing formal design in favor of organizational strategy. Carefully seeding a field with infrastructure and program offered a framework for structuring activity, a loose design approach that might accommodate change and succession over time. The entries pointed towards an emergent urbanism accomplished through the "staging of uncertainty" and "irrigation of territories of potential."[22] Discursive communities like Landscape Urbanism are shaped by the precedents that they talk about.

Its talk of the Koolhaas/OMA scheme for Parc de la Villette suggests that Landscape Urbanism is less concerned with addressing environmental imperatives than it is with using the tropes of environmental systems to inform a practice of urban design. As the landscape architect and urbanist Blake Belanger explains,

> Thinking of cities as ecologies serves two purposes [for landscape architecture students]. In simple terms it provides a useful lexicon that they are already familiar with from natural systems courses, including such concepts as thresholds, cycles and feedback. At a higher level, it helps students to see that cities function ecologically — in terms of flows of energy and information and in the interactions of social, financial, technological and environmental systems.[23]

A critical differentiator between Landscape Urbanism and the long tradition of organicism dating back to Mumford, Geddes and Howard — a tradition that includes many New Urbanists — is Landscape Urbanism's appreciation of recent advances in nonlinear dynamics.[24] Viewing landscapes as "dynamic mosaics" with "shifting nodes of interaction"[25] calls attention not to order but to structuring change.[26]

Landscape Urbanism's real contribution thus far has been translating theoretical concerns into modes of practice, including models of ecological succession[27] and tremendous innovation in diagramming,[28] that in sum suggest roles design might play in addressing multiple dimensions of performance and in structuring dynamic processes of urbanization. This contribution (like the development of form-based codes within New Urbanism) emerges from sophisticated technical talk of the sort that is only possible within an active discursive community whose members share a set of mores governing their discussion.

Discursive Ecologies

Urban design discourses unfold in a dynamic stream of activity in the midst of issues, solutions, actors, institutions, sites and decision situations that are also in the process of unfolding.[29] Urban design discourses engage this stream of activity while already partially formed. They bring the accumulated norms, practices, roles and frames that comprise their discourse with them. This is not to say that discourses impose ready-made solutions; only that they draw the activity they encounter into an already ongoing conversation.

New Urbanism and Landscape Urbanism are rival communities. Exerting similar claims of authority over the city, they compete for attention — from clients, institutions, authorities and acolytes. Like *frenemies*, rivals follow each other, envying each other's successes and becoming piqued by each other's idiosyncrasies. Rival discourses frame our engagement in the talk of urbanism; though we value individual designers, projects and ideas in their own right we also respond to discourses as a whole. We set agendas and orient our perspective in response to particular discourses.[30] Though crude, ideological and often petty, rivalry nonetheless instigates two dynamics that matter to the ongoing development of urban design: the sorting of heterogeneous agents into loose or deep membership in differentiating communities, and the striving of competing communities to win new ground.[31]

New Urbanism and Landscape Urbanism's recent encounters with the environmental moment — whether via the nebulous guise of sustainability or in the more pointed form of Drew Gilpin Faust — are rather like running into an old friend. Environmental ethics informed both movements even before they were formed, but in neither case was environmentalism a prime force in their development. Grounded in talk of community and codes, of program, staging and indeterminacy, New Urbanism and Landscape Urbanism now revisit environment. Through the encounter they may (a) interpret environment through the developed lenses of their communities, (b) re-present their talk to address environmental concerns, or (c) embark on fundamentally new conversations. Though the environmental moment seems to promise a new phase of urban design, it may easily become another passing conversation, part of our culture but largely forgotten.

The recent emergence of Ecological Urbanism has renewed interest in the third ecology — i.e., the "existential ecologies" or "eco-mental system" that inform our interactions with our environment. Drawing on Bateson[32] and the polemics of Guattari,[33] Mostafavi and Kwinter[34] suggest that the environmental dilemmas of the twenty-first century necessitate a new way of thinking, a shift from the mechanistic worldview[35] characteristic of capitalism to one that informs a less destructive pattern of behavior. As Kwinter argues, "the challenges of ecological thinking are found principally in the deepest arenas of our imaginative and intellectual life." A new "ecosophy" is not likely to emerge merely from rational argument, however. Talk of the third ecology will be contingent, complex, ambiguous and contradictory. It will be social and local. It will come into being through tragedies like Stuttgart 21 and Love Canal. Designers interested in development of a third ecology should attend to the cultivation of communicative infrastructure — communities and networks, exemplars and refrains — and to the unseemly political work of framing brute narratives and forging pragmatic but necessary coalitions.

Endnotes

1   Bateson, Gregory. 1972. *Steps to an Ecology of Mind.* New York: Ballantine.

2   Throgmorton, James A. 1996. *Planning as Persuasive Storytelling: The Rhetorical Construction of Chicago's Electric Future.* Chicago: University of Chicago Press.

3   E.g., "Across a range of disciplines, landscape has become a lens through which the contemporary city is represented and a medium through which it is constructed," from Charles Waldheim. 2006. A Reference Manifesto. In Charles Waldheim, Ed., *The Landscape Urbanism Reader.* New York: Princeton Architectural Press.

4   Duany, Andrés and Elizabeth Plater-Zyberk. 1994. The Neighborhood, the District, and the Corridor. In Peter Katz, Ed., *The New Urbanism: Toward an Architecture of Community.* New York: McGraw-Hill.

5   Yaro, Robert D. 2000. Growing and Governing Smart: A Case Study of the New York Region. In Bruce Katz, Ed., *Reflections on Regionalism.* Washington, D. C.: The Brookings Institution.

6   Scully, Vincent. 2000. The Architecture of Community. In Peter Katz, Ed., *The New Urbanism: Toward an Architecture of Community.* New York: McGraw-Hill.

7   Kunstler, James Howard. 1993. *The Geography of Nowhere.* New York: Touchstone.

8   Solomon, Daniel. 2003. *Global City Blues.* Washington, D. C.: Island Press.

9   Diagram by Andrés Duany and Elizabeth Plater-Zyberk, in *The New Urbanism: Toward an Architecture of Community.*

10 Daskalakis, George, Charles Waldheim, and Jason Young, Eds. 2001. *Stalking Detroit.* Barcelona: ACTAR.

11 Berger, Alan. 2006. *Drosscape: Wasting Land in Urban America.* New York: Princeton Architectural Press.

12 Cuff, Dana and Roger Sherman. 2011. *Fast-Forward Urbanism: Rethinking Architecture's Engagement with the City.* New York: Princeton Architectural Press.

13 Corner, James. 1999. Recovering Landscape as a Critical Cultural Practice. In James Corner, Ed., *Recovering Landscape: Essays in Contemporary Landscape Architecture.* New York: Princeton Architectural Press.

14 Treib, Marc. "Nature Recalled" in *Recovering Landscape.*

15 Corner, James. 1997. Recovering Landscape as a Critical Cultural Practice. In *Recovering Landscape;* and Corner, James. 1997. Ecology and Landscape as Agents of Creativity. In George F. Thompson and Frederick R. Steiner, Eds., *Ecological Design and Planning.* New York: J. Wiley.

16 Corner, James. 1997. Eidetic Operations and New Landscapes. In *Recovering Landscape.*

17 Girot, Christophe. 1997. Four Trace Concepts in Landscape Architecture. In *Recovering Landscape;* Mathur, Anuradha. 1997. Neither Wilderness nor Home: The Indian Maidan. In *Recovering Landscape.*

18 Leatherbarrow, David. 1997. Leveling the Land. In *Recovering Landscape.*

19 Kwinter, Sanford. 2002. American Design? *Praxis* 4: 6-9.

20 James Corner. 2001. Landscraping. In *Stalking Detroit.*

21 See, e.g. the essays in Czerniak, Julia, Ed. 2001. *Case: Downsview Park Toronto.* Munich: Prestel Verlag.

22 Koolhaas, Rem and Bruce Mau. 1995. *S, M, L, XL.* New York: Monacelli Press.

23 Blake Belanger, personal communication, January 13, 2012. Belanger teaches in the Department of Landscape Architecture / Regional and Community Planning at Kansas State University.

24 DeLanda, Manuel. 1997. *A Thousand Years of Non-Linear History.* New York: Zone Books.

25 Hill, Kristina. 2005. Shifting Sites. In Carol J. Burns and Andrea Kahn, Eds., *Site Matters: Design Concepts, Histories, and Strategies.* New York: Routledge.

26 Reed, Chris. 2010. The Agency of Ecology. In Mohsen Mostafavi, Ed., *Ecological Urbanism.* Baden, Switzerland: Lars Müller Publishers.

27 Waldheim, Charles and Marili Santos-Munné. 2001. Decamping Detroit. In *Stalking Detroit;* and James Corner and Stan Allen. 2001. Emergent Ecologies. In *Case: Downsview Park Toronto.*

28 Reeser, Amanda and Ashley Schafer. 2002. Approaching Landscapes. *Praxis* 4. Somol, R.E. 2001. All Systems GO! In *Case: Downsview Park Toronto.*

29 Cf. Hopkins discussion of a stream of opportunities in Hopkins, Lewis D. 2001. *Urban Development: The Logical of Making Plans.* Washington: Island Press.

30 One example of many: "But I would also stress that Landscape Urbanism was developed in some ways as a direct critique of New Urbanism"— quote of Charles Waldheim in Stein, Jeff. 2010. Groundswell: The rise of landscape urbanism — Charles Waldheim talks with Jeff Stein AIA. *ArchitectureBoston*: Fall.

31 See Duany's discussion of "plugs" and "power grids" in Duany, Andrés. 2011. New Urbanism: The Case for Looking Beyond Style. *Metropolis:* April.

32 Bateson, Gregory. 1972. *Steps to an Ecology of Mind.*

33 Guattari, Félix. 2000 [1989]. *The Three Ecologies.* Ian Pindar and Paul Sutton, trans. London: Athlone Press.

34 Mostafavi, Mohsen. 2011. Why Ecological Urbanism? Why Now? In *Ecological Urbanism.* Kwinter, Sanford. 2011. Notes on the Third Ecology. In *Ecological Urbanism.*

35 Mumford, Lewis. 1967. *The Myth of the Machine: Technics and Human Development.* New York: Harcourt.

15

Articulating Landscape Urbanism

JUSUCK KOH

LANDSCAPE AS AN IDEA AND PRACTICE has received increasing attention and application during the last three decades among various environmental designers, planners, scientists and policy makers. Landscape Urbanism, however, still remains characterized by practice-directed strategies and methods rather than coherent and grounded theories substantiated by empirical science.

This paper offers a refined, and more theoretically grounded, definition of Landscape Urbanism that is rooted in the distinction between an "architectural approach" and a "landscape approach" to urbanism. I argue that as an emergent project and practice, Landscape Urbanism has yet to be conclusively and coherently defined, in part because it lacks a more nuanced understanding of what distinguishes a "landscape approach." This weakness must be addressed if Landscape Urbanism is to move foreword.

Consider the following two definitions of Landscape Urbanism:

> Landscape Urbanism describes a disciplinary realignment currently underway in which landscape replaces architecture as the basic building block of contemporary urbanism. For many, across a range of disciplines, landscape has become both the lens through which the contemporary

city is represented and the medium through which it is
constructed.[1]

[Landscape Urbanism is an] "inside-out reversal of the city/
landscape relationship ... placing open space concerns at
the core of planning and design of urban areas."[2]

Bunster-Ossa's definition suggests a view of landscape as open space
in and around the city. Waldheim's definition of Landscape Urbanism is
descriptive in that it describes what is happening, and metaphoric in that
it does not build upon science and philosophy.

What is needed is a way of prescribing Landscape Urbanism as an
empirically based paradigm and discipline, one with a coherent theory
and methodology. We should not be content with an operational use of
landscape as an instrument, or the metaphoric use of landscape as an
idea.

A theory of Landscape Urbanism hinges upon what we mean by
"landscape" and "urbanism." Enough theory exists on urbanism, in spite
of Koolhaas' eloquent criticism,[3] and even more rigorous critique by
Cuthbert.[4] The essence of urbanism and the city is diversity, richness,
density, stimulation, trade, interchange and exchange, culture and consumption. An attribute of the ideal city may be contact-maximizing and
travel-minimizing.

In order to define Landscape Urbanism, it is important to clarify
the distinction between a "landscape approach" and an "architectural
approach" in defining urbanism. The latter is characterized as a naïve
conception of the city as big architecture with an accompanying belief
that architects can design cities with the same approach and individual
creativity applied to building design. Sola-Morales in *Terrain Vague* characterizes such an architectural approach:

> Architecture's destiny has always been colonization, the
> imposing of limits, order and form, the introduction into
> strange space of elements of identity necessary to make it
> recognizable, identical, universal. In essence, architecture
> acts as an instrument of organization, of rationalization, and
> of productive efficiency capable of transforming the uncivi-
> lized into the cultivated, the fallow into the productive, the

void into the built …. architecture is forever on the side of forms, of the distant, of optical and figurative, while the divided individual of contemporary city looks for forces instead of forms, for the incorporated instead of the distant, for the haptic instead of optic, the rhyzomatic instead of the figurative.[5]

The early modernist urbanism espoused by CIAM (and its followers until the 1960s) was an architectural approach only relevant to Western culture. There has been no such form-oriented approach and conception of architecture as pure creation in Eastern culture. Western European civilization has always been more centered on urban culture (Watt 1958), and urbanism after the Renaissance and Enlightenment paid heavy attention to form and architecture. The centrality of the market in the European city illustrates and symbolizes this importance in spatial form in Western European culture.

An architectural approach to design as I characterize it here is generally imperial, willful, goal-directed, anthropo- and egocentric, authorial (believing in individual creativity and thus even copyright), and closed to change and modification. Based on vision and form-thinking, it is compositional, representational and geometric, as well as inside-out oriented and centered on architecture. This tradition is inseparable from the very history of Western art itself, which has been patronized by the powerful and wealthy, is associated with power, and was used as tool for the display of wealth, taste, culture and faith in the absolute and divine God.[6] Clearly, the fundamental point of architecture is to colonize, structure and build, rather than to conserve and to protect the environment. And art in the Western sense is about being artificial and man-made, not natural.

In comparison, a landscape approach is community-based. It combines construction with management, development with conservation, and space-based thinking with process-oriented thinking. It combines form design with experience design. It seeks aesthetic engagement, participatory design, and stewardship. This approach is fundamentally rooted in the very concept of land — meaning *land and people*; and in the concept of landscape, *landschap*, meaning shaping, conserving, fellowship or home. It is both physical and poetic, process and experience.[7]

This phenomenological and cultural orientation is missing in the current discourse of Landscape Urbanism.

Landscape Urbanism recognizes landscape as both the material process and the physical product of cumulative, ongoing, dynamic human engagement. It is engagement in the sense of both shaping and managing over time, a practice rooted in agricultural rather than industrial and linear processes. This engagement is cyclic: preparation, seeding, tendering, harvesting, replenishing; again and again.[8]

Ten Defining Characteristics of Landscape Urbanism

If Landscape Urbanism is to be more than an opportunistic and trendy appropriation of the idea of "landscape," we have to appreciate fully the implications of a landscape approach. I offer now ten defining characteristics of Landscape Urbanism, which together provide the basis of a more theoretically coherent notion of what the term actually means. They are: (1) Integrative, (2) Generative, (3) Dynamic, (4) Strategic, (5) Land-economic, (6) Bottom-up, (7) Phenomenological, (8) Ordinary, (9) Postmodern, and (10) Eco-feminist.

Though these characteristics are interrelated and reflective of the contemporary condition of life and epistemology, each deserves a separate elaboration.

1. Integrative design and urbanism

The city as landscape implies spatial and material/process integration between urban and rural areas, or between built-up and open areas. It also means that various functions in the city are integrated and should be designed in an integrative way. The integration in this case is not so much an exclusive internal integration of system itself, but an inclusive integration of a system with other systems and its environment.

This urban and rural integration is already practiced by the planning and landscape disciplines in Western European countries. Yet it is a significant development. The dictionary meaning of urbanism refers to (1) *the conditions or characteristic way of life of those who live in an urban area* and (2) *the study and theory of building and other physical needs in cities or predominantly urban culture.* (Webster's 1976) In Latin, *urbs* connotes city as much as wall. *Urbs* thus refers to a city with a wall and is a reference to the Roman colonizers' outposts with defensive walls. (At the architectural scale Western architecture of the pre-modern period can be characterized as architecture of the wall, separating indoor from outdoor.) This wall effected not only a spatial and physical separation of the urban and rural, but also a conceptual and cultural separation. Furthermore, in the West the city was privileged over the countryside and was the economic, political, cultural and religious center. Church and market occupied a place in the city center. *Urbanite* and *urbanity* implied being well bred and cultured. This is the story and history of western European cities before modernization. How then should a city without physical, conceptual and legal walls look and function? How should a future city look that is no longer defined by a colonial power with defensive needs? Would it look like a conglomerated or networked town, or a city with extensive sub-urbs, or would it perhaps be a "trans-urb"?

The process integration between city and countryside refers to the relationship between production and consumption, entropy and negentropy, oxygen and carbon dioxide, as well as the natural process of water, climate, wildlife, and so on. Given today's globalized living, with a new focus on the localization of food and fuel supplies through urban agriculture and renewable local energy production, landscape can be a multifunctional machine or medium for energy, water, food, and even waste treatment. It also means that open space such as the urban park becomes multifunctional beyond recreation, integrating various functions. Productive land such as an urban farm can be re-creative land, while re-creative land such as an urban park can be productive and functional as a water retention area and wildlife habitat. The majority of cities in the developed countries today have gotten rid of polluting industries and unhealthy workplaces. We don't need the kind of parks and open spaces that are the product of nineteenth-century urbanism, particularly when they are costly to maintain, and scenic but not ecological.[9]

Integrative design also means integrating spatial thinking with time thinking. Landscape changes over space as well as over time. Both in the process and in our experience of landscape, space and time are indivisible and interrelated. There is time in space and space in time. Landscape makes our experience of time much more poignant than architecture or cities. Lynch, in *What Time is this Place?*, points out the important role the park plays in urban living by raising our awareness of time passing and change occurring.

There are ample examples of spatial and process integration of the urban and rural, the natural and cultural, landscape and city: the Chandigarh plan of Le Corbusier; the gardens that were the corner stones of Persian cities;[10] the city plan of Savannah, Georgia, in the US; or Chinese cities following the feng shui principle. If the garden city of Ebenezer Howard was a response to the industrial city, the landscape city of process and space integration can be a postmodern ecological response to modernity.

2. Generative design

A landscape approach to the design of the city means that urban design is searching for emergent form rather than preconceived final form. What is designed and ordered is not so much the form as the process and the process of change. Such dynamic and adaptive design addresses not just growth and development but also shrinking, not just development but recycling and restructuring. Self-organization, life cycle, system development, emergence and evolution are key concepts in generative design. In such an approach, the life of the community contains and necessitates the death of the individual, just as our living body and landscape involve numerous deaths of cells or organisms.

This explains the shift in urbanism from a mega-structure approach to the combination of a mega- and micro-structure approach; from a top-down, linear master plan approach to an incremental, interactive and participatory approach; from a goal-directed (leading to final or ideal form and image of utopia) to a principle-guided approach; from closed design to open design; from conceiving the city as a machine to seeing it as an intelligent, living, learning, self-organizing system; from a market-economy-based efficiency to one which incorporates environmental economy and evolutionary consequences. Generative design conceptualizes city and community as one system, and requires community empowerment, self-design and self-similarity as well as a city-people system as its adaptive structure. Here the initial image of the city is that of an embryo.

Given the scale, complexity, rapidity of change, uncertainty, and inherent indeterminacy of the city and the urbanization process, this seems to me the only sensible approach. The city is not mega architecture. The scale and nature of the problems dictate the methods of design. Methods that work at the building scale do not necessarily work at the city scale. Livable cities cannot be made in one generation. We can think of various examples of generative design in a landscape approach, or landscape restructuring: the regeneration of former coal mine sites in the IBA See project and the "shrinking cities" in eastern Germany; the regeneration of the Ruhr area into Emscher Park; the "growing structure" approach in adapting the enclosure dike and coastal defense line of the Netherlands and the "Room for the River" realignment of its Lower Rhine River zones; or the frequently cited Fresh Kills and Downsview parks in North America. In all these projects the designer's role is less to give a final form and more to create the conditions and kick off the process, letting the community take ownership of the design and management.

3. Dynamic design

Design in Landscape Urbanism is like large-scale landscape design itself. It is not only about the design of dynamic processes but also about designing along these processes as construction and development unfold new problems and opportunities. The city, integrated with landscape's natural processes and the community's social process, is a dynamic and living system. The uncertainty of the future and the risk associated with the outcome of initial provisionary actions require designing with and for time, as much as designing with nature and community. Here a linear approach with a final predetermined image and unshattered confidence . in science do not work. The situation is fluid. The market will change quickly, as will politics. Landscape itself changes and so do governing principles.

Even in a self-organizing system such as an ecosystem, governing principles change: growth and relative uniformity are emphasized in the early phase while distribution and diversification rule when the system reaches maturity and a stable state.[11] This shift finds its parallel in inorganic self-organizing systems: order (conservation of energy) prevails when the system is near equilibrium, and disorder (waste of energy) at the far-from-equilibrium state.[12] Order is not always good, disorder not always bad, and there is some social need and economic justification for disorder as well. Besides, order and disorder are mutually relative and complementary in this world of nested hierarchy. Order at one level can be disorder at another. Thus dynamic design also implies a shifting emphasis between ordering and disordering, and balancing of the top-down approach with the bottom-up approach: top-down when rapid development and economic growth are at stake and bottom-up when social stability and distributional justice and democracy are important. The economist's term for creative destruction, and the Landscape Urbanist's (such as Alan Berger's) recognition of the waste of contemporary cities in America as a sign of a healthy economic process, can be understood in the context of what I call dynamic balancing of order and disorder.[13]

All this means that design of Landscape Urbanism and the city has to be open, resilient and adaptive, with no fixed end vision. Basic guiding principles can be set: sustainability, justice, diversity, identity, community, and so on. Recognition and tolerance of the local and transitional messiness of an in-between state of development (or an early phase of development such as urbanization or industrialization), and of the liberating and informal effect of disorder, are essential. So is providing a creative outlet for this disorderly process, including accidents, uncontrollability and unpredictability, and the ability to design and live with ambiguity and indeterminacy. Design is conceived here as a kind of seeding. It provides a script to be played out with certain improvisation as it proceeds. In this case, the design approach must be planned, both in terms of open-endedness and reiteration. Design thus becomes a verb, designing.

Order and ordering, however, require a constant supply of surplus energy, including human energy. Leaving both city and city design open-ended is the key (to saving energy). Perhaps this dynamic view is best grasped by the ancient Chinese philosophy of yin-yang. Unlike the western concept of static balance and equilibrium of forces, yin-yang refers to the reconciliation of opposing and different qualities in flux. This view is recently vindicated by science's recognition of a non-equilibrium view of the system.[14]

4. Strategic design

Strategy is a game plan. As such it needs to be played out in the face of the unknowability of the opponent's plans, uncertain market forces and political processes, and uncertainty about how different context scenarios will play out. In the past, architects and urban designers often used nature's structure as a strategy for design.[15] Trees, spinal skeletons, spider webs or honeycombs have inspired many architects historically. While we now recognize that "the city is not a tree" and that we are not animals or plants, we can nevertheless use landscape structure and process as strategy for design of the city and region. As for human-made structure, the grid has proved to be an effective organizing strategy for colonized towns as well as for large territorial division in the Midwestern United States — the Jeffersonian grid (which itself is a form of colonization). Yet the grid is essentially a geometric rather than a geographic approach. It works better on homogeneous land or space, reflecting the tabula rasa concept. Landscape is heterogeneous and changing by nature and culture, however. No two places on earth are exactly the same, just as no two persons in the world are exactly the same. Recognizing this fact, the Dutch have come up with the concept of the Casco landscape plan or framework design strategy. This concept is similar to Dutch architect John Habraken's concept of "structure" and "infill" as a way for open-ended design in architecture.[16] But the former is geographic, while the latter tends to be geometric. Ultimately, structuring is our cognitive and perceptual process as much as it is nature's self-organization and mathematical tool.

As a design strategy for uncertainty and adaptability, strategic design economizes necessary but costly and risky pre-investment under uncertainty. It is therefore not to be confused with a minimalist approach under the "less is more" belief in modern architecture. It resembles more the Taoist belief in creating room, a void to be filled and connected with energy flow, and working with an opponent force to your advantage, as is the case in judo. The Chinese game of Go is another wonderful example of a strategy game. It combines spatial strategy with timing strategy. Likewise, acupuncture points are strategic points in our body's nerve and circulation systems. And in the case of feng shui, landscape is conceived as homologous to the body; the positioning of a building in the field of energy is more important and strategic than is the shaping of its form. Feng shui has thus influenced not only the layout of various capital cities of China throughout its long history, but also cities in Korea and Japan. In all of them the positioning of settlement is done without negatively disturbing the energy field of landscape. This fits very well with landscape and the landscape approach. Dutch polder making is also strategic, as much as it is infrastructural landscape. An infrastructural approach with emphasis on efficiency and economy explains well why modernism and Euclidian geometry are so conspicuous in Dutch landscape and architecture.

Strategic design guided by the structure and process of landscape can have various expressions and applications. It follows simple rules such as protecting ridges and valleys, critical and scarce resources, hazardous and vulnerable areas, or access to precious sources of energy, food and water. Greenway design, or the Netherlands' Ecological Main Structure design, the Dutch practice of using the water system to structure the city, or its Room for the River strategy of preventing flooding downstream (where wealth is concentrated and risk is greatest) by expanding upstream flood plain areas and dredging for additional retention capacity, are good examples of strategic, infrastructural approaches to the design of metropolitan landscapes and regions. They all are characterized by open-ended and system design; controlling critical zones for delayed pain, to borrow a medical term. And they all work with time, waiting for the opportune moment to act, and letting community, nature and ecology complete or figure out their respective optimization, and thus take charge and ownership of design. Nature and community are intelligent and creative, often more intelligent and creative than individual designers, in dealing with a situation in flux.

5. Land-economic design

A landscape approach to urbanism recognizes that each piece of land has distinctive ecological as well as experiential values. Valuing land on the basis of the market economy is one thing; valuing land on the basis of its ecological productivity, a sense of home and habitat, society as a whole, and future generations is another matter. In a spaceship-earth economy, environmental economy matters to the valuation of land. In this sense continuing the urban expansion eating up green areas without fully utilizing brownfields or urban wastelands is not land-economical. It is a way of using land as disposable commodity rather than as base for building community. If we cannot formulate urban land use in ways that no waste is transferred to another place or time and that the diverse capacities of the land to provide the food, water, space, access, protection and energy are fully utilized rather than providing a functionalistic layout of land use, the city will become entropic: wasteful, inefficient and unsustainable. It will also become identity-less, lifeless and alienating. Urban sprawl will continue. Greenbelts will not work as long as the market economy remains a driving force, fossil fuel is imported (destroying the environment elsewhere), and waste is exported at less than environmental cost. This allows the city to grow beyond its ecological footprint. Energy and resources can be imported in a global economy, but pollution remains a local matter despite the prevailing NIMBY attitude. Under these circumstances pollution and CO_2 production may eventually become the determining factors. Providing and appreciating the full ecological value of landscape and even agricultural land (not only to avoid such scenarios) is imperative and inseparable from a landscape approach to urbanism. It is instructive that some of the most significant challenges and projects that landscape architects are dealing with today are waste and waste sites.

6. Bottom-up design

The plan view is a top-down view. Likewise, survey and map-based planning, survey-analysis-and-planning sequence, and rational organization of space and territory are all associated with top-down design. Haussmann's plan of Paris and grand designs modeled after the imperial Versailles gardens reflect a human desire to control and confidence in the power of reason and the certainty of science. Many architects care about the skyline, a photographic and iconic image to impress and sell. A landscape approach cares more about the groundline, about how the building touches the site, how the city settles on the landscape. For day-to-day experiences of the city, street level experiences count more. How the city integrates nature counts more. At the ground level, how indoor connects with outdoor counts more. City as landscape can be experienced best on the street level, through movement, time and interaction. Design evaluation and promotion of urban form from a bird's-eye perspective does not do justice to a sense of concreteness and engagement that affects our everyday experience of place. Plan and bird's-eye view show the organization, not the experience, quality, charm, or our emotional attachment to the everyday city.[17]

Landscape is by nature localized, regionalized and contextualized geographically and culturally. It is about the shaping and shape of ground surface as well as the experience of it. If the land use plan is about rational colonization and allocation of space, the landscape plan (or landscape approach to planning) deals with place experience and identity *of* place and identity of self and community with place. Thus "circulation" and "roads" in city planning are travel experience and wayfinding in a landscape approach to planning. The residents of a community know this. For this reason, local knowledge counts. Engaging the community and incorporating local knowledge requires a bottom-up approach to urban as well as regional design. Such engagement is the best way to ensure interactive design and engaging management of the city over a long time.

Landscape as scenery, a framed view, is static, selected and composed. Landscape as region defies such framing and selection. Rivers, shorelines and mountain ridges integrate as much as they separate. A city designed with a landscape approach cannot be fully appreciated from a bird's-eye view or with photography alone. It requires as much as affords immersed and total sensory experience. The charm of incremental growth, the diversity of architectural styles and sense of human scale found in organically grown cities, cannot be found in top-down design. Landscape design cannot be approached without a bottom-up approach. In the Netherlands, a bottom-up and landscape approach combined with the concerted effort of diverse architects are the secret to the apparent liveliness and cared-for appearance of projects such as the EVA Langsmeer sustainable community or the regeneration of Amsterdam East Harbor.

7. Phenomenological design

Designing a city is not just about system, structure, form and function. It is also about experience, particularly the everyday experience of its residents rather than a tourist experience of spectacles. "Experience" is "experiences of the body." And landscape itself is a body in a physiological, spiritual and subliminal sense. Of such sensual experiences, water and the perception of water in particular work wonders. One can think of Amsterdam, Venice or St. Petersburg, defined by and reflected in their canals; San Francisco's hills with a view of the ocean; or Freiburg with its open rainwater channels. The water channels in Beijing's Forbidden City are as poetic and symbolic as the bent column in a tea hut in the Katsura Villa of Kyoto. One can also think of the Kanto region of Japan with Mount Fuji rising elegantly above it, Rio de Janeiro with its towering rock outcrop, Stockholm with its water and exposed bedrock. All of these landscapes enrich our experience of connectedness to the land and nonlinearity of nature. Even the seasonal colors of street trees contribute to our memory and rhythm of, and affection for, the city we live in. If the modern city and architecture are preoccupied with ordering space, the city integrated with landscape provides the ordering of time and our place in time.[18]

The rice paddies in the middle of Japanese cities serve as urban agricultural fields and retention ponds. But more pronounced is their ability to give us a sense of time and of history of place. The Chonggye River restoration in Seoul, in spite of its enormous cost and being less than ecological, has been a great publicity success and a catalyst for the regeneration of surrounding urban areas. But the experience of living water and a vibrant stream in the city also adds the story of journey and the flow of life, a stream being the blood vessel of the landscape.[19] In a landscape approach the city is more than the sum of visual, spatial and formal issues and more than a collection of iconic buildings. It is the experience of inhaling, drinking, touching, tasting and smelling the landscape that counts. Such daily experience confirms that we are alert, alive and refreshed every day. Landscape is in our body as much as our body is in the landscape.

8. Ordinary urbanism

The contemporary city has to be a city of democracy. In such a city it is not so much the monuments or spectacular boulevards that count as the main street, alleys, routes and places that its ordinary citizens experience on a day-to-day basis. Instead of the overall city experienced at a distance as a spectacle or skyline, the places experienced at immediacy and casually lead to fond memories and offer a keen sense of knowing, and dwelling in, the place. A city that is good for residents is not necessarily good for tourists and visitors. Children and adolescents prefer to have backyards and fields where they can mess around instead of manicured landscapes they cannot trespass.

The landscape city provides this quality of living for ordinary residents. The Ramblas with its many vendors in Barcelona, the Gueilin city parks where the local Chinese practice ta'i chí or rest together with their birds brought in cages, the philosophers' paths in Heidelberg and Kyoto where lovers stroll, or the Rhine riverside in Bonn or Cologne with promenades, bicycle paths and restaurants, are all ordinary places that become extraordinary sights. Restoring main streets into pedestrian malls, or providing belvedere lookouts or parks where everyone can mix, see and be seen, makes city life attractive even for tourists, and perhaps more so than the ruins of historical monuments. In the end we relate to life more than to death. The city that offers diverse flowers along the street and highway noise barriers covered with meadows of wild flowers, as in the Netherlands or some parts of Southern California, also gives travelers the benefit of experiencing the richness in life without having to be rich. Ultimately we are not attracted to the city itself but to people living in and enlivening the city. The landscape city, the lived-in city, is a living thing.

9. Postmodern design

Modern architecture has failed most conspicuously in housing, ordinary architecture and city-making. After all, the city is not about a style and objects. A lively city can neither be made by one big master plan nor by a tabula rasa approach. The conception of a site as tabula rasa is geometric rather than geographic. Geometry is a tool for shapes and abstraction, not for place and concretization.

The city builds upon history and the vernacular. Attention to the past and the vernacular is attention to cultural landscapes. Attention to context is attention to landscapes. Landscape is context as well as text. Landscape Urbanism is an urbanism contextualized by landscape. In the modernist view, architecture was figure and icon, landscape was entourage and frame. In the landscape approach architecture becomes the furnishing of the city, a framework for interaction with landscapes. Postmodern designers' attention to sense and sensuality, feeling, time, memory and identity of place, can be accomplished in (the design of) a city integrated with landscape.

The apartment housing in the image of vernacular architecture in the Dutch new town of Almere is a good example. It works both as icon and cultural landscape. If an ecological approach to landscape design is modernistic in terms of its faith in the authority of scientific rationality and social relevance, a cultural landscape approach is inherently postmodern. McHarg is correct in characterizing J. B. Jackson as the Robert Venturi of landscape architecture.

10. Eco-feminist design.

The city in the image of a soaring church tower or high-rise buildings suggests power and masculinity, as much as the aspiration to reach

Heaven and God (imaged as male). It is for the gaze of a distant view. A landscape approach to city building pays attention to horizontality or "horizontal spread." This horizontality as seen in the low-rise urban spread of old Isfahan, Beijing or Kyoto makes the city less (geo)metric and more (geo)graphic, less a spectacle than a field. Being graphic is commonly considered a feminine trait, the rational metric being associated with the male. Though this could risk being seen as cultural stereotyping, image thinking is associated with the emotional brain, logical thinking with the rational brain. In general, women are more in touch with their emotions. Attention to landscape, like attention to ecology and Mother Nature, is eco-feminine. Recognizing land surface (as the rolling hills of Tuscan landscapes or sand dunes in Africa) as sensual, feeling and breathing body surface may be a macho bias. But it is consistent with Chinese feng shui and many other mythologies of traditional cultures.[20]

High-rise architecture and mega cities require enormous energy subsidy. Just as low-rise and high-density housing is the most viable type of living for a family with children, cities with five- to seven-story buildings as Berlin and Paris make sense not only in terms of their ecological footprint but also the experience of landscape they afford. The Dutch female architect Francine Houben may be on to something when she suggests that if they are to be a part of landscape, buildings in the Netherlands should not be taller than tree height, except in particular situations.

The image of ordinary and inhabited landscape is not one of power, reason, control or occupation. These belong to architecture and the modern city. In terms of subliminal association, landscape is more about love, fertility, beauty (not beast), eros (originally meaning "relation" in Greek) and romance. Besides, to be (geo)graphic is to recognize (and complement) the limitation of the metric of Pythagoras and Euclid. It is also to accept chaos, not cosmos, the order in disorder and disorder in order that Poincaré and Mandelbrot discovered in a self-organizing system. These are manifested in fractal geometry, self-similarity and nested hierarchy, without center and central authority.[21] Plato thought that music was the highest form of art, because it is so metric, so close to numeric harmony, mathematics being closest to truth and perfect science. But we don't need to continue the belief that architecture is frozen music with equally high metric quality, be it geometric and symmetric. Besides, true musicality does not come from the metric but from feeling and expressiveness, making music not a form but an experience. It is not by accident that even in the modern period many landscape architects sought asymmetry rather than symmetry as a condition for beauty.[22]

The majority of cities that we consider beautiful and romantic have a strong connection with landscape or waterscape. It is difficult to imagine New York City without Central Park, or Paris without the Seine. It is just as difficult to imagine the ideal house without a garden or landscape view. The landscape city is then eco-feminism asserting itself against the macho quality of early modern architectures and cities. It is, however, not a feminine city but a wholesome integrated and balanced city for humane and cultured living.

Conclusion

In this chapter, I articulated ten characteristics of Landscape Urbanism that together provide a better theoretical basis for Landscape Urbanism. I offered a normative definition of what Landscape Urbanism ought to be — how a landscape approach can contribute to making the city more humane and more sustainable, meeting the fundamental purpose of the city as something that sustains human life.

Landscape Urbanism had started initially with architects and urbanists appropriating a landscape approach and practice: landscape as a looking glass and medium for solutions to contemporary urban and urbanization problems. It addressed such problems as resource depletion, environmental degradation, loss of place identity, and human alienation and shrinking city. It was an appropriation by architects and urbanists at a theoretical and methodological dead end of the architectural approach (design as form-making) and their faith in scientific rationality (a socio-economic policy-based approach to planning).

Landscape Urbanism as it stands now is still a project and a set of operational strategies. It is focused more on the material side of urban and landscape restructuring and regeneration, and less on the experiential side. As such, it does not touch on one important meaning of urbanism: urbanism as a way of living.

The definitional framework provides a way to integrate two paradigms of settlement design: one based on an architectural approach, the other on a landscape approach. The problems inherent in an architectural approach explain why so many architects are struggling today and why they have reached an intellectual and aesthetic dead end in the face of environmental and cultural issues. Landscape Urbanism provides a way foreward. It provides a way for landscape architecture to reach beyond landscape as scenery and beyond design as form.

Endnotes:

1 Waldheim, C., Ed. 2006. *The Landscape Urbanism Reader*. New York: Princeton Architectural Press, p.11.

2 Bunster-Ossa, I. 2001. *Landscape Urbanism*. Washington, D.C.: Urban Land Institute, p. 37.

3 Koolhaas, R. and B. Mau. What Ever Happened to Urbanism?. In Koolhaas, R. and B. Mau. 1995. *S, M, L, XL*. New York: Monacelli, pp. 961–71.

4 Cuthbert, A. R. 2007. Urban Design: Requiem for an Era — Review and Critique of the Last 50 Years. In *Urban Design International*, 12: 177–223.

5 Sola-Morales Rubio, I. de. 1995. Terrain Vague. In Davidson, C., Ed., *Anyplace*. Cambridge, MA: MIT Press, p. 112.

6 Berger, J. 1972. *Ways of Seeing*, London: British Broadcasting Corporation.

7 Motlock, J. 1991. *Introduction to Landscape Design*. New York: Van Nostrand Reinhold. A. W. Spirn, 1998. *The Language of Landscape*. New Haven: Yale University Press.

8 Corner, James, Ed. 1999. *Recovering Landscape*. New York: Princeton Architectural Press. C. Girot. 1999. Four Trace Concepts in Landscape Architecture. In Corner, J., Ed., *Recovering Landscape*. New York: Princeton Architectural Press, pp. 59–68.

9 Koh, J. and A. Beck. 2006. Parks, People and City. *Topos Magazine*, June 2006. Landscape is not just visual scenery to look at but performative and engaged landscaping. In this regard it is instructive that the Chinese concept of open space and void, and for that matter landscape, is not just empty space or scenery but a field full of energy and life. The open court in the center of the Chinese house or the open space around the settlement is a channel through which vital energy flows to connect humans to nature. Likewise, the ponds in Kula city of Bangladesh perform ecological, social and productive functions. In the Netherlands, greenhouse gas emission is now getting integrated into the heating system for housing, just as industrial heat waste on an island in Denmark is harvested to be reused for commercial and residential use. (Hawken, 1993)

10 Javaherian, F. (curator). 2004. *Gardens of Iran: Ancient Wisdom, New Visions*. Tehran: Iranian Institute for Promotion of Visual Arts, p. 22.

11 Odum, E. P. 1971. *Fundamentals of Ecology*. Philadelphia, PA: W. B. Saunders.

12 Prigogine, I., G. Nicolis and A. Babloyantz. 1972. Thermodynamics of Evolution. *Physics Today*, v.25, n.11 &12.

13 Koh, J. 1978. An Ecological Theory of Architecture. Dissertation, University of Pennsylvania.

14 Capra, F. 1975. *The Tao of Physics*. Berkeley: Shambhala.

15 Pearce, P. 1978. *Structure in Nature is a Strategy of Design*. Cambridge, MA: MIT Press.

16 Habraken, N. J. 2000. *The Structure of the Ordinary*. Cambridge: MIT Press.

17 Cullen, G. 1961. *Townscape*. London: The Architectural Press. J. Gehl. 1987. *Life Between Buildings: Using Public Space*. New York: Van Nostrand Reinhold. B. Rudofsky. 1969. *Streets for People: A Primer for Americans*. Garden City: Doubleday.

18 Lynch, K. 1972. *What Time is this Place?* Cambridge: MIT Press. M. Miller. 1993. *The Garden As Art*, Albany, NY: State University of New York Press. M. Miller.1999. Time and Temporality in Japanese Gardens. In Birksted, J., Ed., *Relating Architecture to Landscape*. London: E&F Spon, pp. 43–58.

19 Moore, C. W. and J. Lidz. 1994. *Water and Architecture*, London: Thames and Hudson.

20 Jung, C. G. 1964. *Man and His Symbols*, Garden City: Doubleday.

21 Gleick, J. 1988. *Chaos, Making a New Science*. New York: Viking Press.

22 Imbert, D. 2007. The AIAJM: A Manifesto for Landscape Modernity. In *Landscape Journal*, 26:2: 219–35.

Additional Works Cited

Berger, A. 2006. *Drosscape: Wasting Land in Urban America*. New York: Princeton Architectural Press.

Birksted, J., Ed. 1999. *Relating Architecture to Landscape*. London: E & FN Spon.

Doevendans, K., H. Loerzing and A. Schram. 2007. From Modernist Landscapes to New Nature: Planning of Rural Utopias in the Netherlands. In *Landscape Research*, v.32, n.3: 333–54.

Ellin, N. 1996. *Postmodern Urbanism*. Cambridge: Blackwell.

Frampton, K. 1983. Towards a Critical Regionalism: Six Points for an Architecture of Resistance. In Foster, H., Ed. *The Anti-Aesthetic: Essays on Post-Modern Culture*. London: Pluto Press, pp. 16–30.

Gutman, R., Ed. 1972. *People and Buildings*. New York: Basic Books.

Hough, M. 1995. *Cities and Natural Process*. London: Routledge.

Lang, J. T. 1994. *Urban Design: The American Experience*. New York: Van Nostrand.

McHarg, I. L. 1969. *Design with Nature*. Garden City: Doubleday.

Nisbett, R. E. 2005. *The Geography of Thought*. London: Nicholas Brealey.

Rapoport, A. 1977. *Human Aspects of Urban Form: Towards a Man-Environment Approach to Urban Form and Design*, Oxford: Pergamon Press.

Turner, T. 1996, *City as Landscape: A Post-Postmodern View of Design and Planning*. London: Spon.

Watts, A. P. 1958. *Nature, Man and Woman*. New York: Vintage Books.

Wirth, L. 1938. Urbanism as a Way of Life. *The American Journal of Sociology*, 44:1–24.

16

Landscape Ecology and Its Urbanism

PERRY PEI-JU YANG

MANY OF THE CHAPTERS IN THIS BOOK take the view that Landscape Urbanism has gone too far in articulating a green-centered vision that dominates and even undermines sustainable urban form. In this essay I take a different view: that in fact, Landscape Urbanism has not gone far enough in fleshing out what is needed for a truly ecological structured approach to urbanism. Based on an international design competition for Downsview Park in Toronto, I review three approaches: landscape as picture, landscape as flow and landscape as process. I argue that landscape as an organizational principle tends to be weaker than infrastructure and architecture as the essential building blocks of urban form. It is still unclear how landscape generates urban physical form and structure in intensive urban environments. An alternative, ecology by design, uses ecology and its flows as organizational principles for city development.

Emerging Landscape and Ecology Discourse in Urbanism

The literature on landscape ecology provides extensive empirical evidence that it is important to ensure that ecological flows are horizontally connected in the process of urbanization. Human-driven flows such as traffic, cycling, walking, electricity transmission, and the piping of utilities tend to produce straight lines that disturb ecological processes such as surface runoff, groundwater flow, migration, pollination, plant dispersal, and wind and water erosion — all of which tend to be curvi-linear. Forman used a patch–corridor–matrix to describe "land mosaics," patterns of natural and human-made elements and their relationship to "landscape flow," the flows and movement of plants, water, animal, wind, material and energy.[1] The fundamentally horizontal interactions of land-scape ecology have been interpreted as being suggestive of healing the spread-out urban form of contemporary cities.[2] In this context, urban design and planning are seen as tools to manage the dynamics of spatial patterns and functions over time, i.e., landscape change.

Considering landscape and ecology in the process of urban design and development is not new. Many of these ideas emanated from the regionalism of Patrick Geddes, Benton MacKaye, and Lewis Mumford and their methods on ecological planning.[3] Though often unattributed, recent calls for the integration of landscape and urbanism derive from this regionalist tradition. But they go further. Designers are now using landscape as an essential element for organizing the urban environment, replacing architecture's traditional role as the basic building block of urban design.[4] Landscape is seen as a tool for dissolving the dominant role of buildings, blocks and infrastructure, which have traditionally cut off ecological connection.

Projects and case studies in *The Landscape Urbanism Reader*[5] tend to be located at the interface of city and nature at the urban fringe or "mid-dle landscape." As such, the discourse of Landscape Urbanism tends to be focused on issues of suburban sprawl in an American urban context.[6] Proposals cover urban or suburban development within natural environ-ments, or the ways in which hybrid landscapes interweave infrastructure, nature and city.

Under Landscape Urbanism, development proposals in any context — urban or suburban — must extend beyond the design of geometry for architectural and infrastructural spaces. In other words, the design or redesign of cities, based on landscape and ecology, must involve a reformulation of the idea that cities should be functionally organized as streets, blocks, buildings and lots. From the perspectives of Landscape Urbanism, cities should be designed to respect, as in landscape ecology, surfaces of patches, corridors, matrices and layered systems — but how, exactly, is this accomplished? To what extent can we apply landscape and ecological principles such as horizontal flows and dynamic processes to designing large-scale urban settings? How do we get beyond "object-oriented" city design?

To better understand how landscape and ecology can be taken as organizing principles for an "emergent urbanism," to use Corner's phrase,[7] a case study of large-scale urban landscape design was chosen for examination: Toronto's Downsview Park design competition. The submissions have been reviewed,[8] however insufficiently, but the design concepts produced in the competition provide distinctively different perspectives that illustrate how large-scale urban and landscape design can integrate with contemporary urban environments. A review of these proposals not only helps articulate a critique of Landscape Urbanism,[9] but provides analytical support for a different approach that I call "ecology by design."

Toronto Downsview Park Design Competition

In 1999, a design competition was launched for Downsview Park in Toronto. A 200-hectare military base was to be transformed into a metropolitan open space, and proposals were to address the themes of environmental sustainability, ecological renewal, and celebration of the rich heritage of the site. The finalists' design proposals were exhibited on site in May 2000. The proposals reveal the hybridity of contemporary environmental space and the ways in which a large-scale development might be conceived as working in tandem with ecological and social processes. They also show how a derelict site at the metropolitan fringe can be transformed into a conceptually rich and environmentally complex urban setting.[10]

Three design approaches, which could be labeled landscape as picture, landscape as flow, and landscape as process, can be evaluated to better understand the potential role of design in the making of ecological progress. The first proposition, landscape as picture, contains some conventional ideas about park design and emphasizes the quality of open space for individual recreation. The second proposition, landscape as flow, focuses on the way material, energy, water and species flow across the landscape horizontally. The interweaving of ecological and human flows is used to enhance, in a dynamic way, the quality of park settings. The third proposition, landscape as process, highlights the process of conceiving and implementing landscape design, both of which are treated as being more important than static landscape form.

The proposal to construct a city-wide ecological sound landscape relies on the process of ecologically restoration as well as the mechanism of community participation.

Landscape as Picture

One of the proposals in the Downsview Park competition is the emerging landscape (Figure 16.1). As a fairly conventional park design, landscape is conceptualized as a series of picturesque elements. The design is modernist in the sense that landscape has the quality of openness,

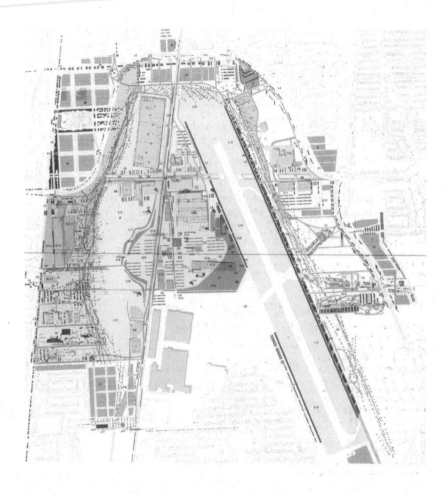

Fig. 16.1: *The emerging landscape proposal by Brown & Storey in Downsview Park competition. (Czerniak, 2001)*

and there is no distinctive boundary. Legibility and centrality are shaped by the geometric arrangement of plants, circulation patterns, and building objects, all of which guide the public toward a core area intended for gathering. Zones are delineated by a secondary green belt linked to pedestrian paths in outer satellite neighborhoods. This inside-out ring pattern and pathway networking fully utilize the potential of landscape as picture. The technique is sometimes used in urban design. The disappearance of boundary and the open plan system allow the central open space of the park to be conceived as part of the neighborhood space. This extends the territory of the park to the adjoining neighborhoods and opens up opportunities for community involvement through common environmental stewardship (Figure 16.2). The design concept implies a

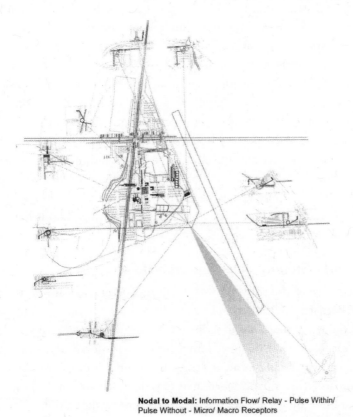

Nodal to Modal: Information Flow/ Relay - Pulse Within/ Pulse Without - Micro/ Macro Receptors

Fig. 16.2: *The disappearance of boundary and the open plan system, diagram by Brown & Storey in Downsview Park competition. (Czerniak, 2001)*

decentralization of power that is to be executed by a participatory mechanism of park management.

Landscape as Flow

Topography as an operational system for flows and visual experience

Landscape as flow constitutes a complex system that interweaves nature,
human movement, and sport activities. An example is the synthetic
landscape for Downsview Park proposed by Foreign Office Architects.
Its landscape configuration is reminiscent of their ferry terminal project at Yokohama. In the proposal, landscape surface and its topography
become an operational system that control all kinds of flows such as
water and pedestrian activity. The interplay of human movement and
land form or topography is meant to generate sequential experiences
and enhance the visual quality of the place. It allows a variety of different modes and speeds of movement to circulate within the park. The
patterns of walking, jogging and biking, together with slopes, loops and
circulation, are used to shape the artificial, human-made topography
(Figure 16.3). These variations of terrain and slope in the site design
are meant to show how hydrology, species and vegetation systems and
flows are being accommodated. The artificial land form is an ecological
metaphor that represents nature as well as its coexistence with human
activities. This landscape setting implies a high level of control, in terms
of both ecological flow and the collective and individual behavior patterns of recreational users.

Synergy of natural shape and urban form

To go beyond the conventional dualism of "city and nature," the architect Bernard Tschumi brought in a new set of narratives, "the digital
and the wilderness," to prescribe a new formula for an ecological urban
landscape. Instead of questioning how urban development suppresses
biodiversity, the provocative design is meant to nurture biodiversity in
an urban environment, where nature is designed and shaped in support
of various ecological functions. The landscape configuration is composed
of natural, urban and digital programs to define clear territories for these
ecological functions to coexist with other human activities. A finger-like
natural shape creates a sharp contrast of distinctive landscape features.

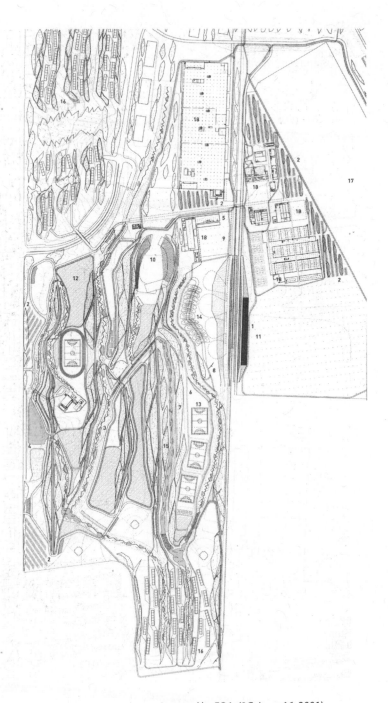

Fig. 16.3: *The New Synthetic Landscape Proposal by FOA. (2G: Issue 16, 2001)*

This convoluted boundary between natural and urban forms creates a micro-terrain that allows the drainage system to flow from interior space to outer fringes and create more interfaces for the interpenetration of flows from both sides (Figure 16.4). A rich and dynamic wetland environment is formed along complex edges.

Some principles of landscape ecology are clearly applicable to the design. The proposition of "aggregate-with-outliers" as the optimum

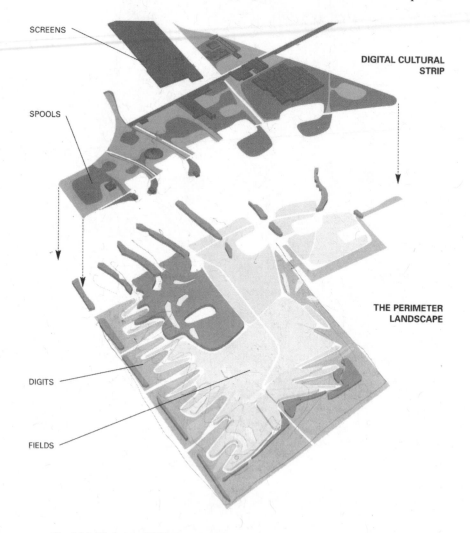

SCREENS

DIGITAL CULTURAL STRIP

SPOOLS

THE PERIMETER LANDSCAPE

DIGITS

FIELDS

Fig. 16.4: *Digital and Wilderness in Tschumi's proposal in Downsview Park competition.* (Czerniak, 2001)

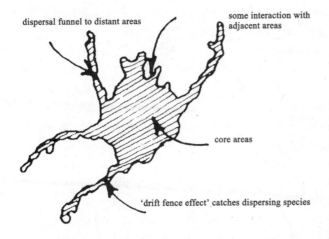

dispersal funnel to distant areas

some interaction with
adjacent areas

core areas

'drift fence effect' catches dispersing species

Fig. 16.5:
The "aggregate-
with-outliers"
as the optimum
arrangement of
landscape pattern.
(Forman, 1995)

arrangement of landscape pattern has been tested by many landscape ecologists,[11] and is evident in the proposal. Such a pattern contains more opportunities for maintaining biodiversity through the horizontal flows of species, vegetation, water and materials. (Figure 16.5) The technique of overlay mapping visualizes the idea by extracting distinctive horizontal layers of landscape elements, translated as the urban, digital and wilderness in Tschumi's Downsview Park proposal. The synergy of urban form and natural shape symbolically represents a future in which city confronts nature and attempts to optimize the relationship. Design is intended as an ecological intervention for reconfiguring and reweaving the natural pattern with the urban fabric.

Landscape as Process
Ecological restoration process

Most urban design is presented as static, or "end-state," built form. Conventionally, both urban and landscape design solutions appear deterministic, and represent a singular outcome. However, many ecological processes are stochastic, and landscape patterns are generated by probability. For example, biodiversity of species responds to habitat fragmentation stochastically.[12] Climatic and hydrological change is also a stochastic phenomenon. Some have argued that we should embrace uncertainty and unpredictability because change and surprise are inevitable in urban–natural systems.[13] We should therefore acknowledge that uncertainty is a critical component of ecological design. That landscape patterns and urban forms change over time means that they both follow and affect ecological processes and dynamics.

In the emergent ecologies proposed by Allen and Corner,[14] ecological site analysis includes the surveying of habitat, soil and water quality. The engineering-level site plan provides great details of contours, drainage and infrastructural systems without making any suggestion for pre-determined landscape features. The landscape design is like a physical spatial framework that provides flexibility and adaptability and accom-modates flows of species, water and materials to occupy and transform the landscape over time. Any subjective design intention is minimized by a very thin programmatic effort. The main drawing is made in a black-and-white line frame that implies a representational strategy of a nearly formless quality in its landscape expression (Figure 16.6). Rather than

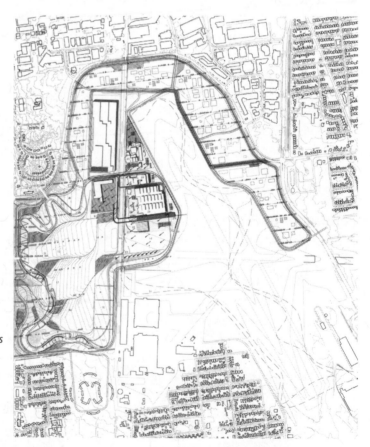

Fig. 16.6: The site plan of the emergent ecologies proposal by Allen and Corner in Downsview Park competition. (Czerniak, 2001)

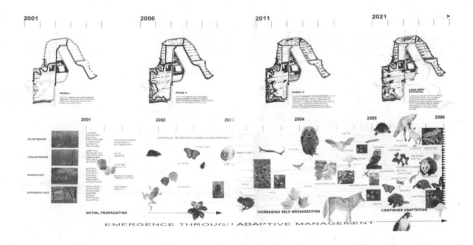

Fig. 16.7: *The evolutionary process diagram, by Allen and Corner in Downsview Park competition. (Czerniak, 2001)*

presenting a final form, a key point of the proposal is that it projects ecological change and evolutional process two decades into the future (Figure 16.7). Urban landscape design thus boils down to the strategic planning of large-scale ecological restoration processes. The management of evolutionary process is more important than final form in determining the quality of landscape design.

Community participatory process for making a pluralistic urban landscape

Koolhaas and Mau's Tree City proposal for Downsview Park attempts to visualize how landscape change can be managed and sustained through a process of local involvement. Tree City is composed of thousands of mosaic-like landscape circles. A thousand paths, provided by the local government and creating a thousand new entries, intended to open the park to the whole metropolitan area. Facing the pressure of urban sprawl from Toronto's outward expansion and the decrease of natural resources in the region, Tree City proposed a radical action by growing landscape circles — trees — from the periphery toward the center. Trees and landscapes would gradually encroach upon the city. Eventually, a new form of low-density green metropolitan development would evolve, moving toward a new conceptualization of city vs. nature (Figure 16.8).[15]

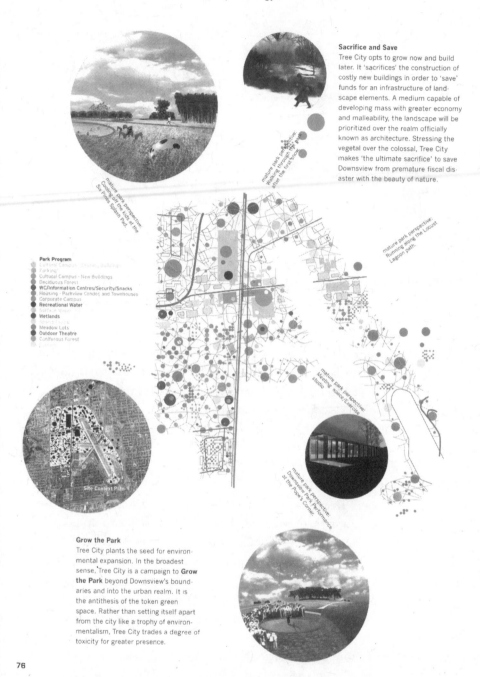

Sacrifice and Save

Tree City opts to grow now and build later. It 'sacrifices' the construction of costly new buildings in order to 'save' funds for an infrastructure of landscape elements. A medium capable of developing mass with greater economy and malleability, the landscape will be prioritized over the realm officially known as architecture. Stressing the vegetal over the colossal, Tree City makes 'the ultimate sacrifice' to save Downsview from premature fiscal disaster with the beauty of nature.

Park Program
Cultural Campus - Existing Buildings
Parking
Cultural Campus - New Buildings
Deciduous Forest
WC/Information Centres/Security/Snacks
Housing - Parkview Condos and Townhouses
Corporate Campus
Recreational Water
Wetlands
Meadow Lots
Outdoor Theatre
Coniferous Forest

mature park perspective:
Walking through the park after the first snow.

mature park perspective:
Running along the Locust Lagoon path.

mature park perspective:
Meeting spatial Exercise studio.

mature park perspective:
Downsview Park Performance at the Pixel & Corner.

mature park perspective:
Cooling off the kids at the Six Piles Splash Pad.

Site Context Plan

Grow the Park

Tree City plants the seed for environmental expansion. In the broadest sense, Tree City is a campaign to **Grow the Park** beyond Downsview's boundaries and into the urban realm. It is the antithesis of the token green space. Rather than setting itself apart from the city like a trophy of environmentalism, Tree City trades a degree of toxicity for greater presence.

Fig. 16.8: A pluralistic landscape, the Tree City proposal by Koolhaas & Mau for Downsview Park. (OMA website, 2011)

The proposal, which went on to become the winning design entry, relied on an underlying process of social participation involving the cultural creation of individual picturesque landscapes. Collectively, these were meant to give form to the "tree city," a "nature's metropolis," representing a mosaic-like, diverse urban society. Although the idea is nurtured from the North American suburban context, the proposal provides a tool for visualization and a process for design that may be applicable in other social and environmental contexts.

There is a similarity between Koolhaas and Mau's Tree City and Corner and Allen's Emerging Ecology in that both emphasize process over static form. There is a difference, however, in terms of what drives those processes. Corner and Allen's ecological restoration approach is about managing the evolution of landscape ecology, whereas Koolhaas and Mau's pluralistic social design sees participation and community involvement as the mechanism for generating Toronto's future landscape. For both, the final form of urban space and landscape is undetermined and, to a certain degree, unpredictable. The future construction of an eco-city or nature's metropolis is supposed to emerge from either the ecological restoration that comes from nurturing nature or from the socially pluralistic design process that emanates from bottom-up community engagement.

From "Ecology in Design" to "Ecology by Design"

Based on this review of design proposals for Toronto's Downsview Park, I have categorized distinct approaches to large-scale urban and landscape design: landscape as picture, landscape as flow, and landscape as process. These constitute three ways of conceptualizing how a large-scale urban landscape can be shaped by the principles of landscape ecology:

Landscape as picture focuses on the visual quality, activities, and environmental legibility of parks by managing the experiential effect of landscape features. Landscape as flow is an approach that interweaves natural pattern, urban form, and human activities and movement. Terrain and land form provide an operational system of flow and visual quality. The manipulation of landscape layers is meant to allow ecological, pedestrian and vehicular flows to coexist.

Landscape as process engages large-scale spatial transformation over time. It emphasizes the design of process and mechanism rather than static landscape form. The process of ecological restoration and community participation drive scenario planning in a long-term and incremental way. The design and development process is intended to be a catalyst for implementing an eco-city in which the reconstruction of city fabric and natural systems rely on micro-scale actions.

The three approaches contain arguments and propositions that seem to diminish the problem of human-nature and city-nature dualism. In this they affirm the existence of "second nature": that there no longer exists an original or pure nature. Nature is a human construct, conceived, designed, planned and shaped by human beings.[16] The interweaving of nature, city and infrastructure has created enormously complex boundary and edge spaces and conditions.

How does a large-scale urban design engage this hybrid landscape, and then create a city-wide ecological effect? The design proposals reviewed here took ideas from landscape ecology, restoration ecology, and ecological modernization in a way that went well beyond conventional thinking about preserving nature and leftover resources, moving away from a defensive approach to planning toward a new understanding about nurturing nature in the context of urban environments.[17]

And yet, proposals rendered under the idea of Landscape Urbanism, within which these design submissions fall, can be faulted for failing to distinguish between ecology in design and ecology by design. Traditional urban and landscape design sees ecology as consisting of natural elements that need to be preserved or added in design, and tends to be deterministic in form-making. Ecology by design aims for design of an ecology-structured urban system, and deals with ecological processes — such as energy and water flows, species movement, and ecological evolution — that are normally stochastic. Ecology is seen as a driving force of urban transformation. Designing an ecological spatial framework allows ecological adaptation and socially incremental processes to drive urban change. Ultimately, this could produce a higher quality of organized complexity and diversity in both urban and natural environments.

Landscape Urbanists have articulated an argument that landscape is an essential spatial element for organizing urban space, attempting, at least rhetorically, to go beyond the proposition of ecology in design. Landscape and its ecology, they argue correctly, is more than bringing in natural elements into in-between urban spaces, it is a form of urban eco-infrastructure.[18]

However, it is the inexplicit articulation of ecology by design, and how it differs from ecology in design, that signals the potential limitations and problems inherent in Landscape Urbanism. First, most practices of Landscape Urbanism are located in the context of an urban fringe, marginal places consisting of hybrid landscapes. It is still unclear how urban — as opposed to low-density, semi-urban form — can emerge from the application of Landscape Urbanist ideas. In fact, examples of how landscape generates urban physical form and structure in intensive urban environments are rarely seen. Further, the reasons why Landscape Urbanism as a proposition for future urban development have been and should be confined to hybrid or peripheral landscapes are not well argued.

Second, despite claims otherwise, in many practices landscape as an organizational principle tends to be weaker than the functional operation of infrastructure and building in the making of urban form. We have to move our focus from designing the peripheral landscape or spaces in between buildings, blocks and infrastructures to the design of urban systems per se. The approach to analysis and design for flows in landscape needs to be extended to flows in cities: how cities at the system level function and operate ecologically in terms of energy, materials, water, species flows and human movement.

Finally, the meanings of landscape are multiple, contentious, and sometimes too broad to lead to any executable operation of planning, design and construction. In fact it is not clear how the recurrent themes of Landscape Urbanism — horizontal extensivity, landscape as infrastructure, forms of process, operational techniques of mappings, and ecology — actually translate. Landscape is seen as a tool or instrument for dissolving the problem of segregated buildings and infrastructure, but, given the visual output that often presents buildings in isolated contexts, it is not clear how the urban agenda of Landscape Urbanism will be accomplished.

The notion of ecology by design provides a more narrowly defined, executable idea than the broad and relatively vague agenda presented in Landscape Urbanism. There is a need to engage design through performance-based ecological analysis of the urban environment, by connecting its geometrical, perceptual, material attributes and processes over time. Indeed this is close to what Allen argued for — the geometrical, material and performative perspectives of landscape[19] — but with a focus on urban systems. We should refine our knowledge and understanding of urban ecologies, adopting more appropriate performance measures and better ways of linking these insights to design.

It is unclear whether Landscape Urbanism has really engaged with the kinds of questions that need to be answered before ecology by design can become a reality. Can urban spaces support and nurture biodiversity? How do we use ecology and its flows as the major organizational principles of cities, and what does this mean for the design of urban spaces? How do we envision an ecology-structured urban system, achieved through a transformative process that connects the urban forms and flows of material, energy, water and organism across system boundaries? How do we design a flexible framework that can accommodate future urban changes, and would break the divide between ecological science and urban design?

These questions override the peripheral positions and landscape strategies used by most Landscape Urbanists or landscape architects. They get to the core question of future urban growth by shifting our attention from the peripheral to central urban questions: how do we analyze flows in cities on top of flows in landscape, and design for an ecology-structured urban system? How do we manage, ecologically, fundamental urban change? Ecology must be the driving force of urban transformation. Landscape Urbanism has gone some way toward articulating that vision. But it has not gone far enough and much more needs to be done.

Conclusion

Landscape and ecology can be seen as tools of urban design, as shown in the review of Toronto's Downsview Park design proposals. The three approaches to large-scale urban and landscape design — landscape as picture, landscape as flow, and landscape as process — provide alternative propositions for resolving the dichotomy of city and nature. They move us away from the defensive position of preserving nature and "leftover resources" toward a more design-oriented approach in which design is seen as an ecological intervention.[20] In this, there needs to be a distinction between ecology in design that defines ecology as natural elements to be preserved or added to a design, and ecology by design in which ecology drives urban transformation more fundamentally.

Landscape Urbanism engages many of these issues, but appears to be too broad and relatively vague to address this specific ecological urban agenda. Ecology by design is a model for designing a flexible framework that accommodates future urban changes in a sustainable way. While ecological urban design should be treated as a strategic planning and design process rather than as a static landscape configuration or urban form, it also shows a potential approach to articulating and understanding ecologically based large-scale urban transformation that focuses on cities as ecology-structured urban systems whose design relies on a transformative process that connects flows in cities over flows in landscape.

Endnotes

1   Forman, R. T. T. 1999. Horizontal Processes, Roads, Suburbs, Social Objectives and Landscape Ecology. In Klopatek, J. and R. Gardner, Ed., *Landscape Ecological Analysis: Issues and Applications.* Basel: Springer Verlag.

2   Allen, S. 2009. *The Practice: Architecture Technique + Representation,* Expanded Second Edition. New York: Routledge.

3   Talen, E. 2005. *New Urbanism and American Planning: The Conflict of Cultures.* New York: Routledge.

4   Waldheim, C. 2006. Landscape as Urbanism. In Waldheim, Charles, Ed., *The Landscape Urbanism Reader.* New York: Princeton Architectural Press.

5   Waldheim, op cit.

6   Weller, R. 2008. Landscape (Sub)Urbanism in Theory and Practice, *Landscape Journal* 27:2–08.

7   Corner, J. 2006. Terra Fluxus. In *The Landscape Urbanism Reader.* Waldheim, C., Ed., Princeton Architectural Press, p. 23.

8   Czerniak, J. Ed. 2001, *Case: Downsview Park Toronto,* Harvard University Graduate School of Design. New York: Prestel Verlag.

9   Waldheim, op cit.

10 Czerniak, op cit.

11 Forman, R. T. T. 1995. *Land Mosaics: The Ecology of Landscapes and Regions.* New York: Cambridge University Press.

12 Ibid.

13 Alberti, M. 2009. Future of Urban Ecosystems. In *Advances in Urban Ecology: Integrating Humans and Ecological Processes in Urban Ecosystems.* Basel: Springer Verlag.

14 Czerniak, op cit.

15 Czerniak, J. Ed. 2001, *Case: Downsview Park Toronto,* Harvard University Graduate School of Design. New York: Prestel Verlag. OMA. 2011. Downsview Park Toronto 2000. oma.eu/projects/2000/downsview-park

16 Cronon, W. 1991. Introduction: In Search of Nature. In Cronon, W., Ed., *Uncommon Ground: Toward Reinventing Nature.* New York: W. W. Norton.

17 Yang, P.P.J. 2009. Questioning Urban Sustainability: Social Sufficiency, Ecological Efficiency and Ecosystems Compatibility. *Journal of Urbanism,* November, Vol. 2, Issue 3.

18 Mossop, E. 2006. Landscape as Infrastructure. In Waldheim, Charles, Ed., *The Landscape Urbanism Reader.* New York: Princeton Architectural Press. C. Reed. 2006. Public Works Practices. In Waldheim, Charles, Ed., *The Landscape Urbanism Reader.* New York: Princeton Architectural Press.

19 Allen, op cit.

20 Hill, K. 2001. Urban Ecologies: Biodiversity and Urban Design. in *Case: Downsview Park Toronto,* Harvard University Graduate School of Design. New York: Prestel Verlag.

Additional Works Cited

2G. 2001. *2G,* issue 16: Foreign Office Architects. Barcelona.

Ahern, J. 1999. Spatial Concepts, Planning Strategies, and Future Scenarios: A Framework Method for Integrating Landscape Ecology and Landscape Planning. In Klopatek, J. and R. Gardner, Ed., *Landscape Ecological Analysis: Issues and Applications.* Basel: Springer Verlag.

Shane, G. 2006. The Emergence of Landscape Urbanism. In Waldheim, Charles, Ed., *The Landscape Urbanism Reader.* New York: Princeton Architectural Press.

Waldheim, C., Ed. 2006. *The Landscape Urbanism Reader.* New York: Princeton Architectural Press.

17

Urbanism — New, Landscape, or Otherwise: The Case for Complementarity

Nan Ellin

WE EACH VIEW THE WORLD THROUGH OUR OWN CULTURAL LENS, a set of ideas and behaviors that are mutually understood, yet constantly changing. Part of that lens is language — shared understandings regarding written and oral communication. Another part is urbanism — shared understandings regarding the arrangement and use of space. These shared understandings regarding language and urbanism provide the stability that allows them to be dynamic, evolving with changing needs and desires over time. When cultures converge, misunderstandings often arise, at times provoking conflict. Cultural convergence can also incite innovation and progress toward improving the human condition when a willingness to learn from one another and collaborate prevails.

Our professions comprise of subcultures that add additional lenses through which we see and act upon the world. Like all subcultures, the professions dedicated to urbanism — principally urban design, urban planning, architecture and landscape architecture — have different languages as well as urbanisms, as do subgroups that form alliances within and between the professions. These subcultural differences have clearly marked efforts to address the shortcomings of modern urbanism.

Like the proverbial blind men and an elephant, these groups have identified different parts of the problem and therefore proposed varying solutions. One group focused on the lack of sense of place, sense of identity, neighborliness, and walkability as well as environmental devastation, urban fragmentation, social isolation, and public health issues. This group — an alliance of architects, planners and urban designers — turned to pre-modern cities for inspiration and introduced Neo-Traditional Urbanism in the 1970s, later renamed the New Urbanism.[1] Another group, comprised primarily of architects and landscape architects, identified the privileging of built objects as the problem, and in response, accorded priority to landscape. Members of this group introduced Landscape Urbanism and then tried to rename it Ecological Urbanism,[2] though the prior moniker has stuck.

Like all subcultures, New Urbanism and Landscape Urbanism have their own languages and urbanisms. For New Urbanism, these largely revolve around built form and how it is experienced, while landscape is the defining element for Landscape Urbanism. New Urbanism continues the humanist tradition of urbanism while Landscape Urbanism draws from a widely appealing blend of the form-making avant-garde and landscape ecology traditions. In the humanist tradition, the role of the professional is to reflect or illuminate (mirror or light). In the form-making avant-garde tradition, the professional is an aesthetic/cultural leader who produces work that may be transgressive (shock), while the landscape ecology tradition calls for understanding and respecting the larger ecosystem (going with the flow). Extending these various traditions, New Urbanism and Landscape Urbanism identify different goals and apply different methods to achieve them.

The convergence of these two subcultures — New Urbanism and Landscape Urbanism — has, not surprisingly, bred misunderstandings and, at times, conflict. It has also produced a creative tension leading each to question assumptions, sharpen skills, and learn from one other to become transformative in the best way. Indeed, the respective contributions of New Urbanism and Landscape Urbanism, as well as the debates their rivalry has engendered, have been integral to a profound change in the conception and construction of places, helping elevate urbanism onto the next rung of sustainability, or what might be called prosperity.[3]

Though there remain potholes and blind corners along the path, we are witnessing propitious changes signaling a redefinition of urbanity. Programmatic density (horizontal and vertical mixed-use) has been emerging in suburban areas and small towns[4] while nature is increasingly being integrated into urban and suburban areas as conservation areas, parks of all sizes, connected greenways, and agriculture. Many new developments, older suburbs, and urban cores have been introducing transit-oriented development, bike trails, permaculture, neighborhood business districts, and other strategies to enhance livability. Whether city, suburb or countryside, local farming may coexist with importing food, local businesses with global ones, and mass transit with the automobile or perhaps even automated personal rapid transit (PRT).

At the same time, the importance of cities to economics and environmental quality has become a given and urban design trends have been aligning fortuitously with political and social trends including the sustainability, smart city, creative city, historic preservation, community garden, urban agriculture, land trust, and public health movements. Around the US, regions and groups[5] have been reviving passenger railroad systems, implementing extensive new mass transit, adaptively reusing existing buildings, creating some great public spaces at all scales, remediating brownfields, adaptively reusing grayfields and redfields, and undertaking significant initiatives to protect air and water quality. Performance- and form-based guidelines, encouraging walkability and integrating nature into the city, are increasingly replacing regulations that focus on traffic flow and risk mitigation. In addition, the overall quality of new development — urban infill as well as greenfield — is far superior to what it was in prior decades.

> Just as complementary medicine looks at the whole person including their physical environment ... "complementary urbanism" looks at the whole environment including people.

Urban designers have been practicing an evolved contextualism whereby geography, history, culture, experiential qualities, and post-occupancy evaluations become significant generators of form. Just as complementary medicine looks at the whole person including their physical environment, this "complementary urbanism" looks at the whole environment including people. The older contextualism, which asked new buildings to be harmonious with surroundings rather than scream "look at me," has also taken stronger root. As Rem Koolhaas recently declared, "an icon may be individually plausible, but ... collectively they form an ultimately counterproductive and self-cancelling kind of landscape. So that is out".[6] Visual representations express this evolved contextualism, a welcome departure from the conventional pristine architectural rendering devoid of people, often from a birds-eye view, as though the viewer is peering down upon a model.

Complementary urbanism has been emerging around the world parallel to rapidly proliferating complementary currencies such as travel miles, time banking and local currencies. Similar to complementary currencies, complementary urbanism *complements* what is already there rather than attempt to replace it or compete with it. In the case of urbanism, what is already there may include existing buildings and infrastructure, market economies, and cultural traditions, as well as theories about which approach may be optimal. In the same way that complementary currencies liberate people from the pyramidal global economy's concentration of power and control along with its excesses and predatory behaviors,[7] complementary urbanism is not bound to the pyramidal urban development process and can benefit from the innovation, dynamism and resilience allowed by leveraging collective intelligence.

In the same way that complementary currencies liberate people from the pyramidal global economy's concentration of power and control along with its excesses and predatory behaviors, a complementary urbanism is not bound to the pyramidal urban development process and can benefit from the innovation, dynamism and resilience allowed by leveraging collective intelligence.

Asset-based and place-based, complementary urbanism builds upon what is integral to people and locales, their "DNA." It supports existing local businesses while also incentivizing innovation and entrepreneurship and providing an attractive place for national and global businesses to establish themselves. It builds upon cultural assets, supporting the rich diversity of communities, including historic buildings and districts, expressive arts and culture, and the wide range of creativity and expertise in any given place. And it showcases environmental assets, often connecting public space systems and integrating more nature into the city.

Complementary urbanism combines strategy with serendipity. In contrast to popular efforts to "conspire with reality," it is not principally tactical. The tactical approach may be that of the spy or double agent, fulfilling an agenda that might be covert and self-serving. Or it may be that of the guerilla community-builder aiming to make specific interventions, usually in their own neighborhoods, skirting political processes.[8] While the tactical approach is typically cynical and sometimes passive-aggressive, complementary urbanism aims clearly and idealistically to enhance places for all people.

The emergence of complementary urbanism is part of what environmentalist and entrepreneur Paul Hawken described several years ago as a worldwide "movement with no name" that will prevail because it is not based on ideology but on the identification of what is humane, behaving like an immune system[9] to heal social and urban malaise. Practitioners of complementary urbanism tend to regard human habitat as part of nature, rather than as a machine for living. They aspire to prosperity for all, rather than aiming principally for power, prestige and profits. Many are developing and implementing important tools for engaging others, unleashed by social media and ubiquitous interactive mobile technologies (Scearce, Leadbeater, Onuma, Collective Intelligence Research Institute). The goal is to render the planning, design and development processes more inclusive, accountable and effective, deeply inflecting the product. For example, the Onuma software system allows real-time collaborative design on a previously unseen scale through BIMStorms that allow users to contribute to a project according to their inclination and regardless of their expertise by using whatever software they have at hand from wherever they may be.[10]

In the course of this shift, the architectural profession has grown more multi-faceted, inspired by ecological flows and minimizing energy usage as much as by form-making. Landscape architecture has entered the urban fray in a big way and planning is becoming more proactive and visionary, rather than reactive and responsive. Each of these fields has been partnering with the others as transdisciplinary teams, as well as approaches, have grown commonplace.

Describing the evolution in planning and urban design, John Landis contends: "Planning is in the midst of a major paradigm change.... Planning's first paradigm, which ran in the US from the turn of the 20th century until the early 1970s, was all about plan-making and regulation: Community plans were developed to lay out future land use and infrastructure patterns, and accompanying land use regulations — typically subdivision controls and zoning — were adopted as implementation tools. Planning's second paradigm, which rose out of the environmental movement during the 1970s, was all about making the planning process more participatory; and then, beginning in the 1980s, more cognizant of uneven power relationships…. The new planning paradigm, call it Planning 3.0, will be all about measuring outcomes and developing implementation models that generate successful outcomes…. Planning 3.0 will be instantaneous in speed, collaborative in nature, and global in scope".[11] For urban design, Landis maintains, this new paradigm "will leave dogmatic labels behind, take on an international bent, and focus on how people actually use public and private spaces, and how they add to the urban livability".[12]

The practice of complementary urbanism begins with an understanding of, and appreciation for, current conditions, rather than ignoring or critiquing them. It then builds upon these existing assets instead of focusing on resolving problems or filling deficits. The latter tendency, which prevailed during the last century, was exemplified by the "hierarchy of needs" introduced by psychologist Abraham Maslow in 1943. This model implied people have deficits that need to be addressed, rather than intrinsic qualities and abilities that may be developed.[13]

Modern urbanism aligned with this view, identifying a need or problem, proposing solutions, establishing goals, and attempting to implement them. Subsequent efforts toward sustainable urbanism, for the most part, did not challenge this conventional approach. Indeed, the most widely applied definition of sustainability includes the word "needs" twice: "Meeting the *needs* of the present without compromising the ability of future generations to meet their own *needs*".[14]

In contrast, complementary urbanists begin by uncovering their own hunches and engaging other stakeholders to consider the assets of a place and how best to leverage them: buildings, neighborhoods, businesses, cultural institutions, natural landscapes, or creative and intellectual capital. Directing attention first to opportunity-finding, this approach counters the tendency to begin with problem-finding by applying *two kinds of vision*: the ability to see things clearly and a vision for a better future. In the process, the greatest problems often become the greatest solutions, revealing blessings that may be disguised and making virtue of necessity.[15]

Just as a good manager builds on the existing strengths of an organization, complementary urbanism builds upon given assets of places and people. Instead of the modernist tendency to begin with a tabula rasa, it begins with a *tabula plena*. This approach cultivates good ideas while leveraging resources and support to realize them. It also sets a generative and dynamic self-adjusting feedback mechanism into motion, enabling communities to build creatively upon their strengths in an ongoing fashion.

Urbanists who are moving beyond sustainability to prosperity — New, Landscape and others — are thereby introducing subtle changes with large impacts. Organizational consultant Otto Scharmer describes the larger context in which this incipient evolution in urbanism is inscribed, saying: "I personally believe that the biggest of all shifts is yet to come. It's a shift that does not deal with a technological transformation but with a social transformation: the transformation of the relationship between business, government and civil society from manipulation and confrontation to dialogue and co-creation." This will occur, Scharmer maintains, with "collective leadership capacity to draw together all key stakeholders and involve them in a process that begins with uncovering common intention and ends with collectively creating profound innovation on the scale of the whole system".[16]

> Just as a good manager builds on the existing strengths of an organization, complementary urbanism builds upon given assets of places and people. Instead of the modernist tendency to begin with a tabula rasa, it begins with a *tabula plena*.

Prospects for Good Urbanism

Thanks to concerted efforts over the last several decades to improve places, there is now a virtual consensus among urbanists about what constitutes good urbanism.[17] This consensus holds that our regions should be comprised of networks of quality public spaces, punctuated and lined by vital hubs of activity. Conversely, good urbanism consists of mixed-use cores (large hubs and smaller nodes) connected by corridors of transit, bicycle, pedestrian and automobile routes and amply interspersed with linked quality public spaces. Key to success is the connective tissue: infrastructure and public spaces. Whether retrofitted or new, for practical purposes or pleasure, the consensus holds that this connective tissue should be multipurpose, beautiful, highly functional and efficient. It should benefit from the most recent technologies and harmonize with its natural and cultural settings.

While there are numerous iterations and a range of foci, most place prescriptions converge on these general principles. Along with this knowledge of the component parts of good urbanism, we also have the will and the tools to achieve those desired ends. Nevertheless, good urbanism still eludes in far too many instances, hence the continued proliferation of prescriptions for healing places and lingering doubts as to the efficacy of professionals dedicated to urbanism, principally architects, urban designers and planners.

With regard to architects, sociologist Nathan Glazer declared: "The long history of the relationship of architects to the design of cities seems to have come to an end, or at least a temporary stop. Architects no longer design cities, and they are not being asked to. A relationship between architects and the design of cities that goes back to the Renaissance and perhaps before, and continued through the American City Beautiful movement and through early modernism, is for the moment in suspension".[18]

Alex Krieger registered a parallel lament about urban designers, saying: "The heroic form-giving tradition may be in decline. After all, the twentieth century witnessed immense urban harm caused by those who offered a singular or universal idea of what a city is, or what urbanization should produce. But our cultural observers remind us that pragmatism and technique cannot be a sufficient substitute, nor can design professionals be mere absorbers of public opinion waiting for consensus to build. One must think and offer ideas as well…. But such deliverers of bold saber strokes (to borrow a phrase from Gideon) are rarer today than they were at the turn of the 20th century, or we heed their visions less often".[19]

Almost two decades ago, James Howard Kunstler queried, "Does the modern profession called urban planning have anything to do with making good places anymore?".[20] More recently, Glazer remarked: "Most observers of the city today would agree that the image of the planner in the public mind is not very defined or compelling, indeed rather dim. City planning, large-scale planning in general, is not in high repute these days…. It is clear the dominant element in the image of the planner is no longer that of the reformer, the bringer of hope, which is what the image of the city planner, I believe, used to be…. The planner today knows many details of many programs and the arguments that support one or another, but larger visions are beyond his responsibility…. And as a corollary, we do not normally think of calling in the professional planner when we consider today what has gone wrong with the city and suburb, and what can be done about it. These days we call him in to help with the details".[21]

Just this past year, Thomas Campanella sounded a similar alarm, asking: "How did a profession that roared to life with grand ambitions become such a mouse?".[22] Campanella posed this challenge: "How can we cultivate in planners the kind of visionary thinking that once characterized the profession? How can we ensure that the idealism of our students is not extinguished as they move into practice? How can we transform planners into big-picture thinkers with the courage to imagine alternatives to the status quo, and equipped with the skills and the moxie to lead the recovery of American infrastructure and put the nation on a greener, more sustainable path? .... We have become a caretaker profession — reactive rather than proactive, corrective instead of preemptive, rule bound and hamstrung and anything but visionary. If we lived in Nirvana, this would be fine. But we don't. We are entering the uncharted waters of global urbanization on a scale never seen. And we are not in the wheelhouse, let alone steering the ship. We may not even be on board."[23]

How can we ensure those specially trained to plan and design cities play principal roles? How to prevent this job from defaulting to private developers in negotiation with city councils and development review boards? How can we, as urbanists, work to achieve good urbanism more reliably?

During a period of rapid urban growth one century ago, Daniel Hudson Burnham sang the praises of big plans, and the creation of numerous city plans and visions ensued for half a century. Widespread disappointment with modern urbanism, however, conspired to diminish such visioning. This disappointment owed to both product and process, the *what* as well as the *how*. With regards to product (the *what*), modern urbanism's principal banes were the separation of functions, the death of the street, and the reliance upon the automobile. In terms of process (the *how*), problems inhered in the imposition of these plans upon places without regard for place (built and natural), history or culture. In the wake of modern urbanism's demise, numerous "open society" and participatory efforts emerged that avoided the heavy hand, but proved largely unsatisfactory in terms of improving places.

The first shortcoming (product) has been ably addressed since then by the emergent consensual prescriptions for good urbanism described above.[24] The second (process), however, has yet to be adequately addressed, severely impairing the advancement of urbanism. Retreating from fully addressing this core issue, the professions dedicated to urbanism largely deflected attention to narrower pursuits, technological preoccupations, and turf wars.

Needless to say, prescribing good urbanism without the ability to heed such prescriptions is insufficient, likely explaining the ongoing lament about the paucity of bold plans ever since the failure of modern urbanism. Throughout history, all the way through modern urbanism, visionary planning and urban design were essentially top-down. The reaction since the 1960s was emphatically bottom-up. Since then, diluted versions of both have characterized most efforts with, for the most part, mixed or underwhelming results.

Complementary urbanism is neither top-down nor bottom-up, but *sideways*. Turning the pyramid on its side, it begins with an idea hatched by one or more people, who invite all stakeholders to participate in refining and realizing the vision. While professional urbanists can catalyze this process, it may also be initiated by political or community leaders, artists, developers, philanthropic organizations, cultural institutions, or anyone else interested in effecting change.[25] Along the way, an entity may be established to oversee the project and institute enabling policy to facilitate implementation and allow others to easily adapt it for other circumstances. Complementary urbanism thereby responds to both shortcomings, process as well as product, enriching (complementing) the conventional approach toward urbanism and moving it beyond sustainability to prosperity.

While the onus previously was on those at the top of the power hierarchy, complementary urbanism often accomplishes the bulk of the work before reaching them. *Instead of diminishing their power, however, this approach actually extends it* because they have enabled the process to occur, or at least sanctioned it, and through co-creation, the process delivers a product that has been polished by the interested parties who have already taken ownership of the project, invested in making it happen, and will feel proud of it when it does. Indeed, so much has already been accomplished by the time it reaches the final decision makers that the process greatly reduces the huge investment typically required to get an idea approved, allocate resources to build it, and obtain necessary support and buy-in. Without this process, these steps are unreliable at best. With it, the project has actually already started happening and the simple rubber stamp of decision makers, now at the side as true civil servants, ensures their popularity and continued support from the community. Plus they can claim bragging rights to a highly successful transformation in their city or town.

While everyone can contribute to produce good urbanism, professional urbanists play a special role by lending a range of expertise while imparting the wisdom to reflect, illuminate, shock, and/or go with the flow. The best urbanism has always drawn appropriately from humanist, avant-garde *and* landscape ecology traditions. Applying the two kinds of vision (seeing clearly and envisioning a better future), we can discern when and where to apply each, and in what combination. The opportunity is ours to be transformative in the best way by continuing to learn from cultural convergence and transmute the creative tensions of contending urbanisms into a complementary one that forges better places for all into the future.

Endnotes

1   For an overview, see Ellin 1999, 93–105

2   Mostafavi, Mohsen and Gareth Doherty. 2010. *Ecological Urbanism*. Baden: Lars Müller Publishers.

3   For those already strongly committed to, and invested in, the pursuit of sustainability, or who do not find the term prosperity particularly appealing, this could just as well be described as a shift to the next level of sustainability.

4   See Dunham-Jones and Williamson.

5   Rapidly proliferating border-crossing organizations are important allies in this general shift. These include the Center for Ecoliteracy [ecoliteracy.org], Design for Health [designforhealth.net], Shaping Footprints [sfpinc.org], Active Living by Design [activelivingbydesign.org], Project for Public Spaces [pps.org], Walkable Communities [walkable.org], Society for Organizational Learning [solonline.org], Well Community Association and Foundation [wellcommunity.org], the Urbal Institute [turnstone.tv/theurbalinstitut.html], Project for Livable Communities [livablecommunities.wordpress.com/], and the Slow Cities Movement [cittaslow.net], among others.

6   Koolhaas, Rem. 2010. Advancement versus Apocalypse. In Mostafavi, Mohsen and Gareth Doherty, Eds., *Ecological Urbanism*. Baden: Lars Müller Publishers, pp. 56–71.

7   Collective Intelligence Research Institute. ciresearchinstitute.org. Accessed January 21, 2012.

8   See Lydon et al.

9   Hawken, Paul. 2007. *Blessed Unrest: How the Largest Movement in the World Came into Being and Why No One Saw it Coming*. New York: Viking Press.

10 Onuma, Kimon. 2010. Location, Location, Location: BIM, BIM, BIM. *Journal of Building Information Modeling* (Fall): 21–22. Accessed July 13, 2011. wbdg.org/references/jbim.php.

11 Landis, John. 2011. Letter from the Chair of Planning. Accessed August 5, 2011. www.design.upenn.edu/city-regional-planning/letter

12 www.design.upenn.edu/city-regional-planning/letter

13 While Maslow recognized that people who are self-actualizing favor "Being-cognition," which focuses on what they have (their own gifts), as opposed to "Deficiency-cognition," which is self-critical, his hierarchy of needs is a model that focuses on deficiencies.

14 United Nations. 1987. *Our Common Future: Brundtland Report.* UN World Commission on Environment and Development. August 4. Emphasis added.

15 I have described this approach as VIDA, Spanish for "life" and an acronym for Visioning, Inspiring, Demonstrating and Advocating (Ellin 2010b).

16 Scharmer, C. Otto. 2010. The Blind Spot of Institutional Leadership: How to Create Deep Innovation through Moving from Egosystem to Ecosystem Awareness. Paper prepared for World Economic Forum Annual Meeting of the New Champion. Tianjin, People's Republic of China, September: 13–15.

17 Zeynep Toker and Henrik Minassians (2011) also suggest this.

18 Glazer, Nathan. 2007. *From a Cause to a Style: Modernist Architecture's Encounter with the American City.* Princeton, NJ: Princeton University Press. p. 290.

19 Krieger, Alex. 2009. Territories of Urban Design. In Krieger, Alex and William S. Saunders, Eds., *Urban Design.* Minneapolis, MN: University of Minnesota Press.

20 Kunstler, James Howard. 1993. *The Geography of Nowhere.* New York: Simon and Schuster.

21 Glazer, op cit., p. 270.

22 Campanella, Thomas. 2011. Jane Jacobs and the Death and Life of American Planning. The Design Observer Group. places.designobserver.com/feature/jane-jacobs-and-the-death-and-life-of-american-planning/25188/. In Page, Max and Timothy Mennel, Ed. 2011. *Reconsidering Jane Jacobs.* Chicago: American Planning Association.

23 Ibid.

24 See Ellin 2012.

25 In *Urban Design Reclaimed*, Emily Talen provides step-by-step instructions for anyone interested in advancing an urban design proposal (2009).

Additional Works Cited

Dunham-Jones, Ellen and June Williamson. 2008. *Retrofitting Suburbia.* New York: Wiley.

Ellin, Nan. 2012. *Good Urbanism.* Washington, DC: Island Press.

_____. 2010b. "Canalscape: Practising Integral Urbanism in Metropolitan Phoenix." *Journal of Urban Design*, Special Issue, 15.4: 599–610.

_____. 2010a. The Tao of Urbanism." In Goldsmith, Stephen and Lynne Elizabeth, Eds., *What We See: Advancing the Investigations of Jane Jacobs.* Oakland, CA: New Village Press.

_____. 2006. *Integral Urbanism.* New York: Routledge.

Krieger, Alex. 2000. The Planner as Urban Designer: Reforming Planning Education. In Rodwin, Lloyd and Bishwapriya Sanyal, Eds., *The Profession of City Planning: Changes, Images and Challenges: 1950–2000.* New Brunswick, NJ: Center for Urban Policy Research / Rutgers University Press.

Leadbeater, Charles. 2008. *We-think: Mass Innovation, not Mass Production.* London: Profile Books.

Lydon, Mike, Dan Bartman, Ronald Woudstra and Aurash Khawarzad. 2011. *Tactical Urbanism.* PDF. pattern-cities.com/archives/175.

Scearce, Diana. 2011. Connected Citizens: The Power, Peril, and Potential of Networks. Knight Foundation and Monitor Institute. knight.box.net/shared/ng70lqn9hb.

Scharmer, C. Otto. 2007. *Theory U: Leading from the Future as It Emerges.* Cambridge, MA: Society for Organizational Learning.

Talen, Emily. 2009. *Urban Design Reclaimed.* American Planning Association.

Toker, Zeynep and Henrik Minassians. 2011. Good Cities and Healthy Communities for a Better Quality of Life. Abstract, ACSP Conference Salt Lake City, UT.

18

A Critique of the High Line: Landscape Urbanism and the Global South[1]

Leon Morenas

O VER THE PAST YEAR, there have been serious attempts to introduce the Indian architecture and planning community to Landscape Urbanism, a fairly recent American landscape movement. *The Journal of Landscape Architecture* (*LA Journal*) dedicated its entire June issue to this subject, while the introductory issue of the international architectural magazine *Domus* in India in November 2011 featured six large glossy pages (with illustrations) on the High Line, which it deemed the most visible success of this movement. The guest editor of *LA Journal* writes that Landscape Urbanism "may play an important role in theorizing and conceiving the character and morphology of its [India's] future development".[2] This chapter attempts to unpack the claims of Landscape Urbanism by examining the writings of some of its earliest progenitors and by presenting the lesser-known narratives of the High Line's "impact" on New York's urban context. Such an analysis is especially timely given the ongoing proposals to replicate High Line-type projects in other American cities, namely Chicago, Philadelphia, Jersey City and St. Louis.[3] The views presented in this chapter are therefore not just relevant for India's future development but urban development within the United States as well.

Landscape Urbanism is a discipline that attempts to leverage the art of landscape architecture towards the ends of urban planning. It has been gaining valence with the success of the environmental movement, since it promises to integrate ecology with the traditional, engineered, infrastructural systems that drive urban development. Some have argued that Landscape Urbanism "has allowed landscape architects to fill a professional void, as planning has largely opted out of responsibility for proposing physical designs".[4] Professional voids may have been filled, but this paper wrestles with a related but perhaps more important question: does Landscape Urbanism fill (or create) other voids left by planning?

This chapter therefore approaches the discipline of Landscape Urbanism with scepticism and offers a critique of Landscape Urbanism's lexis and praxis by examining the writings of its most vociferous proponents and contextualizing the political and economic development of the High Line in Manhattan, New York. The first section lays out the foundations of this scepticism, while the second section details this critique.

Making and Unmaking the Indian Metropolis

> We can not only do a more viable job, but a more Indian job than they could, because I think we can really enter into their spirit. Practically all forward looking Indians have been educated in and dazzled by the Western world, so that for a considerable time to come, they will be doing Western work.

In his "*Report on Master Plan of the New Punjab Capital*" in 1950, American regionalist Albert Mayer envisaged his planning practice in India in the aforementioned words. "Fused with our own [American] simplicity and functional honesty",[5] his plans would ultimately be superior to any indigenous planning attempt, especially given the commonsensical fact that all aspirations of "forward looking Indians" to modernity were Western. In his fifteen years of practice in India, Albert Mayer became one of the most prominent American planners in the country's tryst with modernity. While his most famous projects include the rural development plan of Etawah in the State of Uttar Pradesh, the Master Plan for Chandigarh, and the Regional Plan for Delhi, he was also involved in urban planning of the Indian cities of Ahmadabad, Allahabad, Bombay, Calcutta, Kanpur, and the larger Damadar Valley Development.[6]

I invoke Albert Mayer's work for two specific reasons. First, his words are a striking example of the territorial claims made by Western planners, that irrespective of the vagaries of the Indian context, its Third World condition could be "made modern" through the proper emulation and deployment of Western models of planning and development. While these claims enshrined in the master plans for the city of Chandigarh and the region of Delhi have clearly failed to deliver [Western] modernity to the masses, the faith in Western models and rhetoric still remains. The recent outsourcing of the Bangalore Master Plan 2015, to a French consultancy firm M/s SCE by the Bangalore Development Authority,[7] and the attempts to peddle Landscape Urbanism as a planning panacea mentioned earlier attest to this predilection.

Second, I wish to draw attention to the fact that Landscape Urbanism is not the first attempt to structure the urban environment using landscape and ecology. Other authors in this book explore this history in detail; I have argued elsewhere[8] that in the 1950s, the practice of regional planning was envisaged as the attempt to structure urban development using ecology to create "a fuller quality of life, at every point in the region".[9] Albert Mayer cofounded the Housing Study Guild along with American regional planning pioneers Lewis Mumford and Henry Wright in 1933 and went on to become an active member of the Regional Planning Association of America.[10]

The Delhi Master Plan of 1962 (DMP), produced under the leadership of Albert Mayer using regional planning principles, outlined an "integrated and balanced overall programme of development" for Delhi over two decades.[11] Two Master Plan amendments later, the development in India's capital is increasingly uneven. Close to 66 percent of the city's population lives on a tenth or less of Delhi's urban land and even these pockets are in the most marginalized of areas, while the other third has access to the other 90 percent of good urban land.[12] This inequitable distribution of land is increasing under the neoliberal and laissez-faire policies of the Indian state.

These shortcomings are not just typical of India or Delhi but are evident in the prominent examples of regional planning — and Landscape Urbanism, as we shall see later — within the United States, even before they inspired repetition in India. Despite the rhetoric and assertions of the planners of the Tennessee Valley Authority Project and Radburn,

New Jersey, both projects excluded large sections of the poor, the very people for which they were planned.[13] In the following section, I will be employing a similar method of analysis in examining the contentions of Landscape Urbanists and the impact of their most visible project on the larger New York metropolis, especially on lower-income populations and their neighborhoods.

The View from the High Line

It was a damp day in late July 2009 when I got to experience the $152-million "great West Side story" called the High Line.[14] A third of the High Line to be exact: at that time, only the first phase of the project, approximately half a mile (800 meters) long, had been opened to the public. Since its inauguration by New York's mayor Michael Bloomberg in early June, the High Line had been receiving accolades from the press and my peers. As I stood about thirty feet (10 meters) above the ground among verdant vegetation and planting beds, it was easy to be spellbound by this oasis of green. The park offered panoramic views of the Hudson River in between rundown warehouses with graffiti-embellished walls. I did not know it at the time, but the park was a quintessential example of Landscape Urbanism. To me, there were two particular design features that were alluring: [a] the intelligent use of the train tracks that carved meandering pathways through the planting beds and flora and [b] the creative use of the changing urban context. These two points were linked,

Fig. 18.1:
Urban context of abandoned warehouses around the High Line.
Source: Friends of High Line

and as I eventually found out through my research, told a much larger, more complicated story.

History of the High Line and the Ideology of Landscape Urbanism

Originally designed in 1929 and functioning by 1934, the High Line was an elevated freight railway system thirteen miles (twenty-one kilometers) long used to transport produce from the Meatpacking District without disturbing street-level traffic.[15] At that time, the project cost over $150 million (the equivalent of $2 billion today), but given the growth of inter-state trucking, the High Line lay abandoned from 1980 onwards.[16] Then, in 2004, a non-profit organization called the Friends of High Line selected James Corner Field Operations and Dillier Scofidio+Renfro to design the reuse of this section of the line.

Charles Waldheim, founder of the Landscape Urbanism movement, describes the emergent practice, of which this project is emblematic, as "the use of infrastructural systems and the public landscapes they engender as the very ordering mechanisms of the urban field itself, shaping and shifting the organization of urban settlement and its inevitable indeterminate economic, political and social futures".[17] So how is the reuse and redesign of the abandoned freight line used to "shape" and "shift" the organization of the urban settlement of West Side Manhattan around it? And what kind of "indeterminate" yet "inevitable" economic, political and social future of New York did the High Line engender?

The High Line's designer, James Corner, himself advocates in his article "Terra Fluxus" that Landscape Urbanism "suggests shifting attention away from the object qualities of space (whether formal or scenic) to the systems that condition the distribution and density of urban form".[18] And yet, there is a tendency among those disciplines dealing with "nature" — landscape architecture included — to compress complex phenomena into "a flat, colourless cartoon",[19] ignoring the social, political, economic and cultural particularities of the context involved.[20] Corner himself challenges this view in his article, citing the Marxist geographer David Harvey: "'the struggle' for (landscape) designers and planners lies not with spatial form and aesthetic appearances alone but with the advancement of more socially just, politically emancipatory, and ecologically sane mix(es) of spatio-temporal production processes,

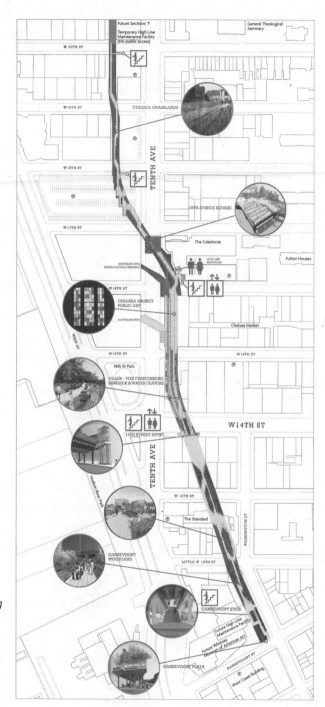

Fig. 18.2: *Plan of Phase I of the High Line. The plan shows the overall planting design of the first phase along with images of the prominent landscape feature.* SOURCE: CITY OF NEW YORK, 2009

rather than the capitulation to those processes, imposed by uncontrolled capital accumulation, backed by class privilege and gross inequalities of political-economic power".[21] In other words, the breathtaking design of the High Line was only part of the job of the Landscape Urbanist; other responsibilities included creating socially just, politically emancipatory, and ecologically balanced designs.

A View of the High Line: the Tiering of New York City's Parks

So did the Landscape Urbanism of the High Line fulfil these other responsibilities? Sadly, not according to me, and certainly not according to the man whom Corner uses to justify the practice of Landscape Urbanism. In 2010, David Harvey commented that "the billionaire mayor, Michael Bloomberg, is reshaping the city along lines favourable to developers ... and promoting the city as an optimal location for high-value businesses and a fantastic destination for tourists..., in effect, turning Manhattan into one vast gated community for the rich".[22] Bloomberg is charged with "leverage[ing] public land and money to turn parks into self-sustaining enterprises," ultimately creating a "two-tier parks system".[23] On one tier are spectacular, exclusive and expensive parks like the High Line,[24] Madison Square Park, and Union Square Park, while on the other are neighbourhood parks like Canarsie and Flatlands in Southeast Brooklyn that provide space for plebeian activities like sports, barbeques, picnics and walks. Their growing alterity is evidenced by at least two mutually reinforcing factors: [a] the lack of public funding of social infrastructure and human resources; and [b] the privatization of successful parks eliminating cross-subsidization to support other parks.[25]

In 1960 — the same year New York's infamous "master builder" Robert Moses retired — the New York Department of Parks and Recreation was the largest urban parks system in the United States. It boasted over 35,000 acres (14,000 hectares) of land and received 1.4 percent of the city's funds for parks' maintenance and operations. Under Mayor Bloomberg's gigantic 2010 city budget of $63.6 billion, the fraction allocated towards the city's parks was a paltry 0.37 percent (or $239 million).[26] These budget cuts have resulted in the downgrading of the park's workforce to around three thousand employees, about half the number that was employed in 1970. So while lower-income parks like

Fig. 18.3: *Detail of planting design.*
Source: Friends of High Line.

Canarsie and Flatlands have just one dedicated maintenance worker for 1,200 acres (500 hectares) of parkland, the 2.9 acres (1.2 hectares) of the High Line are tended to by a team of maintenance workers including gardeners, custodians and bathroom attendants. In the Bronx, 6,970 acres (2,821 hectares) are patrolled by five or six security officers, while the High Line is patrolled by double that number.

In the past, it was customary for parks to pay close to 20 percent of their concession revenues to build and maintain the parks system, but with the increasing reliance on private–public partnership models, "special arrangements" are made so that the percentage of revenues paid to the city is greatly reduced.[27] One "special arrangement" is that the Friends of High Line keep *all* of the money from park concessions. In diverting what was traditionally city income that could have been redistributed to other neighbourhood parks, these profits have ended up as handsome rewards to philanthropically inclined individuals. Robert Hammond, the founder of Friends of High Line, pocketed more than $1.2 million over a ten-year period, raking in $280,000 for his philanthropic work in 2009 alone.[28] Hammond's salary was $75,000 more than what the city's parks commissioner, Adrene Benepe, was paid to oversee more than ten thousand times the park acreage that year.

Conclusion

In focusing on a specific Landscape Urbanism project, the High Line, I have attempted to show that despite its original rhetoric (conceived,

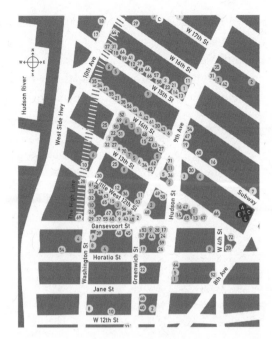

Fig. 18.4: *Meatpacking District. The circles indicate the bars, galleries, boutique shops, hotels, salons and spas that have resulted in the gentrification of the Meatpacking District. The High Line has acted as an unnecesary accelerator to urban redevelopment in this area--presumed to justify its cost.*

SOURCE: MEATPACKING DISTRICT
IMPROVEMENT ASSOCIATION, 2011

likely, with the best of intentions), Landscape Urbanism does not inherently contribute to social justice, political emancipation, or ecologically saner designs. Rather, it could be argued that parts of the movement have contributed to just what Corner wished it would oppose: "uncontrolled capital accumulation, backed by class privilege and gross inequalities of political-economic power".[29] The High Line has in fact become "a huge magnet for development" with more than thirty new projects already commissioned or partially constructed at the time of its inauguration.[30] It is beginning to resemble that predictable form of gentrification where, as Lindsay[31] points out, "shopping malls, multiplexes and box stores proliferate" as part of "a 'new urbanism' movement that touts the sale of community and boutique lifestyles to fulfil (bourgeois) urban dreams."

In his critique of Landscape Urbanism, American urban designer Graham Shane[32] asserts that the movement is a *response* to a particular type of American urbanism, typical to Detroit, characterized by "Henry Ford's myopia, racism and anti-urbanism." In embracing Landscape Urbanism for its small-scale and bottom-up approaches, we should not lose sight of the fact that other cities — in the US and elsewhere — are not organized along these principles and may not require a Landscape

Urbanist response. He goes on to remind us that "the foundations of a true urbanity" are social justice and equality.

As mentioned at the beginning of this chapter, visions for India's urban future have often drawn on models proposed by the West. "Vision–2021" now envisages Delhi as "a global metropolis and a world-class city," and just like in New York, there have been disturbing trends and increasing evidence of the city's poor experiencing growing spatial and social injustice.[33] Before we drink the Landscape Urbanism Kool-Aid that proposes "moving from both modernist and New Urbanist models of ordering the city ... to more open-ended, strategic models",[34] it may serve us well to critically examine — keeping the High Line in view — whose strategies and whose ends are being served, and at whose expense.

Endnotes

1   An earlier version of this essay appeared in *The Economic and Political Weekly*, XLVII (7) in 2012.

2   Paul, Rahul. 2011. Landscape Urbanism. *Journal of Landscape Urbanism* (31): 27–31

3   Taylor, Kate. 2010. After High Line's Success, Other Cities Look Up. *The New York Times*, 14 July 2010. Viewed on 18 Mar 2012. nytimes.com/2010/07/15/arts/design/15highline.html?_r=1&ref=opinion Witold Rybczynski. 2011. Bringing the High Line Back to Earth. *The New York Times*, 15 May 2011. Viewed on 18 Mar 2012. nytimes.com/2011/05/15/opinion/15Rybczynski.html. p. 2.

4   Waldheim, Charles. 2006. Landscape as Urbanism. In Waldheim, C. Ed., *The Landscape Urbanism Reader*. New York: Princeton Architectural Press, p. 39.

5   Mayer, Albert. June 14, 1953. *The Future of India*. New York: Columbia University Avery Archives.

6   Emmett, Robert. 1977. *Guide to the Albert Mayer Papers on India*. Chicago: University of Chicago Press. Viewed on 18 Mar 2012. lib.uchicago.edu/e/su/southasia/mayer.html

7   Jacob, Samuel. 2008. Master Plan Not Legal: PIL in High Court. Citizen Matters in Bangalore, 11 Jul 2008, Viewed 18 Mar 2012. bangalore.citizenmatters.in/articles/view/270-cdp-charged

8   Morenas, Leon. 2010. *Planning the City of Djinns: Exorcizing the Ghosts in Delhi's Post-Colonial Development Machine*. Unpublished Manuscript.

9   Mumford, Lewis. 1925. Regions — To Live In. *Survey*. No 54.

10   Hall, Peter. 1988. *Cities of Tomorrow*. Cambridge: Blackwell Publishing Limited, p. 148.

11   Delhi Development Authority (DDA). 1962. *Master Plan of Delhi*. Delhi: DDA, p. 1.

12   Verma, Gita Dewan. 2002. *Slumming India: A Chronicle of Slums and Their Saviours*. New Delhi: Penguin.

13   Ekbladh, David. Summer 2002. Mr. TVA: Grass-Roots Development, David Lilienthal, and the Rise and Fall of the Tennessee Valley Authority as a Symbol for U.S. Overseas Development, 1933–73. *Diplomatic History*. No 26. pp. 335–74. Peter Hall. 1988. *Cities of Tomorrow*. Cambridge: Blackwell Publishing Limited, pp. 161–164. Daniel Schaffer. 1982. *Garden Cities for America: The Radburn Experience*. Philadelphia, PA: Temple University Press, pp.173–77.

14   As its name suggests, the serpentine, mile-and-a-half-long project is located on Manhattan's West Side. Beginning at Gansevoort Street and progressing through the Meatpacking District, the elevated park is conceived as fairly linear, running between 10th and 11th avenues until West 30th Street. The urban park then loops around the West Side railyards and veers along 12th Avenue close to the Hudson River before terminating on West 34th Street. Robin Pogrebin. 2009. Renovated High Line Now Open for Strolling. *The New York Times*, 08 June 2009, p. 6. Viewed on 01 Jan 2012. nytimes.com/2009/06/09/arts/design/09highline-RO.html

15 Friends of High Line. 2010. High Line History. Viewed on 01 Jan 2012. thehighline.org/about/high-line-history

16 Ibid.

17 Waldheim, op cit., p. 39.

18 Corner, James. 2006. Terra Fluxus. In Waldheim, C., Ed., *The Landscape Urbanism Reader*. New York: Princeton Architectural Press, p. 28.

19 Cronon, William. 1995. Introduction: In Search of Nature. In Cronon, W., Ed., *Uncommon Ground: Rethinking the Human Place in Nature*. New York: W.W. Norton & Company, p. 35.

20 In order to answer the aforementioned questions, I will be drawing from the largely interdisciplinary fields of the humanities, detailed by Cronon in his 1995 work. He reminds us that scholars from the humanities, who include anthropologists, ethnographers and literary theorists, have demonstrated that "the natural world is far more dynamic, far more changeable, and far more entangled with human history" (1995, p. 24) than traditionally acknowledged. So what the humanities offers, in addition to shifting the focus from product to process, is to embed these products and processes within the larger context of human history.

21 Corner, op cit., p. 28.

22 Lindsay, Greg. 2010. David Harvey's Urban Manifesto: Down With Suburbia; Down With Bloomberg's New York. *Fast Company.Com*. 21 Jul. Viewed on 01 Jan 2012. fastcompany.com/1673037/david-harveys-urban-manifesto-down-with-suburbia-down-with-bloombergs-new-york, p. 6.

23 Arden, Patrick. 2010. The High Cost of Free Parks: Do Public-Private Partnerships Save Parks or Exploit Them? *Next American City*. Issue 27. 16 June. Viewed on 01 Jan 2012, p. 6. americancity.org/buzz/entry/2402/

24 Mayor Bloomberg's support of the High Line was instrumental in its creation as part of his larger agenda of encouraging public–private partnerships to renew the city. The High Line, a paltry 2.9 acres (1.2 ha) of a partially completed park, cost a whopping $86 million in city, state, federal and private donations (of which the philanthrocapitalist group "Friends of the High Line" contributed a little over half) (Pogrebin 2009).

25 There is a third factor worth mentioning: this involves the unholy nexus between private interests and elected representatives who reallocate dwindling public funds towards the more exclusive parks. Christine Quinn, the current speaker of the New York City Council and "a leading supporter of the High Line project" during her controversial third-term council reelection, received $54,343 campaign funding from the Friends of High Line board members. While this practice of receiving campaign funding from private parties with vested interests is not considered illegal in the United States, it is perceived as bribery in most other countries of the world. In April 2008, *The New York Times* unearthed a scheme that allowed the city council speaker, who was Christine Quinn, "to hand out funds for pet projects throughout the year." In 2008 alone $4.5 million of public money — and $17.4 million since 2001 — was handed out as political favors, receiving only meek criticism that public funding was being "bestowed without accountability" (*The New York Times*, 2008).

26 Arden also points out that the city of Chicago spends almost $150 million more on approximately 14,000 acres (5,700 hectares) of parkland (2010: 12). Arden Patrick. 2010. The High Cost of Free Parks: Do Public-Private Partnerships Save Parks or Exploit Them? *Next American City*. Issue 27. 16 June, p. 11,12. Viewed on 01 Jan 2012. americancity.org/buzz/entry/2402/

27 Ibid, p. 40.

28 Ibid.

29 Corner, op cit., p. 28.

30 Kilgannon, Corey. 2010. High Line's Next Phase: Less Glitz, More Intimacy. *The New York Times*. 19 Dec. Viewed on 01 Jan 2012. cityroom.blogs.nytimes.com/2010/12/19/high-lines-next-phase-less-glitz-more-intimacy/?sudsredirect=true

31 Lindsay, op cit., p. 5.

32 Shane, Graham. 2003. The Emergence of "Landscape Urbanism": Reflections on Stalking Detroit. *Harvard Design Magazine;* 2003(19) 1–8. Viewed on 01 Jan 2012. crtl-i.com/PDF/GrahamShane_OnLandscape.pdf

33 Dupont, Veronique. 2011. The Dream of Delhi as a Global City. *International Journal of Urban and Regional Research,* 35 (3): 533–54.
34 Corner, op cit., p. 28.

Additional Works Cited

Ciorra, Pippo. 2011. The High Line, New York. *Domus.* 01(01): 76–81.

Editorial. 2008. Ms. Quinn and the Potemkin Accounts. *The New York Times.* 05 Apr. Viewed on 01 Jan 2012. nytimes.com/2008/04/05/opinion/05sat2.html

Mayer, Albert. May 12, 1950,. Report on Master Plan of the New Punjab Capital. *The Albert Mayer Papers on India.* Box 18, Folder 30. The University of Chicago Library.

Index

About the Editors

Andrés **Duany** is a founding principal at Duany Plater-Zyberk & Company (DPZ). DPZ has completed designs for close to 300 new towns, regional plans, and community revitalization projects. Andrés received his undergraduate degree in architecture and urban planning from Princeton University and a master's degree in architecture from the Yale School of Architecture. He has been awarded several honorary doctorates, the Brandeis Award for Architecture, the Thomas Jefferson Memorial Medal of Architecture from the University of Virginia, and the Vincent J. Scully Prize for exemplary practice and scholarship in architecture and urban design from the National Building Museum.

Emily Talen is a Professor at Arizona State University in the School of Geographical Sciences and Urban Planning and the School of Sustainability. She holds a Ph.D in Geography from the University of California, Santa Barbara. She is a Fellow of the American Institute of Certified Planners. She has published over 50 peer-reviewed journal articles and has four books. Her most recent book is *City Rules* (Island Press, 2012). Support for her research has come from artistic agencies, including the National Endowment for the Arts, as well as science foundations, including 3 grants from the National Science Foundation.

About the Contributors

JASON BRODY IS AN ASSISTANT PROFESSOR in the Department of Landscape Architecture / Regional and Community Planning at Kansas State University. He teaches studios as well as courses in urban design, planning history, planning theory, and research design. Jason's research involves historical analysis of the construction and diffusion of urban design knowledge. He is particularly interested in how "big" ideas like sustainability, community, New Urbanism, and Landscape Urbanism shape professional practices and urban form. He holds a Masters degree in City Planning from the University of Pennsylvania and a PhD from the University of Illinois at Urbana-Champaign.

Michael Dennis is a principal of Michael Dennis & Associate in Boston, and Professor of Architecture at MIT, where he teaches Urban Design and Theory. He was the 1986 Thomas Jefferson Professor of Architecture at the University of Virginia, the 1988 Eero Saarinen Professor of Architecture at Yale University, and the 2006 Charles Moore Professor of Architecture at the University of Michigan. In 2011, he was awarded the CNU Athena Medal for his contributions to urbanism. He has lectured widely, and is the author of Court and Garden: From the French Hôtel to the City of Modern Architecture.

Bruce Donnelly is an urban planner, editor, and New Urbanist based in Cleveland, Ohio. His main work involves editing plans and published works, analyzing codes and planning documents, and writing explanatory text to illuminate a range of issues, problems, and solutions related to urbanism. He has been involved in writing codes and comprehensive plans for several SmartCodes, and has worked on the Louisiana Speaks recovery plan and the creation of a Public Works Manual for Taos, New Mexico.

Nan Ellin is Professor and Chair of the Department of City & Metropolitan Planning at the University of Utah where she leads the Salt Lake City Workshop, a seeding ground for placemaking and community-building initiatives. Ellin's new book *Good Urbanism* describes a paradigm shift in urban design and planning moving beyond sustainability to prosperity. She is also the author of *Integral Urbanism, Postmodern Urbanism, Phoenix: 21st-Century City* (with Edward Booth-Clibborn), and the editor of *Architecture of Fear*. Ellin's collection of public scholarship, *Desert Urbanism*, can be found at her university website. Her work has been translated into twelve languages.

Kristina Hill is an Associate Professor of Landscape Architecture & Environmental Planning at UC Berkeley. Her primary area of work is in adapting urban water systems to challenges associated with climate change. She lectures internationally on urban design and ecology, and served as chair of the Landscape Architecture Department at the University of Virginia from 2007-2010. She received her Ph.D. from Harvard University, and was a member of the faculty at the Massachusetts Institute of Technology, the University of Washington in Seattle, and the University of Virginia before coming to California. She is a Fellow of the Urban Design Institute in New York.

Douglas Kelbaugh FAIA, Professor of Architecture and Urban Planning and former Dean of the University of Michigan's Taubman College, was principal in Kelbaugh and Lee from 1977 to 1985, an architecture firm in Princeton that won 15 design awards and competitions. As Chair of the Architecture Department at the University of Washington and principal, he edited *The Pedestrian Pocket Book* and authored *Common Place: Toward Neighborhood and Regional Design and Repairing the American Metropolis.* After his deanship, he was Executive Director of Design and Planning for two years in a development company with projects throughout the Eastern Hemisphere.

Jusuck Koh is Chair and Professor of Landscape Architecture at Wageningen University, the Netherlands, and principal of Oikosdesign. He earned his Ph.D. in Architecture (University of Pennsylvania) with *An Ecological Theory of Architecture,* and practiced as an architect and landscape architect in Korea and USA. Jusuck writes on theory building for ecological design and ecological aesthetics, and on East Asian aesthetics and creativity, currently focusing on a 'Landscape Approach to Design', and a 'Field Theory of Aesthetics and Design'. His recognitions include the Bradford Williams Medal 1985, Distinguished Scholar (US State Department, Fulbright), and an IFLA APR President's Award 2009.

James Howard Kunstler is the author of four nonfiction books and eleven novels. He was born in New York City in 1948. He graduated from the State University of New York, Brockport campus, worked as a reporter and feature writer for a number of newspapers, and finally as a staff writer for Rolling Stone Magazine. In 1975, he dropped out to write books on a full-time basis. His latest book, *Too Much Magic: Wishful Thinking, Technology, and the Fate of the Nation* (Atlantic Monthly Press, 2012) explores the unsustainability of our high-energy lifestyle and the folly of technology as a solution.

Larissa Larsen is an Associate Professor in the Urban and Regional Planning Program (URP) and Natural Resources at the University of Michigan. Larissa's research focuses on identifying environmental inequities in the built environment and advancing issues of urban sustainability and social justice. Most of her current work involves climate adaptation planning and urban heat island studies. Larissa completed her undergraduate and graduate degrees at the University of Guelph, Ontario, and received her Ph.D. in Urban and Regional Planning from the University of Illinois at Urbana-Champaign. She is a registered landscape architect and has a passion for native plants.

Alistair McIntosh is a Fellow of the American Society of Landscape Architects and a member of the Royal Institute of British Architects. He has over 35 years of experience in the practice and teaching of landscape architecture. His practice specializes in the planning and design of public open space in the contemporary city, with a focus on making environmentally situated stages for the practice of contemporary public life. He has taught landscape architecture at Harvard, MIT and The University of Pennsylvania.

Michael Mehaffy is an author, researcher and consultant in sustainable urban development, and executive director of the Sustasis Foundation, a non-profit that works on new solutions for sustainable cities by bringing together leading minds in a range of fields including planning, mathematics, computer science, biology, medicine and economics. Michael has taught at five graduate institutions in four countries, teaching sustainable technology, urban planning, architecture and philosophy. He is on the boards of three internationally active NGOs in sustainable urbanism. He has published papers and articles in many journals, newspapers and magazines, and contributed chapters to 16 books.

Leon Morenas' research engages debates in critical Marxist geography, science and technology studies (STS), urban planning, design and policy, the anthropology of development, post-colonial studies, as well as the history and theory of architecture. His writing examines the technological politics embedded within everyday design objects, focusing on the production of the urban. He has an M'Arch from the School of Planning and Architecture, Delhi and a PhD from Rensselaer Polytechnic Institute. He has taught at schools of architecture, engineering, and urban design in India and the US and is currently Assistant Professor at the School of Design at Ambedkar University, Delhi.

Paul Murrain is an urban design consultant based in London. He was formerly a Senior Lecturer and Graduate Diploma Course Chairman at the Joint Centre for Urban Design in Oxford, England. From 2002 — 2005 he was Senior Design Director at HRH The Prince of Wales' Foundation for the Built Environment. Paul was appointed as Visiting Professor at the University of Greenwich from 2007 to 2010. He has also taught at the University of Miami. Along with his co-authors he recently received a lifetime award in the UK for 'Responsive Environments' an urban design manual published in 1985.

Neal I. Payton is an architect and Principal at Torti Gallas and Partners, Inc. where he created, and directs its Los Angeles office. His work centers on urban design and town planning at a variety of scales including urban revitalization, inner suburban infill and refill, and transit oriented development in emerging development areas. He has received numerous national and international design awards from the AIA and CNU among others. Prior to joining Torti Gallas, Neal served on the architecture faculties of The Catholic

University of America, Rice University, Washington University in St. Louis, and The University of Virginia.

Michael Rios is Associate Professor of Community and Urban Design in the Landscape Architecture Program at the University of California, Davis. Michael has contributed numerous publications on the topics of placemaking, marginality, public space, the ethics of practice, and critical pedagogy. His co-edited book, *Diálogos: Placemaking in Latino Communities* (Routledge 2012), considers how demographic changes in regions, cities, and towns both challenge and offer insight into community planning and urban design practice in an increasingly multi-ethnic world. Michael received his Ph.D. in Geography from Penn State, and Master of Architecture and Master of City Planning degrees from UC Berkeley.

Daniel Solomon, FAIA, is a partner in the San Francisco-based design firm of Mithun | Solomon. His long list of awards and personal recognition includes the Maybeck Award for lifetime design achievement from the California Council, AIA, and the Seaside Prize for contributions to American Urbanism. He is Professor Emeritus at UC Berkeley and Kea Distinguished Professor at the University of Maryland. After receiving a Bachelor of Arts (Honors in Humanities) from Stanford University, Solomon earned a Bachelor of Architecture from Columbia University and a Master of Architecture from the University of California at Berkeley.

Sandy Sorlien is a code writer and photographer who has coordinated Transect-based tools by more than thirty different New Urbanist firms, including the model *SmartCode* and *Neighborhood Conservation Code*. Sandy is a founding member of the Transect Codes Council and a member of the Congress for the New Urbanism. In 2011, in partnership with the Center for Applied Transect Studies, she launched the Transect Collection image resource — built and natural environments that contribute to walkable neighborhoods and land conservation. Sandy has been photographing and writing about American Main Streets since 2001. She lives in Philadelphia.

Perry Yang is an Associate Professor jointly appointed to the School of City and Regional Planning and the School of Architecture at Georgia Institute of Technology. His research engages performance dimensions of urban form and urban design, a method grounded in landscape ecology, industrial ecology and emerging technologies for spatial analysis, energy performance and life cycle assessment. He has been awarded prizes in urban design competitions continuously from 2005, including the 1st prize in international competition of the 2009 World Games Park at Kaohsiung City of Taiwan in 2005, a project recently featured by CNN as an "eco-friendly venue".

If you have enjoyed *Landscape Urbanism and its Discontents*
you might also enjoy other

BOOKS TO BUILD A NEW SOCIETY

Our books provide positive solutions for people who want to
make a difference. We specialize in:

Sustainable Living • Green Building • Peak Oil
Renewable Energy • Environment & Economy
Natural Building & Appropriate Technology
Progressive Leadership • Resistance and Community
Educational & Parenting Resources

For a full list of NSP's titles, please call 1-800-567-6772 *or check out our website* at:

www.newsociety.com